WOMEN, *ABUSE,* AND THE BIBLE

WOMEN, ABUSE, AND THE BIBLE

How Scripture Can Be Used to Hurt or to Heal

CATHERINE CLARK KROEGER
AND JAMES R. BECK,

E D I T O R S

Baker Books
A Division of Baker Book House Co
Grand Rapids, Michigan 49516

Published by Baker Books
a division of Baker Book House Company
P.O. Box 6287, Grand Rapids, MI 49516–6287

Printed in the United States of America

Library of Congress Cataloging-in-Publication Data

Women, abuse, and the Bible : how scripture can be used to hurt or to heal / Catherine Clark Kroeger and James R. Beck, editors
    p. cm.
    Includes bibliographical references (p.).
    ISBN 0-8010-5707-8 (pbk.)
    1. Women—Biblical teaching. 2. Abused women—Biblical teaching.
3. Woman (Theology) I. Kroeger, Catherine Clark. II. Beck, James R.
BS680.W7W54 1996
261.8'32—dc20   96-30240

To Elizabeth Clark Blank in recognition
of her many years of tireless effort and concern
for abused and battered women

And to all those women
who have been abused in their Christian homes,
women whose courage and faith in God have enabled them
to find help in their time of trouble and
to witness an end to their affliction

Contents

Contents

Prologue

When times of social and/or spiritual crisis arise, God raises up prophetic voices to address the society at large as well as God's people in particular. This was true of Hosea, Micah, John Wesley, William Wilberforce, and many others. Sometimes different voices address various aspects of the same problem. Martin Luther, Catherine of Siena, and Teresa of Avila all dealt with the corruption and spiritual degeneracy of the Catholic church, and all were mightily used of God.

Today we are caught in a social and moral maelstrom that calls for God's people to raise their voices anew. In an effort to speak to the rising flood of abuse and violence within church and home, Christians for Biblical Equality, an evangelical organization committed to affirming a biblical basis for the equality and ministry of men and women in church, home, and society, called for papers to be read at a consultation on women, abuse, and the Bible. The objectives were:

> to compel evangelical and other conservative religious groups to acknowledge the existence of domestic violence and abuse within the homes of their own constituencies;

to demonstrate how and why the doctrines of a rigid funda-
mentalism put a family or a congregation at greater risk of
abuse;

to affirm the biblical concepts of headship and submission, but
to present them with exegetical and critical insights that will
lead to the building of more healthy, egalitarian concepts
within the family;

to show how the Bible may be misused to hurt or appropriately
used to heal;

to offer paradigms and possibilities of creative therapy for both
abused and abuser;

to issue a biblically mandated call (1 Cor. 5:1–8) for congregations and wider religious bodies to take responsible action in
known cases of abuse;

to challenge churches and clergy to address honestly the issues
of domestic, clergy, and verbal abuse, emotional cruelty, rape,
and sexual harassment.

Proposals for papers came in from psychologists, sociologists,
pastors, therapists, biblical scholars, theologians, survivors—even
an incarcerated perpetrator. Each had something to tell, some piece
which could add to the puzzle. No one individual could see the
whole picture, but integration of the various pieces was essential.
We simply cannot have pastors insisting on one course of action
while therapists and rescue workers demand another. The fusion
of biblical directive, pastoral concern, and therapeutic mandate
could provide a basis for cooperation in dealing with the problem.

This compilation of some of the papers represents the thinking
of a variety of Christians from many different backgrounds and
professional competencies. Such a book is needed by committed
laypeople within our congregations—the ones who hold the hands,
dry the tears, risk their lives in rescue efforts, drive the victims to
the hospital, care for the children, and try in the wee small hours
to figure out what in the world a Christian ought to do. As laypeople understand more about the many manifestations of abuse and
the many responses that are possible, they will become ever more
valuable players on the team.

This book is intended for Christian professionals as well—pastors, therapists, psychologists, persons in the medical profession and law enforcement agencies. We made an earnest attempt to talk with one another—sociologist with theologian, survivor with biblical scholar, therapist with church leader, and researcher with the one who binds the wounds of battered women and children. At the consultation we asked, "What can we learn from one another about the totality of battering, incest, rape, emotional cruelty, and clergy abuse? How does our view of Scripture trap or free people in abusive situations? What is the role of the wider believing community in all this? How can we minister in Christ's name to both the abuser and the abused? What can we, as the people of God unified in conviction and in purpose, do toward prevention and treatment of the many aspects of abuse?"

Each of us approaches these urgent questions with his or her own particular issues. Many years ago I (CK) loaded a frightened wife into the car and drove out of a storm-ridden North Dakota town. Located as it was on the border of Canada, the community's nearest American police station was forty-five miles away, but I knew I had to try to get her to safety. For any man to accompany me would have greatly heightened the danger from the insanely jealous husband.

An elder from our church fueled my car and remarked, "Not even grown men would try to make it on a day like this." Of course I knew the perils. One blizzard after another had swept down on us that winter of 1956, and the temperature now stood at twenty below zero. The roads were no longer passable, but the Land Army had plowed a track over the open fields. Everyone in town knew that the abusive husband had a gun that he would not be reluctant to use.

Yet none of these considerations caused the terror that gripped my heart. Had I stepped out of God's will? My husband and I had come to this town to proclaim the Word of God. Was I dishonoring the Lord by flouting what the Scriptures said about submission and the permanence of marriage? If I was disobedient, how could I expect God to help this woman who had already sustained such serious injuries at the hands of her husband? Would my efforts to save a life make a mockery of our ministry?

The perplexities that I faced as a young pastor's wife have confronted millions of earnest Christians who long more than anything else to do God's will. How acute has been the puzzlement, and how deep the pain of those who long to reach out to the abused and yet feel checked by certain scriptural statements. Sometimes a misplaced emphasis on certain passages of Scripture has caused us to ignore the "weightier matters of the Law." The legalists of Jesus' day were misapplying the Scriptures, and he asked them, "Which is lawful on the Sabbath: to do good or to do evil, to save life or to kill?" (Mark 3:4 NIV). How often have we misapplied, misread, or misinterpreted the Scriptures?

This collection of papers from the consultation has been prepared for those who seek the wisdom that God has promised to those who ask. It is intended as a help for Christians who long more than anything else to understand God's will and to do it. Constraints of space forced us to leave out many compelling essays with important perspectives. Copies of these additional conference papers may be obtained from Christians for Biblical Equality, P.O. Box 7155, St. Paul, MN 55107-0155.

PART 1

TO HURT

1

Religious Beliefs and Abuse

Carolyn Holderread Heggen

n my early years as a therapist, I was surprised and saddened that many of the perpetrators of sexual abuse and domestic violence I counseled professed to be Christians. I was particularly confused by the many perpetrators who claimed to see no conflict between their behavior and their Christian beliefs. Some even justified their behavior by citing biblical passages and religious principles.

For several years I was baffled. How could people who professed to be devout Christians do such un-Christlike things to others? During this time I found the research and writings of Thomas Adorno and colleagues (1950), who asked similar things about the many religious people who were attracted to Nazism and supported Hitler throughout his violent reign in Germany. I also reread the writings of Gordon Allport (1954), who found that some of the most bigoted, racially hateful people he studied were very religious. But some of the most tolerant, loving people in his studies were also people who claimed that religious beliefs were important to them.

I began listening more carefully when victims and perpetrators of abuse talked of their religious beliefs and motivations. As I have listened to people in my clinical practice and interviewed hundreds of others for various research projects, I have come to identify certain religious beliefs that I believe are related to the abuse of women. I am not suggesting that any of these beliefs alone necessarily causes abuse, but I believe they interact with other factors to create an environment where abuse may occur and where it is less likely that women will effectively defend themselves and their children. What are some of these beliefs?

Four Religious Beliefs and Their Implications

1. God Intends That Men Dominate and Women Submit

The subordination of woman to man is taught in many religious circles as God's divine plan for social relationships. Many religious people interpret the Genesis 2 creation account as establishing woman's secondary and subordinate nature to man because she was created after and from him. They maintain that this account establishes a divinely ordained dominance-submission model of social relationships where men are to be in dominance and authority over women and children. The name for the social organization and set of beliefs that grant and sustain male dominance over women and children is *patriarchy*.

The Bible gives us an accurate picture of fallen humanity. Just because most families in the biblical stories operated according to patriarchal patterns, we must beware of equating this style of family life with God's intentions. In the Genesis 1 creation story, female and male are created as one and given equal responsibility for dominion over the rest of creation. Both are depicted as having been created in the image of God. Both are seen as the pinnacle of God's creative work (cf Genesis 5:1–2). When I read the Genesis 1 account, which emphasizes an integrative creation of male and female and affirms that both reflect the image of God, many of my clients seem genuinely surprised.

Except in religious feminist circles, the Genesis 1 creation account, which supports mutuality and equality, goes relatively unnoticed. Instead, much teaching in churches regarding marriage,

16

family life, and congregational leadership is based on principles extracted from the Genesis 2 account. Even though there does not appear to be legitimate justification for the subservience of woman based on this text, it does get used to support dominance-submission relationships and patriarchy as God's plan.

The inherent logic of patriarchy says that since men have the right to dominance and control, they also have the right to enforce that control. It is this control-over component of patriarchy and its assumptions of ownership of women and children by men that make it vulnerable to violence and abuse—not only against women and children, but also against the earth and its resources. Helfer and Kempe (1968) in their book *The Battered Child* report that the assault rate on children of parents who subscribe to the belief of male dominance is 136 percent higher than for couples not committed to male dominance.

One woman told me that as an abused child she'd cry out to her father, "Why are you doing this to me?" His response as she remembers it was, "Because I am your father." Her deeply instilled belief that he was the head of the home and that she must obey and submit to his authority made it essentially difficult for her to challenge his behavior and stop the abuse.

Another sexually abused child of Christian parents who subscribed to Bill Gothard's (1979) "chain of command" model for families told me some years after the abuse that she actually had the sense that by saying no to her father she was rebuking God. She had been taught that she couldn't trust herself to know what was right or wrong and that her father's will and word should be trusted as God's voice. Even as an adult, she had a hard time realizing that "chain of command" was a military metaphor and not biblical language.

Unfortunately, this is not an isolated, extraordinary incident. When another woman told her pastor about her husband's abusive behavior, the pastor's response was: "No matter what he's doing to you, he is still your spiritual head. Respect those behaviors that you can respect and pray for those that you can't respect. But remember, no matter what, you owe it to him and to God to live in submission to your husband. You'll never be happy until you submit to him." It was at that point she came for counseling. She was unhappy as a battered wife but had been told by her pastor that to be happy she must submit to her batterer. No wonder she called my office initially saying she thought she was going crazy! Even more disturbing was the devoutly religious husband who insisted he battered his wife because she wouldn't submit to his God-given headship. He was convinced that it was better to batter and bruise her in this life than to fail to teach her submission, a necessary requirement for getting to heaven and avoiding eternal torment.

Lenore Walker (1979) has conducted extensive research on battered women. She has discovered that women with strong religious backgrounds often are the least likely to believe that violence against them is wrong. She also has discovered that battered women tend to hold traditional views about sex roles in the home. Not surprisingly, mental health workers and shelter workers tend to report that the religious beliefs of their clients seem to reinforce passivity and are a detriment to the effective confrontation of domestic violence and abuse. In my own clinical practice, I have observed a disturbing tendency for battered Christian women to believe they are ontologically evil and somehow deserving of the abuse they receive.

We live in a violence-prone culture that particularly disrespects and despises the feminine. When such cultural inclinations are reinforced by religious teachings, they become even more influential and dangerous for women. No other human institution has more power to define and control relationships between women and men than organized religion. Particularly, nothing else has the power of organized religion to define "woman's place" and to punish those women who step outside their religiously assigned role and violate the rules of patriarchy.

As I travel and speak, I am questioned about my criticism of patriarchy more than any other issue. But the longer I listen to stories of family abuse, the more I am convinced that we cannot both support patriarchy and stop domestic abuse. To stop violence among our families, we must stop holding up patriarchy as God's intention for us. We must stop honoring the curse of sin on male-female relations by upholding a dominance-submission model. We must teach that the subordination of woman to man's dominance is the result of sin and not an expression of God's intentions. We must look to Jesus for a new way of being together that reflects the new creation. Ephesians 5:21–6:9 reveals a radical shift from patriarchy to mutuality, and it reflects the revolutionary equality in Christ that is summarized in Galatians 3:28: "There is no longer Jew or Greek, there is no longer slave or free, there is no longer male and female; for all of you are one in Christ Jesus" (NRSV).

2. Woman Is Morally Inferior to Man and Cannot Trust Her Own Judgment

Another religious belief I think is related to the abuse of women is that because of Eve's secondary creation and her role in the fall, women are morally inferior to men and should not trust their own judgment as much as a man's.

When a Christian mother confessed to me that she knew her husband had been sexually abusing their daughters for several years, I asked, "Why didn't you stop him?" She replied, "I didn't know how to stop him, but more importantly, he convinced me that it wasn't really wrong." As I tried to understand how she could have been so pathetically manipulated into complicity, it became clear that she had trusted his assessment of right and wrong more than she trusted her own inner moral sense.

Several years ago, I conducted research on Christian women's role beliefs. I found that many women believe they are more likely to be deceived or morally misled than men. These women trust men to determine right and wrong more than they trust themselves. As support for this belief, one woman respondent quoted from family life materials used in her church written by Elizabeth Rice Handford. Handford (1972, p. 17) says, "Women are more often led into spiritual error than men. That is the reason God commanded her not to usurp authority over man, so she can be protected by him, from false doctrine." Handford (1972, p. 28) also writes, "The Scriptures say a woman must ignore her feelings about the will of God and do what her husband says. She is to obey her husband as if he were God Himself. She can be as certain of God's will, when her husband speaks, as if God had spoken audibly from Heaven!"

In both women and men, a connection has been identified between the association of femininity with defectiveness and defilement and the association of masculinity with spirituality and divinity. Woman is generally held accountable for the entry of sin into the world and for distracting man from the spiritual way. Her natural processes of menstruation, childbirth, and lactation often have been viewed as dirty, contaminated, and evil. Because Christ and the twelve named disciples were men, because most names for God connote masculinity, and because male dominance in some denominations is formalized by regulations allowing only men to assume the highest positions of leadership and authority, the link between masculinity and divinity in many people's minds is strong.

Some make the case that Christianity has elevated women to unprecedented heights of honor. Yet there are seemingly contradictory messages for women who are also taught that because of Eve's sin they themselves are morally defective, that they must live in subordination to men's moral authority, and that they are less a reflection of the divine image than are men. In my city, there is a religious radio station that broadcasts a program for Christian women entitled "The Glory of Man." The underlying and oft-repeated tenet of this program is that while man reflects the glory of God, woman reflects the glory of man, though this is not precisely what 1 Corinthians 11:7 says. The program instructs Christian women in ways to submit to and obey their husbands graciously so that as wives they may truly glorify their husbands.

A female who believes she is morally defective and thus unable to trust her inner sense of what is right and wrong, who believes men reflect more of the divine image than women, and who believes it is her Christian duty to obey men may find it hard to confront an abusive man, particularly if he tells her, "You're over-reacting," or, "It's all in your head," or, "Trust me—there's nothing wrong." When females don't trust themselves, they more easily give up their power and lose their ability to confront and resist destructive things done to them or their children.

Psychiatrist Jean Baker Miller (1986) studied the psychological effects of dominance-submission relationships. She observed that people in positions of subordination, in an attempt to survive, develop characteristics pleasing to people in dominance. These traits include passivity, docility, submissiveness, dependency, lack of initiative, and the inability to decide, think, or act for themselves. These are qualities we generally associate with children, not with adults. Some of these are also qualities regarded in some religious circles as desirable for good Christian women.

A colleague and I tested this in a research project. We asked Christian clergy to describe a spiritually healthy Christian woman (Long & Heggen, 1988). We found that indeed clergy from conservative churches described a spiritually healthy woman as "submissive in the home," "gentle and soft spoken," "lets spouse make decisions," "dependent," "passive," "finds identity through spouse," and "withholds criticism." These are not qualities they named as descriptive of a spiritually healthy man. Nor are they qualities that are likely to empower a woman to protect herself and her children from an abusive man.

I have also studied the relationship between Christian women's role beliefs and their level of self-esteem (Heggen, 1989). I found that belief in a traditional, gender-based, dominance-submission model of family life and church were correlated inversely with personal self-esteem. Women who believed in a traditional model of female subordination to men tended to have lower self-esteem scores than did women who believed in equality and partnership between women and men.

Considerable psychological theory and research has focused on the significance of self-esteem and self-acceptance as determinants of behavior. Social scientists have repeatedly found a strong relationship between self-esteem and mental health (Bandura, 1977; Coopersmith, 1967; Pancheri & Benaissa, 1978; and Witmer, Rich, Barcikowski, & Mague, 1983). Self-esteem is important for emotional well-being and self-confidence. Persons with low self-esteem tend to feel unloved and unlovable, isolated, unable to defend themselves, and afraid of angering others or drawing attention to themselves (Coopersmith, 1968). People with low self-esteem are less able to confront offensive behavior in others. Women with low self-esteem may not effectively be able to stop violent behavior against themselves or their children.

In her research with battered women, Lenore Walker (1979) found that battered women tend to have low self-esteem. They believe that Christian women are supposed to be meek and submissive and that to resist the violence against them violates important religious principles. One battered Christian woman expressed the profound dilemma she faced: "I feel like I can't be psychologically healthy and a good Christian wife at the same time. How can I confront his behavior and be submissive at the same time?"

Children in abusive families often perceive their mothers as weak and ineffective. One survivor told me, "Mom didn't even have the authority to decide when she was going into town to do grocery shopping. I knew telling her about my abuse would just add to her frustrations. She didn't have enough power anyway to stop the abuse."

The battered mother of an abused daughter explained, "All those years when my daughter was little and being abused, I was so depressed and emotionally weak that I was totally dependent on my husband. I couldn't think about anything but my own pain. Now I realize that may have been part of his strategy. He must have known that as long as I was depressed and helpless, I wouldn't ever leave. That gave him lots of years of access to my daughter with no one strong enough to question or stop his behavior."

As Gilbert Bilezikian reminds us, it was a "satanic scheme, devised at the fall," to make women feel guilty for being women (1990, p. 211). Any religious teachings that imply woman's moral inferiority to man, that infer she is created less in the image of God than is man, and that cause her to trust man's judgment more than her own are not only a heretical distortion of the gospel message, but are tragically dangerous to her and her children.

3. Suffering Is a Christian Virtue and Women in Particular Have Been Designated to Be "Suffering Servants"

Most Christians regard Christ's death as vital to humanity's redemption from sin. Indeed, the cross has become the central image of Christianity. Because Christ's suffering and death are understood to have salvific meaning, some Christian communities have come to regard all suffering as virtuous. Martyrdom, an extreme form of suffering, has held a special place of honor among Christians since the time of Jesus.

Unfortunately, there has emerged in some Christian circles the doctrine of feminine suffering. Women have generally been considered more capable of enduring great pain than men. In an atmosphere that glorifies suffering, females tend to see suffering as their cross to bear, as their way of identifying with the sufferings of Christ. Females in abusive relationships are sometimes told that by patiently enduring violence against their bodies, they share in Christ's suffering and redemption and may, in fact, save their abuser's very soul. As one client told me, "If my gentle spirit in the midst of his violence finally causes him to see the face of Jesus in me, every blow I have sustained throughout our marriage will have been worth it."

The glorification of suffering may encourage the acceptance of victimization and may result in minimization of the offensiveness of abuse. One Christian woman who had suffered violent battery throughout the thirty years of her marriage said, "The one advantage of my husband's abuse is that I don't expect to spend long in purgatory after I die; I've already been refined and prepared for heaven by my years of hell on earth."

Marie Fortune (1983) and others have helped us understand the important distinction between voluntary and involuntary suffering. Voluntary suffering is freely chosen for the sake of a greater good. For example, Rosa Parks must have known that by sitting in the front of the Montgomery city bus that day in 1955, she would have to suffer. She willingly chose to suffer because she hoped that it might help bring justice and dignity for her people.

Involuntary suffering is not freely chosen and is often the result of another person's sin against us. It does not necessarily yield a greater good. Yes, in both kinds of suffering we may feel God's presence in the midst of our pain. Coming through both kinds of suffering may result in an increased dependence on God and a sense of God's mercy and grace. But we dare not romanticize nor idealize suffering. Many victims of involuntary suffering have crushed spirits and bitter hearts. Some find it impossible to believe in a God who would allow such cruel things to happen to innocent, helpless people, and they are forever broken by their suffering.

Theologian Dorothee Soelle (1975) discusses suffering in a slightly different manner. One form of suffering allows articulation of pain and encourages change. The other is a passive form of suffering that quietly endures pain and abuse and sees them as a natural result of one's role in life. In this kind of suffering, the one who suffers sees her appropriate response to pain as powerlessness and submissiveness. The sufferer fears that challenging the cause of her pain would be an affront to divine order. Soelle calls this Christian masochism.

While we must walk gently with victims of suffering, helping them find existential meaning and God's healing grace in the midst of their anguish, let us not spiritualize their pain nor glorify their suffering. Let us be wary of religious teachings which suggest that females particularly have been designated to carry the wounds of Christ in their bodies, to practice suffering love in a unique way. Let us hold up the crucifixion, not as a symbol of the virtue of suffering, but as the result of Jesus' consistent challenges against the dominating, violent powers of evil. Let's point to the cross, not as proof that all suffering is redemptive, but rather as evidence that Jesus, because of his wounds, stands in compassionate solidarity with all those who suffer.

4. Christians Must Quickly Forgive and Be Reconciled with Those Who Sin against Them

One of the most complicated issues for victims of domestic violence and abuse is forgiveness and reconciliation with their abusers. No other advice appears to be given so consistently to Christian victims of family violence as "You must forgive your abuser." Not only are victims of abuse told to forgive, but they are often pushed to forgive quickly. Those who find they are unable to extend forgiveness toward their abusers are sometimes shamed and condemned by their religious community. A client who had suffered severe sexual and physical abuse by her father told of once sharing her story with her pastor. When he learned that the abuse had ended over twenty years ago, he said, "Only a bitter, self-pitying woman would even remember these things after all those years."

Particularly when both the offended and the offender are members of the same religious community, there is often strong pressure put on the victim of abuse to quickly forgive and be reconciled to the offender. As long as the relationship is broken, the broader Christian community is affected. Because it makes the entire religious community uncomfortable when there is unresolved conflict, it is understandable, if not appropriate, that victims feel great urging to forgive promptly and be reconciled. Quick forgiveness without true repentance on the part of the offender may make the community feel less anxious, but it is not a healing experience for either the victim or the perpetrator of abuse.

Although biblical texts such as Luke 17:3 suggest that repentance by the offender must precede forgiveness, God's unconditional forgiveness of sinful humans often has been held up as the appropriate model for victims of domestic violence. The Lord's Prayer in the Sermon on the Mount (Matt. 6:12; Luke 11:4) is sometimes used to support the belief that God's forgiveness of us depends on our willingness to forgive others. Likewise, the parable of the unforgiving servant in Matthew 18:23–35 is often interpreted to mean that the person who does not forgive cannot repent and be forgiven before God. The examples most frequently used, according to my clients, are God's unconditional love for us before we were even born and Christ's painful death on our behalf before we had repented.

A client whose father sexually abused her throughout her childhood remembers that after each incident he would "confess" the sinfulness of his behavior and beg her to forgive him. When she finally threatened to tell her mother, he warned her that to do so would mean she hadn't really forgiven him and therefore God wouldn't forgive her and she'd go to hell. She sadly concluded as a young child that it was better to try and forgive her father each time he raped her than to report him and risk God's judgment on her own sins, which seemed immense to this shame-filled, defiled-feeling little girl.

Another young woman who had experienced abuse by her grandfather for many years was working hard in counseling to face her abusive childhood and be healed of the resultant emotional and spiritual wounds. Soon after she began counseling, her grandfather suffered several heart attacks, and it appeared he might die soon. Although he had never admitted what he had done to her nor had he asked her forgiveness, her family tried to coerce her into going to his bedside to tell him she forgave him: "If he dies and you haven't forgiven him, God won't ever be able to forgive him! Furthermore, if he dies before you forgive him, God won't ever forgive you," they told her.

A severely battered Christian wife rejected her counselor's suggestion that she leave home and find a safe place for herself and her young children. She found the counselor's suggestion in conflict with the advice of her pastor, who when previously told of her husband's violence had urged her to stay and develop a more loving attitude. She recalls the pastor saying, "If you truly reflect the sweetness and meekness of Christ, he can't possibly keep hurting you. Nothing is more likely to get him to stop than a sweet, forgiving spirit in the face of his rage."

Another Christian wife finally sought pastoral counseling at a Christian agency after years of emotional and physical abuse from her husband. She told the counselor she had decided to take her children and leave home because she feared her husband's escalating violence might result in her death. She didn't trust him to raise the children should she be killed. The pastoral counselor asked her if he'd been sexually unfaithful to her. When she said he hadn't, the counselor told her that adultery was the only biblical grounds for "splitting up a home." Fearful of the censure and rejection of her religious community, she stayed within the violent marriage until she learned some years later that her husband had also been sexually abusing their two daughters.

While the Christian community must continue to uphold the sacredness of the marital covenant, the church must struggle to understand the permissive will of God in instances where the marriage covenant has already been broken by violence and abuse. The importance of marital permanence must not be elevated above the sanctity of individual personhood and safety. We dare not overlook nor minimize the destructive evils of battery and abuse because of our high regard for the permanence of marriage.

Yes, forgiveness and reconciliation are desirable, appropriate goals for victims and perpetrators of abuse. Even nonreligious mental health professionals have increasingly articulated the therapeutic power of forgiveness. Psychotherapists of many varieties are acknowledging that healing for survivors of abuse is not complete until there is the kind of letting go that comes through forgiveness. They acknowledge that there is a personal empowerment for survivors that only comes through forgiveness.

On the other hand, a facile, quick forgiveness that doesn't appropriately hold the perpetrator of abuse responsible for his behavior not only puts others in danger of his ongoing violence, it likewise decreases the likelihood that he will honestly face his sinful behavior, repent, and get the help he needs to understand and change his destructive patterns of behavior. Pushing for quick forgiveness and cheap mercy not only trivializes the victim's depth of pain and woundedness, but may also rob the perpetrator of the opportunity to experience true repentance and redemption.

Conclusion

Any religious teaching that isn't good news for even the most vulnerable among us is a distortion of Jesus' gospel. Teachings that cause women to doubt their own intrinsic preciousness and equal worth with men, that cause them to mistrust their own ability to make moral judgments, or that make them vulnerable to violence and abuse even within their most intimate relationships and homes are surely a blasphemous misrepresentation of Jesus' intentions for us. Teachings that cause both women and men to mistrust and despise femininity damage and diminish all of us.

The Evangelical Debate over Biblical "Headship"

David M. Scholer

On August 17, 1549, a Bible, fundamentally a new edition of the 1537 Matthew's Bible, was published in London by Jhon [*sic*] Daye, edited with notes by Edmund Becke.[1] The most famous of all the notes in Becke's Bible is the one for the phrase "Likewise ye men, dwell with them [your wives] according to knowledge" in 1 Peter 3:7. Becke annotated: "He dwelleth wyth his wyfe according to knowledge, that taketh her as a necessary helper, and not as a bonde servante, or a bonde slave. And yf she be not obedient and healpful unto hym, endeavoureth to beate the feare of God into her heade, that thereby she maye be compelled to learne her dutie, and to do it."[2]

Although Becke's note may be unique in the history of Bible publication, the idea that the Bible may justify and even encourage husbands to compel their wives to obey by force is, regrettably, deep within the tradition and life of the church and has shaped a painful reality for countless anonymous women throughout the last two millennia.

Background and Perspective

Christian Literature on Abuse

It is not my intention here to attempt either a psychological or sociological study of the connection between the abuse of women and the Bible; that is not my expertise, and others will do that. But it is important to note here at the beginning of this biblical study that the connection between the abuse of women and the Bible is a pervasive and constant theme in literature on the sexual abuse of women.

The connection between abuse and the Bible appears to have at least two dimensions, especially within the various strands of the Christian tradition. First, many men who abuse their wives appear to feel that the alleged biblical teaching of "male headship" is warrant, at least in some degree, for their behavior. Second, many abused women, especially those who have been taught the biblical principles of male headship and female submission, have understood the abuse they have received as either God's rightful punishment for their sins or God's will for their lives, even if it involves suffering unjustly.

Not only are these connections between the abuse of women and the Bible important issues, the other painful reality is that the church, and perhaps in particular the evangelical movement within the church, has been embarrassingly and wrongfully silent on these issues. One fears that most of the silence is the consequence of patriarchy and androcentrism, if not misogyny, in human history and within the church. It would appear that the silence has been significantly broken only in our modern period with the empowerment of women to speak for themselves.

One of the early articles on these issues in our own time was the 1981 essay of Susan Brooks Thistlethwaite, "Battered Women and the Bible: From Subjection to Liberation." Thistlethwaite's article was followed by what is now the 1983 classic of Marie Marshall Fortune, *Sexual Violence: The Unmentionable Sin.* Chapter 10 in that book, "Religious Concerns and Pastoral Issues," documents the reality of the use of the Bible to sustain sexual abuse of women.[3]

Much of the Christian literature in the past five years (especially the evangelical publications) on domestic violence and sexual abuse of women contains pointed discussions of the relationship between biblical teachings of "male headship" and the reality of abused and battered women. The third chapter of Rita-Lou Clarke's *Pastoral Care of Battered Women* is on "Theological Issues Related to Battering." These issues are pervasive in Kay Marshall Strom's book *In the Name of Submission: A Painful Look at Wife Battering*, as well as in Margaret Josephson Rinck's *Christian Men Who Hate Women: Healing Hurting Relationships*. Both James and Phyllis Alsdurf's book *Battered into Submission: The Tragedy of Wife Abuse in the Christian Home* and Carolyn Holderread Heggen's book *Sexual Abuse in Christian Homes and Churches*, the two most important evangelical discussions of this issue now available, treat in significant ways these issues of relationship between the Bible and the social reality of the abuse of women.[4]

One recent example of the connection between the Bible and the abuse of women is the popular article by James L. Franklin, "Clergy Vows New Support for Victims of Battering," which appeared in the *Boston Globe* on November 14, 1993.[5] This newspaper article includes a graphic insert on "The Bible on Love and Marriage," in which one column is entitled "Passages Used as Rationale for Abuse," and the other is entitled "A More Positive Message."

It is remarkable to me that the magnum opus of the so-called traditionalist evangelical position—John Piper and Wayne Grudem's *Recovering Biblical Manhood and Womanhood: A Response to Evangelical Feminism*—is so silent on the issue of the sexual abuse of women. The Danvers Statement of the Council on Biblical Manhood and Womanhood states in its Fourth Affirmation that "The Fall introduced distortions into the relationships between men and women." This is then expanded as follows: "In the home, the husband's loving, humble headship tends to be replaced by domination or passivity. . . . In the church, sin inclines men toward a worldly love of power or an abdication of spiritual responsibility."[6] In light of this, I would expect the Piper/Grudem volume to treat significantly and denounce clearly the abuse of women perpetrated by men, especially when it is a corruption of what they see as "loving headship." Yet no article in the volume addresses this question. There are no entries in the index under "abuse," "battering," "sexual violence," or "violence," although three page numbers are given under "wife, abuse." The index has lengthy entries, however, for "authority," "headship," and "submission."

As indicated, there are three references to wife abuse in the Piper/Grudem volume. The first occurs in the chapter called "An Overview of Central Concerns: Questions and Answers," in which, catechism style, fifty-one questions are posed and answered. Question 9 reads: "Don't you think that stressing headship and submission gives impetus to the epidemic of wife abuse?" The short answer is "no." The full answer, which is about one-fourth of a page, stresses that Christlike husbands would not abuse wives. Further, it is stated that "we believe that wife abuse (and husband abuse) have some deep roots in the failure of parents to impart to their sons and daughters the meaning of true masculinity and true femininity."[7] It seems to me that the introduction of "husband abuse" without further comment trivializes the historical and social realities of the tragedy of wife abuse in the history of the church. More critically, the answer does nothing to actually address the reality of the issue or the pain of women.

The second reference to wife abuse in the Piper/Grudem book occurs in one sentence in James A. Borland's article on "Women in the Life and Teaching of Jesus," in which he states that instances of wife abuse recorded in Scripture are not actions sanctioned by God.[8]

The one strong statement in the Piper/Grudem volume comes from Wayne Grudem in a footnote to his article "Wives Like Sarah, and the Husbands Who Honor Them: 1 Peter 3:1–7." The footnote reads: "However, nowhere does Scripture condone or support the abuse of wives by husbands, but explicitly forbids even harsh attitudes . . . and therefore certainly condemns any physical violence used by husbands against wives. Evangelical churches have a strong responsibility to prevent such abuse and to protect those threatened or harmed by it."[9] The importance and value of this statement should not be underrated. Nevertheless, as the one such statement in the 566-page book—and a footnote at that—it appears to me to be too little too late.

The Tradition and Heritage of the Church Fathers

Carolyn Osiek, in her wonderful and powerful book *Beyond Anger: On Being a Feminist in the Church*, makes a disturbing analysis of the message of the cross in the tradition of the church:

> It has been to women and other oppressed groups that the message of the cross has been particularly directed. Women have been exhorted to enter into the destiny and vocation that belong to them through their superior capacity for self-sacrifice, self-denial, and suffering that has been thought . . . to belong to their "proper nature." . . . women have been invited to participate in and conform themselves to the suffering of Christ by remaining passive and powerless because it is these qualities that will humanize the children they raise and the men for whom they provide a home. . . . This persistent portrayal of women as demonstrating heroic but fitting sacrifice by submitting passively and silently to pain and abuse . . . leads directly to the image of the battered woman. She is the victim not only of the rage of her abuser but the blindness of a whole society that in the name of the sanctity of home and family will do nothing to rescue her. . . . women are to imitate the victim Christ while at the same time they are denied any possibility of fully identifying with him. Doomed to be like him in suffering and humiliation, they are equally doomed to be unlike him in power, authority, or exaltation.[10]

Such a pattern is found in the famous fifth-century spiritual classic, Augustine's *Confessions*, cited in Elizabeth A. Clark's *Women in the Early Church*. Here the greatest theologian of the ancient church expresses eloquently the story of his spiritual pilgrimage, including his devotion to his mother, Monica. In one passage about Monica and her pagan husband, Patricius (who converted at the end of his life), Augustine talks explicitly about certain features of their relationship:

> She was given to a husband whom she served as a lord. . . . Moreover, she thus endured the wrongs to her bed. . . . Indeed, more than this, just as he was an excellent person when feeling well-disposed, so he was raging when he was angry. She learned not

32

to resist a wrathful husband, not only in deed, but not even by a word. . . . In short, while many married women with milder husbands nonetheless bore on a dishonored face the traces of beatings, women who would in friendly conversation betray their husbands' lives, she would censure their tongues. . . . She would tell them that from the time they heard read aloud those matrimonial tablets, they should consider them instruments by which they had been made servants; accordingly, remembering the conditions of the marriage contract, they ought not to take the upper hand against their masters.[11]

It is not really surprising that Augustine could lift up his mother's submission even to abuse as a model for all women and their husbands. Augustine, in line with the traditional understandings of Scripture held by the early church fathers, held a rather negative view of women. For example, Augustine reflects on the creation of the woman in Genesis 2:

If it were not the case that the woman was created to be man's helper specifically for the production of children, then why would she have been created as a "helper"? Was it so that she might work the land with him? No . . . a male would have made a better assistant. One can also posit that the reason for her creation as a helper had to do with the companionship she could provide for the man. . . . Yet for company and conversation, how much more agreeable it is for two male friends to dwell together than for a man and a woman! . . . I cannot think of any reason for woman's being made as man's helper, if we dismiss the reason of procreation.[12]

Augustine further understands Genesis 3 to show the inferiority of women:

That a man endowed with a spiritual mind could have believed this [the lie of the serpent] is astonishing. And just because it is impossible to believe it, woman was given to man, woman who was of small intelligence and who perhaps still lives more in accordance with the promptings of the inferior flesh than by the superior reason.[13]

Augustine applied his understanding of male headship and female submission to a specific instance in which he wrote to Ecdicia, a Christian woman, about her problems with her husband. According to Augustine, her lack of submission to her husband led him to commit adultery; she had asked her husband for intercourse after they had agreed to continence, and she had given away some of her clothing and jewelry to the poor without consulting him. Augustine wrote to her:

> In his great anger at you, he was destructive to himself. . . . This great evil occurred when you did not treat him with the moderation you ought . . . you as the wife ought to have been subject to your husband in other things, accommodating yourself to the marriage bond, particularly since both of you are members of the body of Christ. And certainly if you . . . had had a husband who was not a believer, it would still have been proper for you to act in a submissive manner. . . . You ought to have yielded to him in your domestic association with great humility and obedience. . . . Furthermore, you ought to have consulted with your husband . . . and not despised his wishes. . . . I have written this to you . . . because I am saddened by your husband's behavior, behavior that came about by your unruly and reckless action. You ought to think earnestly about recovering him, if in truth you want to belong to Christ. . . . Write to him, making amends, begging his forgiveness for the sin you committed against him.[14]

Of course, Augustine is not alone in his attitudes. Two other well-known church fathers may serve to confirm the patterns of thinking in the early church about male headship and female submission. Tertullian, about A.D. 200, talks about what women have inherited from Eve: "I mean the degradation of the first sin and the hatefulness of human perdition." Tertullian continues:

> God's judgment on this sex lives on in our age; the guilt necessarily lives on as well. You are the Devil's gateway; you are the unsealer of that tree; you are the first foresaker of the divine law; you are the one who persuaded him whom the Devil was not brave enough to approach; you so lightly crushed the image of

God, the man Adam; because of your punishment, that is, death, even the Son of God had to die.[15]

John Chrysostom, the great fourth-century preacher and scholar, also had a negative view of women. He argues that only the man has the image of God:

The "image" has rather to do with authority, and this only the man has; the woman has it no longer. For he is subjected to no one, while she is subjected to him. . . . Therefore the man is in the "image of God" since he had no one above him, just as God has no superior but rules over everything. The woman, however, is "the glory of man," since she is subjected to him.[16]

Chrysostom elsewhere argues that:

If the more important, most beneficial concerns were turned over to the woman, she would go quite mad. Therefore God did not apportion both duties to one sex. . . . Nor did God assign both to be equal in every way. . . . But taking precautions at one and the same time for peace and for decency, God maintained the order of each sex by dividing the business of human life into two parts and assigned the more necessary and beneficial aspects to the man and the less important, inferior matters to the woman. God's plan was extremely desirable for us . . . so that a woman would not rebel against the husband due to the inferiority of her service.[17]

The early church fathers set a pattern for the history of the church, which certainly continued to be a pattern in the patriarchal structures of the medieval church. Ruth Tucker and Walter Liefeld point out that Thomas Aquinas, the greatest medieval theologian, believed that women were inferior, dependent, dominated by sexual appetites, and unfit for any important role in society or in the church. Thus, Thomas Aquinas argued, as did all medieval male theologians, that women should be subordinate and submissive to men in virtually all matters.[18]

The implications of such views meant that women were often demeaned, harassed, and abused. Both civil and church law codes permitted wife beating, although church law often stressed that such physical punishment should be done only with reason. Although extreme, the 1486 *Witches' Hammer* represents the ultimate denigration of women as completely inferior and as willing to cohabit with demons. As Tucker and Liefeld observe, "Indeed, the witchcraft frenzy of the late Middle Ages was one of the most sexist atrocities to have occurred in all of history."[19]

Contemporary Expressions of the Evangelical View of Male Headship

It is not possible here to give a complete survey of various expressions of the contemporary evangelical view supporting male headship and female submission, nor is it necessary. Some of the major proponents of this view will serve to express it well and clearly.

Robert D. Culver's essay "A Traditional View: Let Your Women Keep Silence" is a forthright presentation of the evangelical traditionalist view. Culver finds that the New Testament strongly supports male headship and leadership, concluding the New Testament section of his article with a citation of H. D. M. Spence in the nineteenth-century Ellicott commentary on the Bible: "The catastrophe of Eden is the beacon for all generations when the sexes repeat the folly of Eve and Adam, and exchange their distinctive position and function."[20] Culver finds that the Old Testament supports male leadership and sees Deborah as "no precedent," and the few prophetesses, whom he does not name, as "exceptional."[21] Near the end of his article, Culver makes several general comments arising out of his mention of the phrase "he shall rule over thee" in Genesis 3:16 (KJV):

> With occasional exceptions, this is the way it has always been and likely always will be. . . . it is a statement of fact, which neither the Industrial Revolution nor the feminist movement is likely to overturn. . . . The radical feminists should give up and quit. Normal, universal, female human nature is against them. Most women prefer things the way they are, at least wherever biblical norms have prevailed. . . . Male ascendancy in most affairs is not a legal ordinance to be obeyed; it is a fact to be acknowledged. . . . Ordinarily the authority of adults over other adults *ought* to be by men and almost certainly will be. The

scriptural standard for male leadership of churches is even stronger.[22]

Susan T. Foh's essay "A Male Leadership View: The Head of the Woman Is the Man" also supports male headship and female submission, although she explicitly attempts to distinguish her view from that of Culver.[23] Foh's view of Genesis 1 and 2 stresses the complementary view of the relationship of men and women. She wants to stress what she calls "ontological equality" or "equality in being"; thus, she argues that Genesis 2 does not establish the inferiority of women. What Genesis 2 does establish is a difference of function and male leadership. She supports this with two observations: first, man was created first, which means that woman is dependent upon man; and second, according to her reading of Genesis 2:23, man named woman, establishing male authority. Foh then writes:

> Is God's arrangement fair? Our objections, whether philosophical or emotional, to this hierarchical system arise because we do not know what a sinless hierarchy is like. We know only the tyranny, willfulness and condescension that even the best boss-underling relationship has.[24]

I cannot help but wonder at this point in her argument what redemption and new creation in Christ ought to mean even now in the church; must it always and only be even there "tyranny, willfulness and condescension"? Foh's essay continues with a long survey of New Testament texts that she understands to support her perception of ontological equality and male headship coupled with female submission existing at the same time in the relationship of men and women in the church. Her view of Paul's remark that "there is no longer male and female" in Galatians 3:28 is that "the male-female distinction is . . . fundamental; God established it at creation, and it cannot be removed. . . . [Thus,] Galatians 3:28 does not annul the passages that teach the submission of women in the church or in marriage."[25]

I consider James B. Hurley's book *Man and Woman in Biblical Perspective* to be the single most important book on the New Testament by a New Testament scholar in defense of the traditionalist evangelical view of male headship and female submission. In my estimation, the most critical juncture in the whole book for the understanding of male headship occurs in Hurley's struggle with Paul's phrase "but the woman was deceived" in 1 Timothy 2:14 and its use of Genesis. Hurley states that "we may similarly dismiss the likelihood that Paul was saying that all women are gullible . . . and therefore are untrustworthy teachers."[26] Yet, and I struggle to be fair with Hurley, it seems that he goes on to present an argument which says, in essence, that all women are indeed gullible. Hurley states that Paul's point in 1 Timothy 2:14 could be paraphrased as follows:

> The man, upon whom lays responsibility for leadership in the home and in religious matters, was prepared by God to discern the serpent's lies. The woman was not appointed religious leader and was not prepared to discern them. She was taken in. Christian worship involves re-establishing the creational pattern with men faithfully teaching God's truth and women receptively listening.[27]

I find it difficult to understand this in any other way than as an assertion of male headship and female submission that is based on a view that God created women in such a way that they are gullible. In Hurley's words, "not appointed religious leader and . . . not prepared to discern . . . [the lies of the serpent]."[28]

A final example here would need to be, of course, the virtually official interpretive book of the Council of Biblical Manhood and Womanhood, *Recovering Biblical Manhood and Womanhood: A Response to Evangelical Feminism*, edited by John Piper and Wayne Grudem.[29] The editors wish to identify their position as one of complementarity, which I understand to be the position of Susan Foh described earlier. This position is held in distinction from what these persons identify as the traditionalist position, which they see as wrongly arguing for the inferiority of women. For example, the title of chapter three, written by Raymond C. Ortlund Jr., may be paradigmatic for this perspective: "Male-Female Equality and Male Headship: Genesis 1–3."

Nevertheless, as I read the Piper/Grudem/Council position, its view of male headship and female submission is certainly the traditional view in the history of the church. This volume develops these themes in careful detail through twenty-six essays divided into the five sections of the book. In my judgment, however, the most revealing comment in the entire volume about these issues comes in John Piper's opening essay entitled: "A Vision of Biblical Complementarity: Manhood and Womanhood Defined According to the Bible." Near the end of the chapter, Piper gives an illustration meant to clarify the "brink of contradiction" between his biblical-theological point about male headship and leadership and the social reality of women's leadership, or what Piper seems to want to call influence:

> It is simply impossible that from time to time a woman not be put in a position of influencing or guiding men. For example, a housewife in her backyard may be asked by a man how to get to the freeway. At that point she is giving a kind of leadership. She has superior knowledge that the man needs and he submits to her guidance. But we all know that there is a way for that housewife to direct the man that neither of them feels their mature femininity or masculinity compromised.[30]

It is difficult to comment on this. It seems far removed from the *biblical* issues and concerns about the relationship of men and women. In short, the comment seems to trivialize the issue.

Biblical and Hermeneutical Foci of the Debate

It is my judgment that the male headship/female submission issue in biblical interpretation, especially within the evangelical tradition, revolves primarily around a series of five separate (but clearly related) topics and texts.[31] These are, in what I perceive to be the order of their importance in the discussion and debate, the following: (1) the meaning of the term *kephale* (head; the term understood traditionally to indicate authority or headship), which also involves 1 Corinthians 11:2–16 and Ephesians 5:21–33, the two New Testament texts in which *kephale* is used with reference to the relationship of men and women; (2) the meaning of *authentein* (usually translated in Bibles as "to have authority

39

over") and its use in 1 Timothy 2:12 within the 1 Timothy 2:8–15 passage; (3) Genesis 1–3 and its interpretation with respect to the relationship of men and women; (4) the biblical examples of women in positions of some type of authority, including women in the Old Testament, the life of Jesus, and within Paul's ministry circle of leaders; and (5) the meaning of submission and silence for women mentioned in 1 Corinthians 14:34–35, and the place of that passage itself in the debate. It is not possible in this context, of course, to discuss all of these topics and texts; rather, this essay will focus only on the first two issues of these five, since they have involved the most intense, careful, and technical debates within evangelical circles. Further, it is not possible to discuss here all the interpretive issues in the biblical texts in which the terms *kephale* and *authentein* occur; the emphasis will be only on those precise points on which the so-called headship debate rests.

The Meaning of the Term Kephale

The modern discussion of the meaning of *kephale* for passages in the New Testament about the relationship of men and women goes back to the 1954 article of Stephen Bedale, who suggested that the metaphorical meaning of the term *kephale* could be "source" in some instances rather than the traditional sense of "authority over" or "leader."[32] Probably the first introductions of this perspective into the evangelical discussions came in the 1971 commentary of F. F. Bruce on 1 and 2 Corinthians and in the early evangelical feminist book of Letha Scanzoni and Nancy Hardesty, *All We're Meant to Be: A Biblical Approach to Women's Libera-tion*, published in 1974. Perhaps the most dramatic presentation of "source" as the understanding of *kephale* in these texts came with the two articles of Berkeley and Alvera Mickelsen in *Christianity Today* in 1979 and 1981.[33]

The challenge from the traditional side, arguing that *kephale* means "authority over" came from Wayne Grudem in 1985, with his famous article covering 2,336 examples of *kephale* in Greek literature. Grudem argues that *kephale* clearly means "authority over" or "ruler," and that it never means "source" or "origin."[34]

The next year, 1986, saw further escalation of the debate. Berkeley and Alvera Mickelsen's major article on *kephale* was published in the summer, with responses by Ruth A. Tucker and Philip Barton Payne. These were papers that had been presented at a conference in October 1984, so they do not enter into dialogue with Grudem's 1985 article. Essentially, the Mickelsens argue in detail for the meaning "source" or "origin" (and other nuances which do not come into the authority category). Tucker raises objections from the writings of theologians throughout the history of the church; Payne agrees with the Mickelsens but attempts to broaden, deepen, and refine their arguments.[35]

The 1986 meeting of the Evangelical Theological Society (its 38th annual meeting) was held in a suburb of Atlanta, and devoted considerable time to a debate over the meaning of *kephale,* with Wayne Grudem, Gilbert Bilezikian, and Catherine Clark Kroeger participating. *Christianity Today* reported on the meeting in a news article entitled "The Battle of the Lexicons." Grudem utilized his 1985 material. The presentations of Kroeger and Bilezikian were subsequently published in 1987 and 1990, respectively. Both Kroeger and Bilezikian argue as extensively for the meaning "source" as Grudem had for the meaning "authority over." Bilezikian's article responds to each one of Grudem's examples from Greek literature, text by text.[36]

Gordon D. Fee's thorough and excellent commentary on 1 Corinthians in the Evangelical New International Commentary on the New Testament series appeared in 1987. Fee includes a brief but sophisticated discussion of *kephale* under 1 Corinthians 11:3, utilizing the critical evangelical literature in the debate published to that time, even Kroeger's 1987 article. Fee concludes that *kephale* means "source," or "source of life."[37]

In 1989, Richard S. Cervin joined Kroeger and Bilezikian in critique of the work of Grudem. Cervin's work was published in *Trinity Journal,* in which Grudem's 1985 article had also appeared. Cervin also responds to each one of Grudem's examples text by text, and concludes against Grudem. He shows that *kephale* does not mean "authority over" in most cases cited by Grudem, and that it can mean "source." But Cervin concludes that in the New Testament texts at stake in the discussion, *kephale* has the meaning "preeminence," which he contends is its basic Hellenistic meaning. Cervin also responds to a 1989 article of Joseph A. Fitzmyer, which concluded independently of and without knowledge of Grudem that *kephale* means "authority over" in Greek literature and in 1 Corinthians 11.[38]

Grudem then responded in great detail to Cervin in the *Trinity Journal* in 1990, strongly reaffirming his 1985 position. There also appeared in 1990 an unpublished thesis on *kephale* by Terrence Alexander Crain at Murdoch University in Perth, Australia. Crain's work is not generally known. His findings, often in considerable dialogue with Grudem, generally support the meaning of "source" rather than "authority over" for *kephale*. Andrew T. Lincoln's interpretation in the *Evangelical Word Biblical Commentary* on Ephesians also appeared in 1990. In connection with Ephesians 5:23, Lincoln comments very briefly on *kephale*, noting only Grudem's 1985 article and the contributions of Fee and Kroeger. He concludes that *kephale* probably contains a mixture of the concepts of "source" and "authority over," concluding that it means "authority over" in Ephesians 1:22, 4:15, and 5:23. Finally, Craig Keener in 1992 discussed *kephale* in his book on Paul and women. Keener mentions most of the literature and provides a summary of Fee's conclusions, with which he expresses his agreement.[39]

What is the result of this two-decades-long debate within evangelical circles over the meaning of *kephale,* and how does it relate to the interpretation of 1 Corinthians 11:2–16 and Ephesians 5:21–33?[40] It is not likely that further progress can be made now in the analysis of the Greek word *kephale*; the evidence is in and has been sifted from various perspectives. It seems clear to me that the evidence shows the metaphorical meaning of *kephale* can be varied, including "authority over," "preeminence," and "source." It is, however, especially important to note that the Septuagint evidence rather clearly indicates that the Greek *kephale* was not normally used to translate the Hebrew *rosh* when the Hebrew term meant a ruler, leader, or someone in authority. This considerably weakens the argument that *kephale* in Hellenistic Greek means "authority over" or "ruler." In my judgment, Bilezikian and Crain have made this case especially well. Further, it seems clearly established that *kephale* can mean "source," as many (such as Kroeger, Fee, and others) have shown. Perhaps Fee has given the most succinct statement of the basic evidence.

However, and this is a very important point that so much of the *kephale* debate seems to ignore or to put aside, the determinative evidence for the meaning of *kephale* is its use and function in particular contexts. Thus, proving a range of meanings for *kephale* is important, especially against the undue limits argued by Grudem, but the critical issue is how *kephale* functions in 1 Corinthians 11:2–16 and in Ephesians 5:21–33.

Although 1 Corinthians 11:2–16 (especially in the allusions to Genesis 2 in verses 7–9) does reflect to some degree the traditional Jewish understanding of androcentrism, the passage as a whole provides considerable support both for an understanding of *kephale* as "source" and also for a genuine equality and mutuality between men and women in the church. The christological issue in the words "and God is the head of Christ" (11:3 NRSV) is better served in Pauline theology by the understanding "source" rather than by "authority over." Further, even the Genesis argument (11:7–9) fits very well with understanding *kephale* as "source." Paul's strong balancing statement (11:11–12), introduced by the emphatic adversative *plen*, makes clear that his intent "in the Lord" is for the mutuality (or equality) of men and women. Further, the clear recognition that women as well as men participate in prayer and prophecy (11:5) also underscores this understanding. Finally, the fact that Paul states (11:10) that women in the Lord who wear the proper cultural head covering do have active, positive authority (*exousia*) makes clear the authoritative participation of women in worship.[41]

Ephesians 5:21–33 certainly reflects the general Jewish and Greco-Roman understandings of marriage in which wives were understood to have the responsibility to submit to their husbands in all things, as Ephesians 5:24 indicates. However, it is clear that this cultural understanding of marriage is significantly qualified for those in Christ, so that the passage teaches an overarching concept of mutual submission. In this context, *kephale* hardly means "authority over," especially in the leadership and authority-bearing sense for husbands over wives given to it by so many of the traditionalist and complementarian interpreters. *Kephale* may mean "source" here, although it could just as likely mean "authority over," especially in light of the use of *kephale* in Ephesians 1:22 and 4:15.

43

Whatever *kephale* might precisely signify in Ephesians 5:21–33, the context makes it clear that it carries for those in Christ no authoritarian sense for men. The opening sentence (5:21 NRSV) is *the* theme of the passage: "Be subject to one another out of reverence for Christ." In addition, husbands are three times commanded to love their wives, an injunction that was not typical in first-century Mediterranean cultures. This injunction is explicitly modeled on Christ's relationship to the church, which is described totally and only in terms of self-giving activity. Thus, what Christ is to the church is the archetype for behavior within the believing community—subjection to one another out of reverence for Christ, a wife's submission to her husband as to the Lord, and a husband's love for his wife.[42]

The use of the term *kephale* in the New Testament texts about the relationship of men and women, understood in their own contexts, does not support the traditionalist or complementarity view of male headship and female submission as described by those authors noted earlier. Rather, this data supports a new understanding in Christ by which men and women are viewed in a mutually supportive, submissive relationship through which either men or women can bear and represent authority in the church.[43]

The Meaning of Authentein and 1 Timothy 2:8–15

The King James (Authorized) Version translated the verb *authentein* in 1 Timothy 2:12[44] as "usurp authority over" (see also the New English Bible translation: "domineer over"). The word *authentein* has frequently been understood as a general term for authority. Thus, the phrase "I permit no woman to teach or to have authority over a man; she is to keep silent" in 1 Timothy 2:12 has traditionally been understood as strong support for the male headship and female submission viewpoint. Such an understanding is replete in the literature surveyed earlier representing the traditional position within the evangelical tradition.

Whether 1 Timothy 2:8–15 supports a male headship view has, in the evangelical debate of the last fifteen years, revolved primarily around the discussion of the meaning of *authentein*. Although other significant issues are relevant—especially the use of Genesis in 2:13–14 and the nature of the heresy combatted in

1 and 2 Timothy and its bearing on the interpretation of the teaching and character of the passage (whether it is normative/universal or contingent/particular)—attention here will be focused on the *authentein* debate, which it turns out has been rather dramatic, especially in the last decade.[45]

What needs to be noted is that *authentein* is a very rare verb. Its only occurrence in the New Testament is at 1 Timothy 2:12. It is rare, too, in the Greek language outside of and prior to Paul, with less than forty examples of its use given in the standard New Testament Greek lexicon of Walter Bauer. It is only within the last few years on the basis of the Thesaurus Linguae Graecae (TLG) computer database project (which contains virtually all three thousand ancient Greek authors from Homer to A.D. 600) that we now know that this rare term and its cognates occur about 330 times, which means that it is still a relatively rare word.

The current evangelical debate may well have been initiated by Catherine Clark Kroeger's 1979 popular article in the *Reformed Journal*. Although Kroeger's article suggested a possible sexual connotation for *authentein* (a meaning that has never been adequately or significantly documented in my judgment), her article correctly and powerfully noted that *authentein* was not the usual word for positive authority, and that there was substantial evidence that it had a negative connotation, thus developing the alternative (second) translation of "domineer" given in Bauer's lexicon. Kroeger developed her discussion further in an article written in 1984 but published in 1986.[46]

Between 1981 and 1984, three studies appeared defending the traditional interpretation of *authentein*, understanding 1 Timothy 2:12 as a prohibition of normal, positive authority in the church to women. Two studies, those by A. J. Panning and C. D. Osburn, were relatively minor. However, the study of George A. Knight III published in 1984 in the prestigious *New Testament Studies* was a major contribution to and very strong defense of the traditional interpretation.[47]

Four years after Knight's article appeared, Leland Edward Wilshire published an article on *authentein* in the same *New Testament Studies*.[48] Wilshire's article was the first study to be able to use the TLG database, and so constituted for the first time a study of virtually all the evidence. This alone gave Wilshire's study great significance. The findings of Wilshire are critical and determinative for the discussion.

Wilshire found that in the classical Greek period (sixth to the fourth century B.C.) the word group almost exclusively means "a perpetrator of a violent act, either murder or suicide." In Hellenistic Greek, the period of Greek in which the New Testament was written, Wilshire found that "the word continues its meaning of murder or murderer. There is also beginning to appear a wider usage of the word, still revolving around personal involvement in a crime." Wilshire notes that with the church fathers, the term *authentein* begins to take on the meaning of "have authority over" without the negative connotations. He then observes: "There are authors, roughly contemporaneous with Paul (Apollonius Rhodius, Polybius, Diodorus Siculus, Flavius Josephus, Appian of Alexander, Philo Judaeus, LXX-Wis), who use the word almost exclusively with the meaning of 'to murder/murderer' or 'to perpetrate a crime/perpetrator of a crime.'"[49]

Thus, Wilshire's study and summary of the evidence clearly and strongly supports the view that *authentein* carries almost exclusively a negative meaning in Paul's Greek context, which would support the idea of "domineer," "usurp," or some such translation. Consequent upon this, the case is very strong on the basis of this term alone that 1 Timothy 2:8–15 is addressing a particular problem of abuse in the church, undoubtedly related to the false teaching/teachers opposed in 1 and 2 Timothy (as I argued in my 1986 article).

What struck me as strange and inexplicable when I read Wilshire's article in 1988 was the fact that, beyond his summaries of the evidence given above, his conclusions did not seem to flow out of his own evidence. At one point, he cautiously says that: "The conclusion by Knight that the recognized meaning for first century BC and AD documents is that of 'to have authority over' is increasingly to be questioned."[50] Rather than "increasingly to be questioned," I would have expected something like "shown to be incorrect." In the closing pages of his article, Wilshire seemed to give some weight to the view of the church fathers on *authentein* as if it were legitimate context for the meaning in 1 Timothy 2:12. He then finished the article with what seemed to me to be a very ambiguous statement about the meaning of *authentein* in 1 Timothy 2:12.

Paul W. Barnett, an Australian, was the first person known to me to use the work of Wilshire on *authentein* in a published article. Barnett, who is a strong evangelical supporter of the traditional position (excluding women from authority and leadership in the church), used Wilshire in support of his traditional position and interpretation of *authentein*, even though that is actually against the evidence Wilshire presented, as shown above. Barnett only briefly, and in my view quite inaccurately, summarizes the evidence presented by Wilshire, and then states:

> What, then, is Wilshire's conclusion? With due caution this scholar suggests that . . . it is the notion of 'authority' [meaning normal, positive authority] which is in the apostle's mind. In other words, Wilshire, while rejecting Knight's generalizations based on the small sample available to him, nonetheless appears to have reached the same conclusion, though this is implied rather than stated outright.[51]

Barnett has, in my judgment, done two things: He has actually misrepresented the evidence presented by Wilshire and yet he has correctly noted Wilshire's own ambiguities in drawing conclusions.

Barnett's work drew two fairly immediate responses, both from other Australians, published in 1990. Kevin Giles's response, actually presented at the same 1988 conference at which Barnett's paper was originally presented, correctly recognizes that Wilshire's data disproves Knight (and the traditional rendering of *authentein*), thus correcting (indirectly) Barnett's reading of Wilshire. Further, Giles also identified clearly Wilshire's own problematic conclusions: "All of the information needed to refute Knight is found in Wilshire's article, but his presentation of the data is at times hard to follow and his conclusion that we should take *authentein* in 1 Timothy 2:12 to mean 'authority' . . . can hardly be taken seriously."[52]

The other response came from Timothy J. Harris and was published in the same journal in which Barnett's article originally appeared. Harris calls attention to Knight, Wilshire, and to Barnett's use of them, but in rather brief terms. Without explicitly naming Wilshire, Harris criticizes the utilization of the church fathers' use of *authentein* in determining Paul's meaning of the term, which is what Wilshire appears to do.[53] Harris goes on to criticize Barnett at another, related, point. Barnett has a section in his 1989 article headed "Other Exegetical Approaches." Nevertheless, Barnett mentions for a short page and a half only Payne, Kroeger's first article on *authentein,* and Padgett; Harris scores Barnett for not also engaging Kroeger's later work, Fee, and Scholer.[54] By omitting these perspectives, the real nature of the debate is skewed.

In 1992, Richard Clark Kroeger and Catherine Clark Kroeger published their long-awaited book, *I Suffer Not a Woman: Rethinking 1 Timothy 2:11–15 in Light of Ancient Evidence.* Part 2 of this book features a lengthy study of *authentein.* The Kroegers, who mysteriously and unfortunately do not mention at all Wilshire's 1988 study (as well as several other articles on the 1 Timothy passage), conclude that *authentein* has at its core the concept of "origination" or "source." They translate 1 Timothy 2:12, then, in this way: "I do not permit a woman . . . to represent herself as originator of man."[55] They understand the cultural-social context to be a fusion of gnostic and pagan "feminism" in Ephesus, which promoted the idea that woman was, in fact, the source of man. Thus, Paul attempts to correct that false teaching in 1 Timothy 2:13 by reference to Genesis 2 and the priority of man's creation. It is very debatable, in my judgment, whether or not the social-cultural construction of the Kroegers is correct. Although their discussion of *authentein* is fascinating, it does not appear to have marshalled the evidence in as convincing a way as has Wilshire.[56] Of course, the ultimate thrust of the Kroegers' book I believe to be correct—1 Timothy 2 is a culturally limited text and does not exclude women from the legitimate exercise of authority in the church.

In 1993, at least three more evangelical publications dealt with the *authentein* debate. A. Wolters, in a review of the Kroegers' book, uses the 1988 article of Wilshire, understanding it (incorrectly) to support the traditional understanding of *authentein* as legitimate authority.[57]

A. C. Perriman also published a substantial article on *authentein* in another evangelical journal.[58] Perriman notes the problem of Wilshire's ambiguous 1988 conclusions, as well as noting the

Barnett/Wilshire 1989/1993 exchange with Wilshire's clarifications. Perriman argues that "authorship" not "authority" is at the heart of the meaning of *authentein* (but in a sense different from that argued by the Kroegers, whom he extensively critiques). Perriman understands that in 1 Timothy 2:12, *authentein* refers to women "initiating" or "perpetrating" something on men, which he understands, correctly I believe, to be the heretical teaching that 1 Timothy was written to oppose. Thus, 1 Timothy 2 is not an exclusion of women from the exercise of legitimate authority in the church. Perriman has made a good case, but it is not clear to me whether the distinctions he draws are actual or substantial differences from the evidence as presented by Wilshire in 1988.

Finally, Leland E. Wilshire published in 1993 a "correction" to his 1988 article in the same journal in which the Barnett and Harris articles appeared. Wilshire was now responding explicitly to the use of his landmark 1988 study. For our purposes here the first section of his article may be the most interesting; it is entitled "Misunderstandings." Wilshire says that Barnett "has made me say something that I scrupulously did not say," quoting the same section of Barnett on Wilshire's conclusions quoted earlier in this paper. Wilshire goes on to say: "Barnett has taken my utmost caution in dealing with philology to arrive at conclusions unwarranted by the evidence and neither stated, explicitly or implicitly, by myself." Wilshire finally says that his study differed from Knight's at all crucial points and that, therefore, "it is a grave misunderstanding to think that we arrived at the same conclusions."[59] I continue to think that Wilshire himself is the cause of some of the misunderstanding of his 1988 article, but I am delighted that he has now made it explicitly clear that he was misunderstood, and that Barnett's use of his study was a misrepresentation of the evidence and of his intention.

Wilshire goes on in his 1993 article to speak clearly about the meaning of *authentein*—its specific meaning in 1 Timothy 2:12, and its implications for the headship debate and the place of women in the church. He concludes for the term *authentein* and its cognates that "the preponderant number of citations . . . have to do with self willed violence, criminal action, or murder or with the person who does these actions."[60] He notes that the infinitival form of *authentein*, which is used in 1 Timothy 2:12, does not occur in Greek literature prior to Paul. The meaning of *authentein* in 1 Timothy 2:12 Wilshire gives as "instigating violence."[61] Wilshire is unclear on the precise social and rhetorical intent of the term in its context, but does suggest one major option, which happens to be my own conclusion, that the widows of 1 Timothy 5 who were speaking on behalf of the false teachers are here told not to instigate violence in the church, but to be silent. Wilshire notes other readings and comes to no firm conclusion. Wilshire does, however, draw a clear application based on his study:

> Does the term *authentein* in I Tim. 2:12 have to do with exercising ecclesiastical power or ecclesiastical authority? The answer is probably not. . . . Both men and women are created good, are to be received with thanksgiving, and by being consecrated by the word of God and prayer, are set free to serve their Lord in the church and in the world.[62]

The "final" chapter in this debate (for now) is Paul W. Barnett's 1994 brief counterresponse, in the same journal, to Wilshire's "correction." Here Barnett reaffirms his previous reading of Wilshire's 1988 article (again clearly noting Wilshire's ambiguity), recognizes that Wilshire's 1993 article explicitly and clearly supports a negative meaning for *authentein,* and rejects that interpretation.[63]

This interpretive survey of the recent debate on *authentein* virtually speaks for itself. I am convinced that the evidence is in and that it clearly establishes *authentein* as a negative term, indicating violence and inappropriate behavior. Thus, what Paul does not allow for women in 1 Timothy 2 is this type of behavior. Therefore, the text is not a transcultural, normative establishment of male headship and leadership with the concomitant view of female submission. I understand the impact of these further studies of *authentein* to support and establish more clearly the view I and many others have expressed that 1 Timothy 2 is opposing the negative behavior of women, probably the women mentioned in 1 Timothy 5:15 who follow and represent the false teachers 1 and 2 Timothy are dedicated to opposing.

Conclusion and Implications

In full recognition of the complexity of the exegetical and hermeneutical issues relevant to the so-called headship debate within evangelical circles, I am fully convinced that the Bible does not institute, undergird, or teach male headship and female submission, in either the traditionalist or complementarian forms of evangelical thought, which exclude women from equal participation in authority with men within the body of Christ, whether in ministry or marriage or any other dimension of life. Rather, the Bible affirms, supports, and teaches by precept and example a mutuality or equality in Christ for women and men, both in ministry and in marriage. This is what is rightfully called evangelical feminism, although I fully realize that the term "feminism" creates conceptual and emotional difficulties for some people.

Because the Bible, and in particular the New Testament, affirms, supports, and teaches a genuine mutuality and equality in Christ, I believe this position should actively, even aggressively—in the Pauline sense of gospel obligation—be taught and acted upon in the church. This requires commitment and understanding, sensitivity and patience, love and forgiveness, humility and courage.

The exceedingly difficult bridge to cross is whether or not this commitment is *part* of the gospel. In other (radical) words, drawing the analogy of the assessment of apartheid in South Africa, is the lack of this commitment only ethical misunderstanding and moral failure, or is it heresy, a perversion of the gospel? I am dedicated to understanding this commitment as part of the gospel, especially on the basis of the inclusion of women in the call and ministry of both Jesus and Paul. In saying this, I am fearful of placing myself in the position of judging others without humility or sensitivity; that I do not want to do. In other words, I would call no one a heretic, but I would call an expression of the gospel that excludes women in any way or sense from equality with men in Christ in status, response, action, and ministry a misguided form of the gospel as presented in the New Testament.

Given these convictions, I believe it is critical within the evangelical debate over male headship and within the social context in which we live to commit ourselves with gospel vigilance to speak out, to act fearlessly against the abuse of women, and to do all within our ability to make certain that biblical misinterpretation and misrepresentation is never used or allowed to be used—even indirectly, implicitly, or unconsciously—to justify, by men or women, the abuse of women anywhere, but especially within the household of faith.[64]

Notes

1. This Bible was also printed in 1551. For the technical data see A. S. Herbert, *Historical Catalogue of Printed Editions of The English Bible 1525–1961* (London: The British and Foreign Bible Society; New York: The American Bible Society, 1968), entries 74 (pp. 40–41) and 93 (p. 52); and William J. Chamberlin, *Catalogue of English Bible Translations: A Classified Bibliography of Versions and Editions Including Books, Parts, and Old and New Testament Apocrypha and Apocryphal Books,* Bibliographies and Indexes in Religious Studies 21 (New York: Greenwood, 1991), 5–6.

2. The citation of the note is taken from F. F. Bruce, *The English Bible: A History of Translations from the Earliest English Versions to the New English Bible,* 2d ed. (New York: Oxford University Press, 1970), 83–84. Bruce gives only the 1551 publication date; see also the reference to Becke's note in Geddes MacGregor, *A Literary History of the Bible: From the Middle Ages to the Present Day* (Nashville: Abingdon, 1968), 134 (the publication date is incorrectly given as August 16, 1549).

3. Susan Brooks Thistlethwaite, "Battered Women and the Bible: From Subjection to Liberation," *Christianity & Crisis* 41, no. 18 (16 November 1981): 308–13. Also Marie Marshall Fortune, *Sexual Violence: The Unmentionable Sin* (New York: Pilgrim Press, 1983), 191–217; see also Fortune's *Keeping the Faith: Questions and Answers for the Abused Woman* (San Francisco: Harper & Row, 1967), 13–21; and her *Is Nothing Sacred? When Sex Invades the Pastoral Relationship* (San Francisco: HarperSanFrancisco, 1989).

4. Rita-Lou Clarke, *Pastoral Care of Battered Women* (Philadelphia: Westminster, 1986), 61–85; see also her article "The Bible and Battered Women," *Daughters of Sarah* 15, no. 3 (May/June 1989): 18–19.

Kay Marshall Strom, *In the Name of Submission: A Painful Look at Wife Battering* (Portland: Multnomah Press, 1986), 49–58.

Margaret Josephson Rinck, *Christian Men Who Hate Women: Healing Hurting Relationships* (Grand Rapids: Zondervan, 1990), 71–75, 81–86.

James and Phyllis Alsdurf, *Battered into Submission: The Tragedy of Wife Abuse in the Christian Home* (Downers Grove, Ill.: InterVarsity Press, 1989); see especially chapter 6, "Wife Abuse and the Submission of Women," 81–95.

Carolyn Holderread Heggen, *Sexual Abuse in Christian Homes and Churches* (Scottdale, Pa.: Herald Press, 1993); see especially chapter 5, "Religious Beliefs and Abuse," 82–97.

See also Elizabeth S. Bowman, "When Theology Leads to Abuse," *Update: Newsletter of the Evangelical Women's Caucus* 12, no. 4 (winter 1988/1989): 1–4; and Sarah J. Couper, "Prelude to Equality: Recognizing Oppression," in *Gender Matters: Women's Studies for the Christian Community,* ed. June Steffensen Hagen (Grand Rapids: Zondervan, 1990), 249–63, especially 256–63. The literature cited in this article from the last fifteen years is, of course, not an attempt to provide a complete bibliography. Rather, I have noted the most important contributions both from the Christian church in general and the evangelical movement in particular.

5. James L. Franklin, "Clergy Vows New Support for Victims of Battering," *Boston Globe,* 14 November 1993, p. 1, 28.

6. John Piper and Wayne Grudem, eds., *Recovering Biblical Manhood and Womanhood: A Response to Evangelical Feminism* (Wheaton: Crossway Books, 1991), 470.

7. Ibid., 62.

8. James A. Borland, "Women in the Life and Teaching of Jesus," in *Recovering Biblical Manhood and Womanhood,* 113–23. The specific sentence is on p. 114.

9. The footnote is number 13 on p. 501 (and is referred to again in note 19 on p. 502); the article is on pp. 194–208.

10. Carolyn Osiek, *Beyond Anger: On Being a Feminist in the Church* (New York/Mahwah: Paulist, 1985). The quotations here are from pp. 68–70.

11. Augustine, *Confessions* 9.9, quoted in Elizabeth A. Clark, *Women in the Early Church,* vol. 13, *Message of the Fathers of the Church* (Wilmington, Del.: Michael Glazier, 1983), 252–53.

12. Augustine, *Literal Commentary on Genesis* 9.5, quoted in Clark, 28–29.

13. Augustine, *Literal Commentary on Genesis* 11.42, quoted in Clark, 40.

14. Augustine, *Letter 262,* quoted in Clark, 65–69.

15. Tertullian, *On the Dress of Women* 1.1.1 for the short quotation; 1.1.2 for the long quotation, quoted in Clark, 39.

16. John Chrysostom, *Discourse 2 on Genesis* 2, quoted in Clark, 35–36.

17. John Chrysostom, *The Kind of Women Who Ought To Be Taken As Wives* 4, quoted in Clark, 37.

18. Ruth Tucker and Walter Liefeld, *Daughters of the Church: Women and Ministry from New Testament Times to the Present* (Grand Rapids: Zondervan, 1987), 164–65.

19. Ibid., 165–70. The quotation is from p. 166.

20. Robert D. Culver, "A Traditional View: Let Your Women Keep Silence," in *Women in Ministry: Four Views,* Bonnidell Clouse and Robert G. Clouse, eds. (Downers Grove, Ill.: InterVarsity, 1989), 37; quoting from Charles John Ellicott, *A Biblical Commentary for English Readers,* vol. 8 (London: Cassell, n.d.), 188.

21. Culver, "A Traditional View," 38.

22. Ibid., 41–42.

23. Susan T. Foh, "A Male Leadership View: The Head of the Woman Is the Man," in *Women in Ministry,* 67–105; see her critique of Culver in the same volume, pp. 53–54.

24. Ibid., 73.

25. Ibid., 89.

26. James B. Hurley, *Man and Woman in Biblical Perspective* (Grand Rapids: Zondervan, 1981), 215. On the same page Hurley similarly writes, "I think it very unlikely that Paul meant to say that . . . all women are too gullible to teach." See my essay review of Hurley: "Hermeneutical Gerrymandering: Hurley on Women and Authority," *TSF Bulletin* 6, no. 5 (May/June 1983): 11–13.

27. Ibid., 216.

28. I have discussed this point concerning Hurley, as well as articles by Douglas Moo ("1 Timothy 2:11–15: Meaning and Significance," *Trinity Journal* 1 [1980]: 62–83;

and "The Interpretation of 1 Timothy 2:11–15: A Rejoinder," *Trinity Journal* 2 [1981]: 198–222), in my "1 Timothy 2:9–15 and the Place of Women in the Church's Ministry," in *Women, Authority, and the Bible,* ed. Alvera Mickelsen (Downers Grove, Ill.: InterVarsity, 1986), 193–219. The specific discussion of Hurley and Moo is on pp. 211–12. See also Philip B. Payne's critique of Moo in "Libertarian Women in Ephesus: A Response to Douglas J. Moo's Article, '1 Timothy 2:11–15: Meaning and Significance,'" *Trinity Journal* 2 (1981): 169–97.

29. Piper and Grudem, eds., *Recovering Biblical Manhood and Womanhood.* The copyright is held by the Council on Biblical Manhood and Womanhood.

30. Ibid., 50. The entire chapter 1 covers pp. 31–59.

31. I have treated some of these issues before in a very brief article: "Male Headship: God's Intention or Man's Invention?" *WATCHword* 12, no. 1 (February/March 1988): 3–4, 7.

32. Stephen Bedale, "The Meaning of *kephale* in the Pauline Epistles," *Journal of Theological Studies* 5 (1954): 211–15.

33. F. F. Bruce, *1 and 2 Corinthians,* New Century Bible (London: Marshall, Morgan and Scott, 1971), 103, with credit to Bedale.

Letha Scanzoni and Nancy Hardesty, *All We're Meant to Be: A Biblical Approach to Women's Liberation* (Waco: Word Books, 1974), 30–31, 100. The second edition appeared in 1986 as *All We're Meant To Be: Biblical Feminism for Today* (Nashville: Abingdon), where the parallel pages are pp. 42–46, 121–22. The third edition appeared in 1992 with the same title as the second edition (Grand Rapids: William B. Eerdmans), where the parallel pages are pp. 33–37, 149–50.

Berkeley and Alvera Mickelsen, "Does Male Dominance Tarnish Our Translations?" *Christianity Today* 22 (5 October 1979), 1312–18; and "The 'Head' of the Epistles," *Christianity Today* 24 (20 February 1981), 264–67.

34. Wayne Grudem, "Does *kephale* ('Head') Mean 'Source' or 'Authority Over' in Greek Literature? A Survey of 2,336 Examples," published as appendix 1 in George W. Knight III, *The Role Relationship of Men and Women: New Testament Teaching,* 2d ed. (Chicago: Moody, 1985), 49–80. Knight's first edition was entitled *The New Testament Teaching on the Role Relationship of Men and Women* (1977). Grudem's article was also reprinted in *Trinity Journal* 6 (1985), 38–59.

35. Berkeley and Alvera Mickelsen, "What Does *kephale* Mean in the New Testament?" in *Women, Authority, and the Bible,* 97–110, with Ruth A. Tucker's response (pp. 111–17) and Philip Barton Payne's response (pp. 118–32). The October 9–11, 1984, conference was held in Oak Brook, Illinois, and was organized by Stanley N. Gundry, Catherine Clark Kroeger, and David M. Scholer.

36. David Neff, "The Battle of the Lexicons," *Christianity Today* 31, no. 1 (16 January 1987), 44–45. Catherine Clark Kroeger, "The Classical Concept of *Head* as 'Source,'" Appendix 3 in Gretchen Gaebelein Hull, *Equal To Serve: Women and Men in the Church and Home* (Old Tappan, N.J.: Fleming H. Revell, 1987), 267–83; Gilbert Bilezikian, "A Critical Examination of Wayne Grudem's Treatment of *kephale* in Ancient Greek Texts," appendix in Gilbert Bilezikian, *Beyond Sex Roles: What the Bible Says About a Woman's Place in Church and Family,* 2d ed. (Grand Rapids: Baker, 1990), 215–52.

37. Gordon D. Fee, *The First Epistle to the Corinthians,* New International Commentary on the New Testament (Grand Rapids: William B. Eerdmans, 1987), 502–3.

38. Richard S. Cervin, "Does *kephale* Mean 'Source' or 'Authority Over' in Greek Literature? A Rebuttal," *Trinity Journal* 10 (1989): 85–112. Joseph A. Fitzmyer,

"Another Look at kephale in 1 Corinthians 11:3," New Testament Studies 35 (1989): 503–11. Fitzmyer's article has been reprinted as "The Meaning of kephale in 1 Corinthians 11:3," chapter 6 in J. A. Fitzmyer, According to Paul: Studies in the Theology of the Apostle (New York: Paulist, 1993), 80–88 (in which he does take note of Grudem and Cervin). Fitzmyer has reasserted his view in another article, "Kephale in 1 Corinthians 11:3," Interpretation 47 (1993): 52–59. Fitzmyer, a prominent Roman Catholic scholar, discusses kephale in the work of various non-evangelical New Testament scholars, some of whom also have argued for the meaning "source."

39. Wayne Grudem, "The Meaning of kephale ('Head'): A Response to Recent Studies," Trinity Journal 11 (1990): 3–72. This is reprinted as appendix 1 to the Piper/Grudem volume (1991), 425–68. Richard S. Cervin has prepared a response (1991), which has not been published (I have the 39-page manuscript copy from Cervin).

Terrence Alexander Crain, "The Linguistic Background to the Metaphoric Use of kephale in the New Testament." (I was the external examiner for this thesis, which explains my acquaintance with it. It has not yet played a role in the public scholarly discussion.)

Andrew T. Lincoln, Ephesians, Word Biblical Commentary 42 (Dallas: Word, 1990), 368–69; and Craig S. Keener, Paul, Women, and Wives: Marriage and Women's Ministry in the Letters of Paul (Peabody: Hendrickson, 1992), 33–34.

40. See the useful summary presentation of views on headship given in an appendix to her book by Elaine Storkey, What's Right with Feminism (London: SPCK, 1985/Grand Rapids: William B. Eerdmans, 1986), 180–83.

41. For details of exegesis on 1 Corinthians 11:2–16, see the commentaries of Fee (pp. 491–530) and of Bruce (pp. 102–8). Bruce's comment on 11:10 is worth citing: "In Christ she received equality of status with man: she might pray or prophesy at meetings of the church, and her veil was a sign of this new authority" (p. 106).

42. See R. Wall, "Wifely Submission in the Context of Ephesians," Christian Scholar's Review 17 (1988): 272–85.

43. For some further discussion of 1 Corinthians 11:2–16 and Ephesians 5:21–33, see my "Feminist Hermeneutics and Evangelical Biblical Interpretation," Journal of the Evangelical Theological Society 30 (1987): 407–20, especially pp. 415–17. This article was reprinted in the Evangelical Review of Theology 15 (1991): 305–20, and was abbreviated as "How Can Divine Revelation Be So Human? A Look at Feminist Hermeneutics," Daughters of Sarah 15, no. 3 (May/June 1989): 11–15.

At the April 15–16, 1994 conference, A. C. Perriman (currently from Amsterdam, The Netherlands) gave me copies of two of his articles on kephale, unpublished at that time: "The Head of a Woman: The Meaning of kephale in 1 Corinthians 11:3" and "Headship and Submission: Disputing the Excuse for Abuse." In these articles, Perriman argues that kephale is best understood in the sense of "prominence," a conclusion very similar to that of R. S. Cervin. Perriman argues strongly for the equality of men and women in the church and all forms of its ministry; he also directly confronts the abuse of women in the name of alleged understandings of kephale.

44. See my extensive article of a decade ago on this text: "1 Timothy 2:9–15 and the Place of Women in the Church's Ministry," in Women, Authority, and the Bible, 193–219; abridged as "Women in the Church's Ministry: Does 1 Timothy 2:9–15 Help or Hinder?" Daughters of Sarah 16, no. 4 (July/August 1990): 7–12.

45. In addition to my own article cited in the previous note, for other representative evangelical discussions of the issues of the use of Genesis and of heresy and the consequent nature of the passage, see the articles by Moo and Payne mentioned in note

28; Douglas Moo, "What Does It Mean Not To Teach or Have Authority Over Men?: 1 Timothy 2:11–15," in Piper/Grudem, 179–93; Hurley, 195–223; Gordon D. Fee, "Issues in Evangelical Hermeneutics, Part III: The Great Watershed—Intentionality and Particularity: 1 Timothy 2:8–15 as a Test Case," *Crux* 26, no. 4 (1990): 31–37, reprinted as "The Great Watershed—Intentionality and Particularity-Eternality: 1 Timothy 2:8–15," in Gordon D. Fee, *Gospel and Spirit: Issues in New Testament Hermeneutics* (Peabody: Hendrickson, 1991), 52–65; A. Padgett, "Wealthy Women at Ephesus: 1 Timothy 2:8–15 in Social Context," *Interpretation* 41 (1987): 19–31; Keener, 101–32; and Richard Clark Kroeger and Catherine Clark Kroeger, *I Suffer Not a Woman: Rethinking 1 Timothy 2:11–15 in Light of Ancient Evidence* (Grand Rapids: Baker, 1992).

46. Catherine Clark Kroeger, "Ancient Heresies and a Strange Greek Verb," *Reformed Journal* 29, no. 3 (March 1979): 12–15. Catherine Clark Kroeger, "1 Timothy 2:12—A Classicist's View," in *Women, Authority, and the Bible,* 225–44, with pp. 229–32 particularly devoted to *authentein.* Kroeger does mention the 1984 article of Knight, but it had appeared too recently for her to have taken full account of it in this article. See also Kroeger's "Women in the Church: A Classicist's View of 1 Timothy 2:11–15," *Journal of Biblical Equality* 1 (1989): 3–31. See note 55 for extensive, further work on *authentein* by Kroeger.

47. A. J. Panning, "*Authentein*—a Word Study," *Wisconsin Lutheran Quarterly* 78 (1981): 185–91; and C. D. Osburn, "*Authentein* (1 Timothy 2:12)," *Restoration Quarterly* 25 (1982): 1–12. George A. Knight III, "*Authenteo* in Reference to Women in 1 Timothy 2:12," *New Testament Studies* 30 (1984): 143–57. Knight mentions only briefly his own study and the study of Wilshire in his *The Pastoral Epistles: A Commentary on the Greek Text,* New International Greek Testament Commentary (Grand Rapids: William B. Eerdmans/Carlisle: Paternoster, 1992), 141–42.

48. Leland Edward Wilshire, "The TLG Computer and Further Reference to *authentein* in 1 Timothy 2:12," *New Testament Studies* 34 (1988): 120–34.

49. The three citations in this paragraph are from Wilshire, 122, 123, and 130.

50. Ibid., 124.

51. Paul W. Barnett, "Wives and Women's Ministry (1 Timothy 2:11–15)," *Evangelical Quarterly* 61 (1989): 232. The article is reprinted in a virtually identical form as "Women in the Church with Special Reference to 1 Timothy 2," in *The Bible and Women's Ministry: An Australian Dialogue,* ed. Alan Nichols (Wanniassa, ACT: Acron Press, 1990), 49–64, without any mention of the *Evangelical Quarterly* form of the article. The article was first presented as a paper in May 1988 in Kurrajong, New South Wales, at a conference of the Evangelical Fellowship in the Anglican Communion (Australia). The *Evangelical Quarterly* article was also reprinted in the *Evangelical Review of Theology* 15 (1991): 321–34.

52. Kevin Giles, "Response," *The Bible and Women's Ministry,* ed. Nichols, 65–87; the specific discussion of *authentein* and the quotation are from p. 75. For the record, it should be said that Kevin Giles and I had discussed Wilshire's article in early 1988.

53. Timothy J. Harris, "Why Did Paul Mention Eve's Deception? A Critique of P. W. Barnett's Interpretation of 1 Timothy 2," *Evangelical Quarterly* 62 (1990): 342–43. Harris had earlier critiqued very briefly Knight's 1984 article on *authentein* in his (Harris's) "The Buck Stops Where? Authority in the Early Church and Current Debate on Women's Ministry," *Interchange* 41 (1987): 21–33, especially p. 32.

54. Ibid., 350–51.

55. Richard Clark Kroeger and Catherine Clark Kroeger, *I Suffer Not a Woman: Rethinking 1 Timothy 2:11–15 in Light of Ancient Evidence* (Grand Rapids: Baker, 1992), 103. Part 2, "The Prohibition" (1 Tim. 2:12), constitutes pp. 77–113 of the book.

56. See my review of the Kroegers' book in *Themelios* 20, no. 2 (January 1995), 30–31. Other reviews of the book, basically by evangelicals, are those of R. H. Finger, *Daughters of Sarah* 19, no. 4 (fall 1993): 50–52; R. Oster, *Biblical Archaeologist* 56 (1993): 225–27; J. F. Watson, *Ashland Theological Journal* 24 (1992): 121–22; A. Wolters, *Calvin Theological Journal* 28 (1993): 208–13; and R. W. Yarbrough, *Presbyterion* 18 (1992): 25–33. See also the article of A. C. Perriman, cited in note 58, especially pp. 132–34. See also L. E. Wilshire cited in note 62.

57. A. Wolters, *Calvin Theological Journal* 28 (1993): 208–13, especially p. 211.

58. A. C. Perriman, "What Eve Did, What Women Shouldn't Do: The Meaning of *authentein* in 1 Timothy 2:12," *Tyndale Bulletin* 44 (1993): 129–42.

59. Leland E. Wilshire, "1 Timothy 2:12 Revisited: A Reply to Paul W. Barnett and Timothy J. Harris," *Evangelical Quarterly* 65 (1993): 44 (all three quotations).

60. Ibid., 47.

61. Ibid., 48.

62. Ibid., 52–53. It may be noted that Wilshire has a brief addendum at the end of his article (pp. 53–54), in which he gives his critique of the Kroegers' book on 1 Timothy 2 (see note 55), especially objecting to the fact that it does not utilize his 1988 article on *authentein*, but also noting that there is much to commend in the book.

63. Paul W. Barnett, "*Authentein* Once More: A Response to L. E. Wilshire," *Evangelical Quarterly* 66 (1994): 159–62.

64. This essay, here in a slightly revised form, was prepared as an invited paper, presented on April 16, 1994, for the "Women, Abuse, and the Bible" consultation sponsored by Christians for Biblical Equality, April 15–16, 1994, Chicago O'Hare Marriott, Chicago, Illinois.

3

Clergy Sexual Abuse

Diane Langberg

T he topic of sexual abuse as perpetrated by members of the clergy is relatively new. I do not believe that the occurrence of such abuse is new, but rather the disclosure and discussion of that abuse is new. I do not want simply to repeat what has already been written, but rather to build on it. I would like to step back a little and consider this topic through a broader lens.

I come to this subject with a heart that is heavy for the body of Christ, as well as for both the perpetrators and the victims as they are very, very broken indeed. And if you believe God's Word to be true as I do, then you and I are profoundly affected by that brokenness. God's Word says, "If one member suffers, all the members suffer with it" (1 Cor. 12:26 NASB). Therefore, it is for the sake of the church of Jesus Christ that I approach this sad and complex subject, with humility and with dependence on God's Spirit for wisdom, for we are talking about something very near to his heart.

We would be naive to assume that this is simply a male problem. Women are just as fallen as men, and when placed in leadership positions are just as capable of abusing their followers. For the most part, women have been protected from the abuse of power because we have not held positions of power. Still, we must not assume that women are immune to those abuses.

Good physicians do not assume that the part of the human body that is experiencing pain or failing to function properly is necessarily the cause of the difficulty. Medicine has realized that focusing on symptoms alone, or on a dysfunctional part in isolation from the rest of the body, will, at best, bring short-term relief. Aristotle pointed this out many years ago when he suggested that many diseases escape us because we never see the whole.

We are in danger of making a similar mistake of being so focused on the clergy who abuse their congregants that we miss those larger contributing factors of which clergy sexual abuse is symptomatic. The abuse is so devastating and horrifying to most of us that we run the risk of jumping in to deal with the perpetrator and his victim (who obviously need our immediate response) while excluding those factors that will breed yet another repetition of the problem.

In my own field of psychology, family systems theory says that to try to "cure" a person in isolation from his or her family is as problematic as transplanting an organ into a body whose chemical imbalance will destroy the new one as effectively as it did the old. If the church is repeatedly experiencing abuse by its shepherds, certainly something is wrong with those shepherds who perpetrate such abuse. However, to stop there is naive and ultimately damaging to the church, for the church that produces and breeds such shepherds is also sick.

Several factors help create a fertile environment for sexual abuse to occur within the body of Christ, and so I think we need to consider what we might call the components of that environment. When plants fail, there are many points along the way that need to be evaluated as possibly contributing to that failure. To find sexual abuse perpetrated by a shepherd in the church of Jesus Christ toward some of the sheep is indeed a crop failure. Many things must be wrong for such an appalling, heartbreaking phenomenon to occur. I believe one of the problems is poison in the soil. As we look at three factors of that poison that I believe make clergy sexual abuse more likely, keep in mind that there are many other valid angles from which we might approach this problem. It is my hope that what is said in this paper will be enlarged upon and worked into the broader topics of abuse, incestuous family dynamics, and other closely related areas.

The three areas that I would like us to consider are: first, how we in this society have come to define the role of leader; second, how our current understanding of power coupled with our definition of leadership fosters pathology; and third, how a scriptural understanding of leadership and power are safeguards against clergy sexual abuse. And finally, because I believe that the ultimate victim of clergy sexual abuse is the church itself, I want to challenge the body of Christ.

Defining the Role of the Leader

We live in a society that has certain expectations for those in leadership, and sadly, much of the church has adopted the world's definition of a good leader. Edwin Friedman (1985) maintains that good leadership is defined by two qualities today: expertise and charisma.

Expertise

We will first consider expertise, which is the quality that forces those in leadership positions to define themselves in terms of their abilities. A good leader is someone who is an expert, who is perpetually acquiring more information and demonstrating it by ever-increasing proficiency. A pastor, then, is one who demonstrates expertise in teaching, preaching, counseling, budget planning, administrating, socializing, and mediating. The more adequate he appears in these areas, the more he is declared a success. Leadership is reduced to a never-ending treadmill of acquiring better and better skills.

Again according to Friedman (1985), this definition of leadership as expertise creates a secondary problem. If the person in the position at the top is the expert, then the followers tend to abdicate much of their own power. To be an expert, by definition, means to know more than others. This seduces both the leader and his followers. The leader functions as though the followers do not know what they are doing and probably would not change but for his or her efforts. The followers function as though it is only the leader who "knows"; they therefore become passive participants who lean heavily on the leader. Both parties assume that if change or success is not forthcoming, it is because of a problem with the leader. When success does not occur, the leader (with the assent and even encouragement of the followers) responds by trying harder. The pressure on a leader in such a position is obvious.

Charisma

The second quality good leaders are expected to demonstrate is charisma, that strongly magnetic personality that certain people have. Leaders with charisma can unify divided bodies, infect others with enthusiasm, and galvanize others to action. In short, charismatic leaders produce a "high" in their followers.

Like the quality of expertise, charisma results in secondary problems. Magnetic leadership is most appealing to followers who need to rely on a motivator outside themselves. Such followers demand that their leaders "move" them. So again, we are breeding passivity in the body. At the same time, charismatic leadership is not healthy for the leader. The leader is perpetually forced to overfunction, and so lives in a chronic state of stress.

Both expertise and charisma give unhealthy power to an isolated person at the top, breed passivity in those who follow, and result in the leader being responsible for the entire family—a heavy load indeed. What a breeding ground for abuse! Given such a scenario—which I believe is an accurate portrayal of much of today's church—it is amazing to me that the problem of clergy sexual abuse is not even more rampant than our worst fears believe it to be.

Understanding Power

It is not hard to see that a leader in a position such as we have described would desperately want power. To feel responsible for an entire system, never to feel adequately prepared, to feel isolated, and to exist in a chronic state of stress produces many reactions. Such a leader would feel overwhelmed, inadequate, in fear of being discovered a fraud, alone, and anxious. A sense of impotence, a feeling of chaos, and the need to deceive all grow readily in such an environment.

Passivity

On the one hand, God our creator called us to rule and subdue. We are by our very natures called to have impact on this world and on each other. But like all other things said by God to be good, this created aspect of who we are has been twisted, distorted. Some have been twisted in the direction of excessive passivity. We do not act on our world or others for good; indeed, we do not act at all. We have abdicated our responsibility, and we meet our need for influence or significance by putting ourselves into the hands of someone who appears to be in control.

Power-Seeking

Others of us have been twisted in the direction of power-seeking. In our frenzied efforts to quell our feelings of impotence, we are driven toward omnipotence. The goal is never achieved, of course, and that failure produces greater isolation, which causes our need for omnipotence to increase. Marguerite Shuster defines power as "the ability to produce desired, intended effects in the world" (Shuster, 1987, p. 156). To live under the demand to be expert and charismatic creates a strong push toward power-seeking. Power-seeking is a natural response to felt powerlessness.

Hidden Anxiety and Psychopathology

The drive for power is often a cloak for terrible anxiety. Anyone who has studied introductory psychology has come across studies demonstrating the high anxiety produced in subjects whose actions have no effect in achieving a desired goal. Unmanaged anxiety leads to pathology. The more isolated, insignificant, and ineffective one feels, the greater the need for power.

Dr. Shuster (1987) points out that both loneliness and grandiosity are characteristic of psychopathology. Let us consider that statement for a moment in light of what we said earlier about leadership. How much lonelier does it get than to be the person at the top who is expected to carry the entire family, motivate them, galvanize them, and inject them with enthusiasm? And what is better fodder for grandiosity than demanding expertise in myriad areas? The leader is to be the one who knows, the carrier of truth, the decider of right and wrong, the holder of all important information. It was Alfred Adler who said, "The loftiest goals are to be found in the most pathological of cases—that is, in the psychoses" (quoted in Shulman, 1968, p. 170). Failure becomes intolerable, and the psychotic responds to it by denying one's finitude or limitations.

Certainly one way evil appears in those who are isolated and seeking omnipotence is in the form of sexual abuse of a parishioner. Often, because of the excessive demands and expectations leaders buy into, they end up consumed by the aim of hiding and remedying their felt deficiencies. Failure is intolerable, for failure means to be thrown out. To achieve, or never to disappoint, is to succeed, but to succeed requires deceit, a denial of reality. Reality says that the leader has limitations, deficiencies, and weaknesses—all of which are threats to his or her existence as leader. Our most successful leaders (at least by the definition of this paper) are often our most pathological. As long as we continue to define leadership as the world does—a position demanding expertise and charisma—we will breed leaders who feel isolated and desperately seek omnipotence. Leaders such as these will be broken off from a reciprocal relationship with the body they are called to serve. Once reciprocity has broken down, then good is defined not as what is good for the body, but rather what is good for the isolated self. This climate is a perfect set-up for the abuse of others.

How often I have found that clergy who have sexually abused women in their congregations are attempting to remedy a terrifying sense of isolation and powerlessness by resorting to violence. Violence is defined as the abusive or unjust exercise of power, and so when one who is in a position of authority abuses one of his sheep, then we must name it violence.

What is the remedy for a disease that is both systemic and individual in nature? If we deal with the individual aspects of the problem, we are in great danger of inadvertently maintaining a system that is sick. Without question, we need to deal with the individual clergy who perpetrate such abuse against their parishioners, and we need to deal with the individual women who are abused. I think we also must be alert to the fact that we do not want to foster a system that encourages women to be passive and find power only by aligning themselves dependently on those who appear to be in leadership. But we must go even further. We must consider the church as a whole.

A Scriptural Understanding of Leadership

Many of us have not brought the Word of God to bear on the idea of leadership. We are turning out leaders in the world's mold. We have bought the "separate and above" concept of leadership. Many of us in the pews have quit thinking and instead demand to be taught. We have quit serving and demand to be taken care of. We have quit relentlessly pursuing God for ourselves and demand he be given to us on Sundays with feeling. We put leaders up above and far apart from the rest of us and then wonder why they don't follow the rules. We teach systematic theology (and we should), but we forget that our Lord thought his disciples needed to be taught how to pray. We teach church growth and forget personal repentance and confession. Is it any wonder that the shepherds are hurting the sheep and the sheep are hurting the shepherds? If we want to prevent sexual abuse of the sheep by their shepherds, then we must go back to the Word of God for an understanding of what it truly means to lead, and what it truly means to follow.

Leadership as Personal Example

According to the Word of God, the practice of leadership is mainly a matter of personal example, of living out the qualities that make for Christian leadership. In response to the disciples' dispute about who among them was to be the biggest and the best, Jesus' response was emphatic—"It will not be so among you!" (Matt. 20:26 NRSV). Christ said that the rulers of the Gentiles (those who do not know him) lord it over those they rule. To lord it over is to domineer, to tyrannize, to oppress. To lord it over someone is to use authority so as to weigh heavily upon them, to overwhelm them, to crush them, to put them under a yoke. According to Luke

22:25, this tyrannical power was cloaked by calling those who exercised it by the name "benefactors." The name "benefactor" means one who gives aid, who helps. But in this case the name is given to one who oppresses, who lives in a fashion diametrically opposed to the name of benefactor. It is a situation very much like what we are considering, for to pastor, to shepherd is to be one who tends, guards, and cares for his sheep. In the case of clergy sexual abuse, however, the name "shepherd" is given to one who abuses, oppresses, and lives in a fashion diametrically opposed to his name.

Leader as Servant—the Organic Model

Christ went on to reverse the whole conception of leadership: The leader was to serve. Those who wish to be chief are to be as those who serve. Christ demonstrated the only model of leadership that will result in healthy leaders and equally healthy followers. It is an organic model, a reciprocal, connected model. It does not breed isolation or omnipotence. No domineering, oppressing, seeking to profit, competing for place or position, or striving for power are found here. It is also a model that does not foster unhealthy dependency, mindlessness, or passivity in its followers. For if the leader is to practice leadership by example, then it follows that those who are being led are to emulate that example. Hence, the shepherd tends, guards, and cares for his sheep, while the sheep tend, guard, and care for each other *and* their shepherd.

Another beautiful illustration of this reciprocity is in 1 Thessalonians 2:7, where Paul says that though he and his associates might have asserted their authority, instead they proved to be gentle as a nursing mother. If that is not a model of connectedness, then I don't know what is. Paul goes on to say in verse 11 that they exhorted, encouraged, and implored as a father would his children—again a model of care and connection. Paul then says that the purpose of such a leadership was "that you may walk in a manner worthy of the God who calls you" (1 Thess. 2:12 NASB). Sheep who walk worthy of God love their shepherd, hold him to the highest, tend his wounds, and seek to minister to him. This living, breathing reciprocity is stated simply and beautifully for us in John

10:14, where Jesus says: "I am the good shepherd; and I know My own, and My own know Me" (NASB).

A family systems perspective also does not create this polarity between leader and follower. The family systems concept of leadership looks at how leader and follower function as part of one another. Paul says, "For even as the body is one and yet has many members, and all the members of the body, though they are many, are one body" (1 Cor. 12:12 NASB). This concept of leadership says that the responsibility of the leader ceases to be for the entire family. Instead the leader must focus on responsibility for self. The basic concept is this: If the leader will take primary responsibility for self, while staying in touch with the rest of the body, there is a more than reasonable chance that the body will follow.

Friedman (1985) describes the concept as an organic one. For any part of an organism to have a continuous or lasting effect, it must stay connected to the organism as a whole. However, it must be connected without being swallowed up. It is a differentiated, yet connected position. How like the body imagery in Scripture. The hand is not the eye is not the foot. Each is differentiated one from the other and yet vitally connected. Christ is the head, "from whom the whole body [leaders and followers], being fitted and held together by that which every joint supplies, according to the proper working of each individual part, causes the growth of the body for the building up of itself in love" (Eph. 4:16 NASB).

A Scriptural Understanding of Power

Power as Derivative from God

What does Scripture say about our second area of focus, power? First and foremost, we are told that all power is derivative. There is nothing that can continue except it do so by the power of God. Jesus said at the close of his earthly ministry, "All power is given unto me in heaven and in earth" (Matt. 28:18 KJV). Anyone in leadership only exercises delegated authority. It is by virtue of this fact that the leader is not only connected to the body he or she serves, but also to the one who is sovereign over all. The leader is not isolated, but connected, not omnipotent, but subject to God's power.

Whenever a leader is disconnected and not subject to God, the resulting search for power will have devastating consequences. To search for power in any place other than from God is to find and exercise power that is destructive. Shuster says, "Any power not in active communion with God is not neutral or harmless but demonic" (1987, p. 112).

Power in Acknowledged Weakness

Power that is sought for the purpose of eliminating felt deficiencies and weaknesses leads to a denial of rationality. Leadership that is not subject to God is irrational. To understand power from God's point of view is to live within the constraints of reality, to honor one's weaknesses and limitations. To live outside that reality is to fight against what is true. It is to despise and deplore weakness, to deny failure and impotence. It results in being lured by a false power that devours what it hooks and never delivers what it promises.

The pursuit of such power and its accompanying denial of weakness has devoured many leaders of the church today. While many of us cheer them on to their destruction, giving them the message that weakness is unacceptable in the pulpit, we, like them, live in denial of that truth which says that "power is perfected in weakness" (2 Cor. 12:9 NASB). We live as if weakness were cured by the pursuit of power. In doing so, we are at variance with the truth of God, and our victims, both perpetrators and abused, are many. The problem is that we *are* weak and limited. Leader or follower, we cannot escape this truth. Have we forgotten that the God of the universe, with whom resides all power, has chosen this very weakness in which to manifest his glory? And if we remember this, then why do we demand that those who lead us be without weakness? And having demanded the impossible, why are we shocked at the abuses?

All who lead are weak. Some of that weakness is simply due to finitude, some is due to sin. Whether we lead or follow, weakness due to human limitation is cause for rejoicing, for it is the arena in which God manifests who he is. Weakness due to our own sin is cause for repentance, for we serve a God who brings life out of

67

death. True power in the church of God will come from acknowledged, not denied weakness.

The world says that leadership is demonstrated by expertise and charisma. Jesus says that leadership means to be the servant of all, to wear the mark of the girded towel. To rule then, is to be unlike Christ himself. To serve in truth and grace is to be like Jesus.

Challenge to the Body of Christ

The problem of clergy sexual abuse is not simply about sex, or about men and women and their cultural roles. It is not even just a problem of violence, though admittedly sex, gender roles, and violence are all pieces of this difficult and complex issue. Ultimately, it is about a church whose members have abdicated their responsibilities. It is about a body whose parts have atrophied. It is about a people who have been blinded by the gods of expertise and charisma. The result is a demand for leaders who are not godly, but pathological. The position of leadership, as it is often defined by the church, has the potential to attract those who are not connected with God or with their people. Leadership of this sort often appeals to those who see themselves as above others, unaccountable, ambitious, and full of knowledge, or else to those who feel beneath others and want the self-enhancing benefits of title and position. We then end up with those who are in a position of authority but possess little spiritual authority. We have leaders who are so terrified by their own impotence that they strut and puff and use clever gimmicks to deceive those who follow. Their feelings of impotence and isolation leave them desperately hungry for connectedness. It is fertile ground for the abuse of power in search of intimacy.

Does this excuse those who so horrendously violate their sheep? No! Are they responsible for the terrible abuse of their power and position? Without question! When that abuse occurs, should the church seek justice and a conformity to the truth? May it never settle for less. But we, the church, are not off the hook. God has called each part of the body to function interactively.

Those of us who lead are called to mutuality and weakness. We are to be under the authority of the one who has all power in every arena of our lives, public and private. We are to be present as one who serves. We are earthen vessels, that the surpassing greatness of the power may be of God and not of ourselves. We are not to deceive ourselves, but are continually to confess, repent, and be taught to pray by the one who emptied himself for our sakes. We are to know our sheep and be known by them. If we follow this way, abuse of a sheep will be out of the question, for the slightest stirring of selfish interest will send us to our knees and to our sheep for accountability and support.

Those of us who follow are no less called to be imitators of God. Paul says we are to walk in love, and that immorality, impurity, and greed should not even be named among us. This is not just about leaders; it is about all of us. Where, then, have the followers been when one of their own was suffering abuse at the hand of a shepherd? Paul's words to us in Ephesians 5:6 are relevant: "Let no one deceive you with empty words" (NASB). How we have swallowed the empty words defining what a leader should be. As Paul goes on to say, "Do not participate in the unfruitful deeds of darkness, but instead even expose them" (Eph. 5:11 NASB). Do we know of abuse and pretend it is not there, saying, "After all, it is up to the leadership to handle"? In the words of Paul again, "All things become visible when they are exposed by the light" (Eph. 5:13 NASB). It is just as much the responsibility of the follower to bring light where there is darkness. "Awake, sleeper, and arise from the dead, and Christ will shine on you" (Eph. 5:14 NASB).

Characteristics of the Incestuous Family

Jackie J. Hudson

ncest is a human tragedy. It destroys that all-important element that is basic to healthy relationships—trust. The following scenario is not uncommon; it is certainly not as uncommon as a majority of the population tends to believe.

The family patriarch, Ralph Smith, and his wife, Betty, have eight children who now range in age from twenty to forty. The Smiths are churchgoing, God-fearing people who say they tried to give their kids a good childhood—that is, a good childhood marred with the molestation of all eight of their children, both males and females.

Lisa, one of their now-adult children, reports that her parents frequently engaged in sexual activity in her presence, and when she turned twelve, her father began having intercourse with her, a practice he continued for many years. When Lisa protested, her father used the Bible to support his actions, claiming that the Bible said it was okay for parents to have sex with their children. He quoted the Book of Job (Vanderbilt, 1992). In a professional capacity, I have heard many firsthand accounts similar to this one in which Scripture passages on the obedience of children and the submissiveness of wives were used to support abusive behavior.

The shattering of basic trust, the very cornerstone to healthy human development, and the long-term effects of incestuous child abuse have been widely documented (Alexander & Lupfer, 1987; Cole, Woolger, Power, & Smith, 1992; Harter, Alexander, & Neimeyer, 1988; Herman & Hirschman, 1981; Jackson, Calhoun, Amick, Maddever, & Habif, 1990; Jehu, 1990; Trepper & Barrett, 1989). These effects include poor social adjustment, sexual problems, low self-esteem, depression, self-destructive tendencies, distorted body image, parenting problems, and many other characteristics that to the adult survivor of incest are much more than a list of words on a page. They are a painful, daily reality carried inside that takes considerable and profound effort to overcome.

Current data indicates that all forms of child sexual abuse against females in the United States are rampant. Studies reveal that from 27 percent to 54 percent of all females have experienced some form of child sexual abuse (Jehu, 1990; Russell, 1983). However, those figures could be substantially higher, according to some researchers. It is possible that these figures are low because of limitations incumbent upon accurate research (DeMause, 1987). It is estimated that there are thirty-four million adult women in our country today who were molested as children (Benson, 1994). Statistics on child sexual abuse against males are less available. Most researchers believe that this abuse rate is also high; however, because of the stigma attached to having been molested, males are less likely to report their abuse.

Although child sexual abuse and incest in particular have been documented in historical literature from ancient times (Kahr, 1991), estimates of incest have risen from one child in a million in the 1950s to one out of every three children in the 1980s (Trepper & Barrett, 1989). It is uncertain whether the cause for such a low estimate of incestuous abuse in the 1950s was due to mass denial, the unavailability of research on this topic, or the fact that only 2 percent of the cases of incestuous abuse were ever reported (Russell, 1983). More current data suggests that in the 1950s incidents of incest were much higher than the one-in-a-million estimate (Kahr, 1991; Russell, 1983).

Sibling incest is the most common, followed by father-daughter and stepfather-stepdaughter incest, which accounts for three-fourths of all reported cases of incestuous abuse. It is reported that stepfathers are five times more likely than natural fathers to abuse their children (Trepper & Barrett, 1989). However, one study revealed that in conservative Christian homes, there is a higher prevalence of sexual abuse by biological fathers than by stepfathers (Gil, 1988). Further research needs to be conducted in order to determine why this may be true. Other types of incest (father-son, mother-son, mother-daughter) are being reported in increasing numbers. One study of polyincestuous families reported that more than a third of the sample consisted of female abusers— mothers abusing together with male partners (Faller, 1991).

As difficult as the problem of incest is to face, it must be addressed because no one is immune—neither the Christian nor the nonbeliever. Incest crosses every socioeconomic, religious, and cultural line. And in fact, some research indicates that the religious right promotes attitudes toward women that allow for a tolerance of sexual abuse in our society today (Hull & Burke, 1991). This contention places the problem at the doorstep of the Christian community, even though it may be unpleasant to face. It must be remembered that Jesus was quick to welcome the children and chastise any who would hurt or harm them (Matt. 19:13–15; Mark 9:42; Luke 17:1–2). Today, he does no less through those who follow him.

This paper is an initial attempt to investigate the relationship between the traditional interpretation of Scripture regarding marriage and the family and the known characteristics of the incestuous family. Many of the traditional (not necessarily scriptural) values taught regarding marriage and the family correlate with many of the characteristics of the incestuous family. The contention is that these values are not wrong in and of themselves, but when rigidly adhered to, they have the potential of putting a family at risk for incestuous abuse to occur.

Although this information may support an egalitarian rather than hierarchical approach to marriage and the family, it is never wise to evaluate Scripture from what we see in society. There are sound biblical scholars, holding to the inerrancy of Scripture, who have presented arguments to support both an egalitarian and a traditional hierarchical approach to marriage and the family. The jury is not in on this highly controversial issue. This paper is one additional piece of information to factor into the equation as we in the Christian community humbly seek God for clarity on issues concerning women. May all who are diligently seeking clarity from the Spirit of God on these issues remember the words of a renowned scholar: "An obstinate outlook will effectually hinder God from revealing anything to us. If we have made up our minds about a doctrine, the light of God will come no more to us on that line, we cannot get it" (Chambers, 1935, p. 98).

Review of the Traditional Interpretation of Scripture

The primary passages from which traditional interpretations are usually made about women are 1 Corinthians 11 and 14, 1 Timothy 2, Colossians 3, Ephesians 5, and 1 Peter 3. These have been traditionally interpreted in the following ways: (1) There is a God-ordained hierarchy in creation that extends to marriage and the family, placing the man at the top with authority (leadership, responsibility) over the woman. More specifically, the husband is the head, the leader, the authority over the wife and children, with the wife also having authority over the children. However, final authority always belongs to the husband. (2) There are specific roles in the marriage. The husband is to be the loving leader and the wife is to be the submissive follower. The role of leader often carries the connotation of the husband being responsible for the spiritual welfare of the family. (3) Although the husband and wife may discuss major decisions to be made, the husband has the final decision-making power. (4) The husband's role primarily involves being the breadwinner of the family, and the wife's role primarily involves staying home and raising the children. (5) Children respecting and obeying parents is a primary goal.

Comments from current popular Christian publications appear to substantiate the above statements. *Growing a Healthy Home*, a book published by Focus on the Family, is a compilation of articles by numerous authors. One author describes ten ways a husband can say "I love you." His advice is for husbands to give their wives a night away from home for "no employer expects a worker to spend 16 hours every day of the week at the office" (Yorky, 1990, p. 48). Another popular author comments that "God seems to have designed within a woman the very talents that make her an invalu-

73

able resource in the home" (Smalley, 1989, p. 8). He continues by saying, "God has built into every man the natural ability to be the very loving leader his family needs" (p. 96). And he continues, "Let me state something clearly. Valuing his wife's differences . . . does not transfer leadership or responsibility away from the husband and place it onto the wife" (p. 53). He makes it clear that the husband is the head of the home. In a later book, the same author teams up with another popular writer. Their interpretation of the fall is as follows: "Because of the fall, woman would be faced with a constant temptation to take control and exercise authority over her husband. This really comes out of a woman's self-centeredness" (Smalley & Trent, 1992, p. 109). They devote a whole chapter to solving this problem of a "woman's tendency to take over and ram through her own agenda" (p. 109). In reference to raising children, Dr. James Dobson refers to the development of respect for parents as the critical factor in child management. He emphasizes how to control children without nagging (Dobson, 1994).

The above excerpts are only parts of well-written books containing many valuable insights regarding relationships. All of these authors are Christ-centered and say what they do in a context of love. These particular parts were selected only to highlight the "traditional" view of marriage and child rearing being taught.

Characteristics of the Incestuous Family

The incestuous family often has the outward appearance of being "normal," functional, and well adjusted (Cohen, 1983). Common remarks when incest has been newly discovered in a family usually go something like this: "He doesn't look like a child molester." "It seems like such a normal family."

Recently, I took a team of people from the sexual abuse treatment center where I work into a classroom at the local university to speak to graduate students in the mental health field. The team consisted of a father who had molested his daughter, a mother whose daughter had been molested by her husband, and an adult survivor of incest. All three were at advanced stages in their treatment and were trained for this community service aimed at breaking the cycle of child sexual abuse in our country.

74

Walking across campus, the offender commented that perhaps he should put on his trench coat before reaching the classroom. Although said tongue-in-cheek, the offender recognized that many people think the child molester is the stranger lurking around street corners in a trench coat. But in reality, he is the "man next door." It is true, however, that most people believe this trench coat theory because the cases of sexual abuse that capture public attention are those which represent the extreme. Sadly so, those cases represent only a small percentage of the actual accounts.

General Characteristics

Most children are molested by a family member or someone they know (Benson, 1994; Russell, 1983). The fathers I work with who have molested their children include Christians, non-Christians, pastors, professors, blue-collar workers, professionals, those who are educated, those who are uneducated, Caucasians, African-Americans, Hispanics, and Chinese. In most cases the family is very important to them.

In the incestuous family, each family member joins in a "conspiracy of silence," either consciously or unconsciously. By keeping silent, they maintain a defense against the family disintegrating (Cohen, 1983). Secrecy and denial are hallmarks of the incestuous family. The family uses denial to protect itself and to attempt to keep itself together at any cost (Sirles & Lofberg, 1990).

Father-daughter incest is associated with very traditional family values. These values include women being subservient to males and children being subservient to adults (Alexander & Lupfer, 1987; Herman & Hirschman, 1981; Trepper & Barrett, 1989). However, with sexual abuse perpetrated by extended family members or outsiders, these families did not necessarily exhibit these same values (Alexander & Lupfer, 1987).

Incestuous families have also been characterized as rigid, a feature that is exhibited by their extremely traditional power structure and their resistance to change (Alexander & Lupfer, 1987; Harter et al., 1988; Herman & Hirschman, 1981; Trepper & Barrett, 1989). What might be indicative of family rigidity would be a firm and unquestioning adherence by the daughter to the rule "do whatever daddy says" (Trepper & Barrett, 1989).

75

In all families there is a strong positive relationship between conflict and the potential for abuse (Mollerstrom, Patchner, & Milner, 1992). In the sexually abusive family the findings are similar. In addition to these characteristics, the incestuous family is not very cohesive (Alexander & Lupfer, 1987; Finkelhor, 1984; Harter et al., 1988; Herman & Hirschman, 1981).

Another characteristic of incestuous families appears to be troubled communication patterns. These patterns include secretiveness, mixed or confused messages to one another, few discussions about feelings, little attentive listening or empathy, and a lack of ability to resolve conflict (Trepper & Barrett, 1989). More specifically, in conservative Christian homes where incest occurred, the fathers were not generally considered warm or effective in communication. The daughters most vividly recalled that the suppression of their feelings was a direct result of the communication patterns of their fathers (Gil, 1988). This would be a natural response when passages about "honoring" or "obeying" your parents have been taken to an extreme and prevent a child from questioning a parent's abusive behavior. In fact, they may even think it is normal or "God-ordained."

Found more generally in the incestuous family are parents who are not empathic toward their children, and children who are reluctant to disclose the abuse. This observation shows the depth of the emotional disturbance typically seen in an incestuous family (Alexander & Lupfer, 1987). There is evidence of parental discord, the marriage is typically conflictual, and the family environment is often one of abandonment. The victims constantly live in fear that they will be "left" by important family members. The children in these families lack the basic emotional qualities of love and support, which may make them more vulnerable to exploitation by any adult who seems to meet those needs (Jehu, 1990).

Father Figures

The descriptions of incestuous fathers are not always consistent (Trepper & Barrett, 1989). Some are rigid, conservative, and moralistic, while others are family oriented and appear more conventional. Some are more emotionally reserved, while others are alcoholics and prone to anger. However, all of these fathers are not very emotionally mature. They tend to control the lives of the other family members by threats, different forms of bribes, or even seduction (Cohen, 1983). In one study, the two major methods of inducement the fathers used while molesting their daughters were the exercise of adult authority and the use of threats or physical abuse (Jehu, 1990).

In a study reported by Jehu (1990), male dominance was found in the family of origin of over half of the victims. Around half of the father figures exhibited anger, hostility, and violence toward spouse and children (Jehu, 1990). Other researchers describe these incestuous father figures as autocratic, patriarchal, or dictatorial (Finkelhor, 1984; Herman & Hirschman, 1981; Hull & Burke, 1991; Jehu, 1990). In many cases, the offending father has a sense of ownership toward his daughter and views her as his property (Cohen, 1983; Jehu, 1990). Often, these fathers believe very strongly that women and children should be subordinate to men and that children should be obedient to parents. Jehu (1990) argues that this patriarchal family structure has a power imbalance where no one can challenge the father, thus leaving the daughter unprotected. These fathers all seem to have an inability to meet their own emotional needs with other adults in a nonsexual way (Cohen, 1983). In one study of sexually abused daughters from conservative Christian homes, the data revealed characteristics similar to those found in the general population. In addition, these Christian fathers were viewed as emotionally "problemed" and legalistic (Gil, 1988).

Despite the sometimes contradictory descriptions of incestuous fathers, there are a number of common personality traits. These include the lack of impulse control, very little guilt, the demand for immediate gratification, little tolerance to stress, and trouble showing empathy toward others (Trepper & Barrett, 1989). In the program where I work treating incestuous families, it is not uncommon for it to take six months to two years before an offending father develops empathy for his victim. He usually enters the program in a great deal of pain, but that pain is primarily associated with his own predicament and losses. It is not until the initial trauma passes (i.e., removal from the home, possible incarceration, involvement with the legal system, possible public humiliation, loss of job, and so on) and he settles into the treatment program that he is willing to drop his defenses enough to feel empathy for his victim. If this never happens, the risk of recidivism is high.

Mother Figures

Jehu (1990) reports a finding that mothers of incest victims tend to be "overdependent, oppressed, and depressed" (p. 18). Their social skills are lacking and they are unassertive. This correlates with their low self-esteem and sometimes poor physical health (Herman & Hirschman, 1981; Jehu, 1990). Other researchers describe the nonoffending mothers as submissive and somewhat weak. Some may tend to be promiscuous (Cohen, 1983). The picture of a subservient, incapacitated mother figure is a common finding (Herman & Hirschman, 1981; Jehu, 1990; Trepper & Barrett, 1989). Further studies point out the mother's passivity and her somewhat incompetent behavior as an adult, which may include a role reversal with her daughter (Cohen, 1983; Trepper & Barrett, 1989). Rigid adherence to biblical injunctions for wives to submit themselves to their husbands can lead to an abdication of personal power resulting in the above characteristics.

Although many mothers deny knowledge of the incest, studies suggest that most mothers had some kind of knowledge of what was occurring. Because they were afraid the father might abandon the family, they did not confront the abuse. Perhaps this is why most incest reports are exposed by the daughter and not the mother (Cohen, 1983). One exception to this was found in families where the disclosure of the incest was followed by divorce. These mothers appeared to possess enough personal power and autonomy to break their passivity. In most cases they reported the abuse (Sirles & Lofberg, 1990).

In citing these statistics, I want to be clear that this is in no way sending the unintentional message that the mother is somehow responsible for the abuse. The mother may have contributed to the dynamics that make a family vulnerable to incest, but the offending father is always responsible for his sexual behavior. To subtly imply "mother blame" and suggest that the father must have his sexual needs met (if not by his wife, then he will turn to his daughter) puts responsibility on women for men's sexual acting out and suggests men have no control over their sexual drives.

This is an insult to women as well as men (Howard, 1993). The important issue here is how the socialization of women to be subservient to their husbands may contribute to a family system that is vulnerable to incestuous abuse.

The Multiple Systems Model

There are many theories explaining the cause of incest. The multiple systems model (Trepper & Barrett, 1989) is an attempt to integrate the important features of various models. It suggests that there are many factors that affect the problem of incest. The operating assumption is that "There is no one cause of incestuous abuse. Instead, all families are endowed with a degree of vulnerability based upon environmental, family, individual, and family-of-origin factors, which may express as incest if a precipitating event occurs and the family's coping skills are inadequate" (Trepper & Barrett, 1989, p. 22). For example, in researching sexual abuse in conservative Christian homes, Gil (1988) not only described characteristics found in the offending fathers (as mentioned earlier), but he also found that the social context at the time of the abuse included significant external pressure, the most significant being financial problems.

One framework the multiple systems model uses for assessing family structure in the incestuous family is based upon Munuchin's structural family therapy (Trepper & Barrett, 1989). This theory suggests a functional structure in which there is a separation between the parental generation and the children's generation by boundaries that are firm, but not rigid. A healthy family is one in which the mother and father stay in one generation and the children stay in another.

```
F   M          F = father
------------   M = mother
C C C C        C = child
```

Dysfunction occurs if the parents and children end up in each other's generation. Trepper & Barrett (1989) identify five types of family structures that are particularly vulnerable to the develop-

79

ment of father-daughter incest. The key element is that the father and the child somehow end up in the same generation, as sex can only occur within the same generational boundary. What usually happens is that the father "falls down" into the daughter's generation or the daughter is "pulled up" into the father's generation. These five structures are not necessarily all inclusive.

Father-Executive

This structure suggests a family where the father is dominant and holds all the power in the family. He parents the mother along with each of the children and is the primary decision maker. The mother is dependent on her husband and is somewhat passive. Eventually the mother and daughter exchange roles as the child is "parentified" and begins taking care of the mother and the other children. If the father confuses affection with sex, incest may occur.

F
- - - - - - - - - - - - -
C C C C M

Mother-Executive

In this structure, the mother is the most powerful figure in the family, and she parents the father along with the children. She tends to be the primary decision maker. Often the father acts like an adolescent by staying out all night and drinking with his friends. The mother may feel isolated from the husband.

M
- - - - - - - - - - - - -
C C C C F

Third Generation Mother-Executive and Third Generation Father-Executive

In these structures, there is a combination of the previous two. In the first, the father is a generational step below the mother. The father still manages to parent the children even though the marriage has all the problems mentioned in the mother-executive structure. The father's sexual abuse of the daughter may include an overtly parental action to obtain sexual favors.

In the second, the mother is a generational step below the father. She still seems to parent the children effectively. The father has to meet the daughter halfway to have sex with her. The daughter and the mother may be rivals for the affection of the father.

```
        M                      F
  - - - - - - - - - -     - - - - - - - - - -
        F                      M
  - - - - - - - - - -     - - - - - - - - - -
      C C C C              C C C C
```

Chaotic

All family members are in the same generation in this structure. No one seems to be in charge and it fluctuates as to who takes the lead. The father may feel more like the daughter's peer. Sibling incest and extended family incest are common in this structure.

```
      - - - - - - - - - -
      F M C C C C
```

Estranged Father

In this model, the father is not emotionally involved with the family. When he temporarily reenters the family, he does so in the daughter's generation. He can be very demanding in nature.

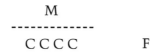

```
            M
      - - - - - - - - - -
      C C C C          F
```

These models for assessing incestuous family structures have been derived from theory and extensive clinical experience. Future research will help clarify and/or modify this theory. Percentages were not cited as to which structure had the highest rate of incest.

Also, it should be noted that there are families that exhibit the above characteristics where incest does not occur. The above structures only represent one factor that might put a family at risk for incest to occur. However, it does appear that incest was *not* found in families where there was not a hierarchy (one parent above or below in power, authority, and decision-making) and the father and mother worked together as a team in parenting the children.

Families at Risk

The more the characteristics above are present, the more a family increases its vulnerability to incest. Trepper & Barrett (1989) suggest that an example of a family that could be highly vulnerable may include one

> 1. that is relatively isolated from others; 2. that lives in a community which tolerates the male domination of women and children, at least tacitly; 3. that adheres to rigid sex roles; 4. that sexualizes much of their routine interactions; 5. that displays extreme rigidity with regard to change, a high value to strict adherence to rules, and yet is extremely enmeshed with regard to their emotional bondedness; 6. where secrecy in communication is tolerated and encouraged; 7. where the father has poor impulse control, has a sense of total entitlement concerning his children, and has a sexual fantasy of total sexual power and possession; 8. where the mother has a passive-dependent personality style, and where she has a greater felt-need for personal protection and sustenance than for protection of her children; 9. where the daughter has a great need for affection, has a conflictual relationship with her mother and close emotional alignment with her father, and is psychologically estranged from her other siblings; and 10. where the father was emotionally abused and neglected during his childhood, and the mother was sexually abused and/or emotionally neglected in her childhood. (p. 25)

When these characteristics are present in a family, and the coping mechanisms of the members are inadequate, then the family is at high risk for incest to occur when an external stressor (such as financial stress) presents itself (Gil, 1988; Trepper & Barrett, 1989).

Although it may be apparent by now that rigid adherence to a traditional interpretation of Scripture regarding marriage and the family correlates with many of the characteristics that contribute to a family being vulnerable to incest, some further comparisons are in order. Holding rigidly to the concept of a hierarchy in marriage and the family with the husband/father having ultimate authority corresponds with the "father-executive" or "third generation father-executive" family structure mentioned earlier. When the final power for decision-making is in the hands of one person, others can be left with a feeling of powerlessness and lack of control over their own personal lives. This leaves them open to being controlled and victimized.

An unbending insistence on the male-authority view may lead to the male dominance found in many incestuous families. Rigid adherence to traditional roles within marriage (where the husband is the leader and breadwinner, the wife is submissive and a homemaker) can lead to an unhealthy dependence on the part of the wife and an unequal balance of power within the home. Rigidly stressing obedience with children and respect for parents (and all adults) can lead to an environment where children never question, and ultimately do not learn to discern good and evil, which is a part of maturity. This may also promote an atmosphere of secrecy. All of these elements make a family vulnerable for incestuous abuse to occur. Many other comparisons could be made, but these are the major ones.

All of this has implications for us in the Christian community. Trepper & Barrett (1989) indicate that many incestuous families identify themselves as religious. Some even use their religious beliefs to support their abusive behavior. The perpetrator of incest has been described as a man "who is devout, moralistic, and fundamentalist in his religious beliefs, coming from a background in which morality was preached in public and breached in private" (Hoorwitz, 1983, p. 516). In a large research study done on incarcerated sex offenders, more than half of all incest offenders were found to be devout in their religious practice (Gebhard, Gagnon, Pomeroy, & Christenson, 1965).

Hull and Burke (1991) found a relationship between sexual abuse and traditional (they used the word "negative") attitudes toward women. Men who had perpetrated sexual abuse and women who had been victims of sexual abuse more readily believed that men and women should maintain traditional sex roles, that women's rights (political, economic, and social) should be limited in relationship to men's, that women should take care of the children and the housework, and that men should have more authority than women in the family. Their conclusion is that "the pervasiveness and power of a world view based on a particular religious orientation may well lead to greater tolerance for sexual abuse" (Hull & Burke, 1991, p. 9).

Conclusion

Once every thirteen weeks the children in our program who have been molested meet with the adults for what is called a "conjoint" session. The children range from eleven to seventeen years old (younger children are not allowed to participate). The evening is carefully supervised by therapists and is for the purpose of helping the children get answers to their questions concerning what has happened to them. They can ask the offenders, the nonoffending parents, or the adult victims any questions they want. It is often a very emotional and healing time for the children. Invariably, the first question out of a child's mouth to an offender in the room is: "Why? Why did you molest? Didn't you know it would hurt someone? Why, if you were molested, did you turn around and molest someone else?" No matter how honest and vulnerable an offender might choose to be, the answer is usually not enough to satisfy the hurting heart of the child. Yet it is a helpful part of their process to sort out their feelings, to be believed, to be heard, and ultimately to integrate an understanding of the insanity and cruelty of incest. This type of process should be encouraged rather than seen as dishonoring to their parents. Not allowing children to question and evaluate promotes secrecy and increases the risk for abuse to occur.

May we in the Christian community do no less than these children in trying to understand and stop the cycle of incest in our country, in our communities, in our churches, in our homes. This is a monumental task that will take considerable time, prayer, and effort to accomplish.

One way to approach this task is to continue the healthy process of examining the controversial passages concerning women and marriage. The Scriptures are inerrant, but our translations and interpretations of troubling passages may not always be accurate. We would be wise to discern between what is truth and what is tradition. Second, whether we hold to an egalitarian or a hierarchical view of women and marriage, it is imperative that we have an accurate understanding of the biblical use of authority. Nowhere does Jesus equate authority with power and control, but rather with servanthood. If this misuse of biblical authority was dealt with as quickly and severely as any other form of sin in the body of Christ, we would be less likely to wound and damage those God has given us the privilege of serving.

Finally, we may not all believe the same things about certain passages of Scripture, but we can all be aware of what dynamics make a family vulnerable to incest and take responsible action to prevent this human tragedy.

5

How Evangelical Women Cope
with Prescription and Description

Alice P. Mathews

n *All the King's Men*, Robert Penn Warren speaks of the problem of living in a house with a great big promise (1946). For
many Christian women, hierarchically structured marriage
poses the problem of living in such a house. The promise is
that, in exchange for the self-surrender or submission implicit
in asymmetrical gender roles, a wife will be "absorbed into a caring, gratifying entity, both powerful and dependable" (Turner,
1976, p. 1005). Popular Christian proponents of hierarchy in marriage stress a rich return for such self-surrender:

What does the woman gain by submission to her own husband?
Only the infinite security of yielding to the duly constituted
chain of authority in the universe; only the deep joy of living
with a real man who grows stronger every day; only the fulfillment of fully participating in a genuine love relationship; only
the completing of what is partial in her human nature; only the
opening of her yielded being to the influence of God's Spirit, who

comes where humble and yielded spirits are seeking Him. (Miles, 1975, p. 42)

To be submissive means to yield humble and intelligent obedience to an ordained power or authority [the husband]. . . . God did not give this law of wives being submissive to their husbands because he had a grudge against women; on the contrary, he established this order *for the protection of women and the harmony of the home.* He means for a woman to be sheltered from many of the rough encounters of life. Scripture knows nothing of a 50–50 "democratic marriage." The wife is 100% a wife, the husband 100% a husband. . . . A wife's primary responsibility is to give of herself, her time, and her energy to her husband, children, and home. (Christenson, 1970, pp. 32–33, 40)

In spite of the promised "rich return" for a wife's submission, self-surrender for women often leads not to the promised fulfillment, but to alienation. Sociologist Miriam Johnson reports:

The symbolism of wife is apparently well understood in the United States today. In an article for *Working Woman,* Kathleen Fury reacts to the *New York Times* report of a poll showing that only 6 percent of their respondents checked "being a wife" as one of the two or three most enjoyable things about being a female—well behind both career and motherhood. Fury suggests that women still very much want an egalitarian relationship of friend, lover, and life companion (the egalitarian marriage); being a wife, however, suggests inequality, taking a back seat, economic dependence, being a provider of personal service, and loss of self. (1988, p. 41)

When the complaints of husbands and wives about their marriages were compared, researchers learned that it is wives, not husbands, who are dissatisfied with their marriages. Johnson further notes:

The decision to divorce is more often made by wives than by husbands. . . . Wallerstein and Kelly found in their California study that in 75 percent of the couples they interviewed, it was the wife who wanted the divorce. . . . A study comparing the

87

complaints of husbands and the complaints of wives found that wives, not husbands, are dissatisfied with their marriages. . . . Moreover, women are less likely than men to remarry. (1988, p. 243)

These findings are present in spite of the fact that, according to Weitzman, men experience a 42 percent improvement in their postdivorce standard of living, and women experience a 73 percent decline (Johnson, 1988).

Within traditional hierarchical marriage, a significant number of conservative Christian women experience a gap between the promise of a rich return for self-surrender and the reality of self-estrangement or alienation. This gap places increasing pressure on such marriages, leading to marital dissatisfaction, uneven efforts at realignment of relational structures, and even marital dissolution in families once considered impervious to breakup.

Many conservative Christian authors defending gender-based hierarchy as essential to the protection of "family values" deny the reality of this estrangement (Allen & Allen, 1985; Bacchiochi, 1987; Dillow, 1977; Elliot, 1976; Gothard, 1979; Hurley, 1981; LaHaye, 1976; Piper & Grudem, 1991). Such authors insist that proper submission on the part of a Christian wife insulates a marriage from the erosion common to marriages of non-Christians or of Christians in egalitarian relationships. Is this true? Or is it possible that hierarchical marriage structures work against marital success? To probe these questions, this paper will draw on insights from the fields of epistemology, sociology of religion, and sociology of self.

Epistemology

The work of William Perry (1970) and of Mary Belenky and her colleagues (1986) uncovered "ways of knowing," with important implications for understanding how women "know" what they know.

Our basic assumptions about the nature of truth and reality and the origins of knowledge shape the way we see the world and

88

ourselves as participants in it. They affect our definitions of ourselves, the way we interact with others, our public and private personae, our sense of control over life events, our views of teaching and learning, and our conceptions of morality. (Belenky, Clinchy, Goldberger, & Tarule, 1986, p. 3)

Perry's research with Harvard male undergraduate students resulted in four epistemological perspectives: (1) The position of *basic dualism* assumes that everything in the world is dichotomized as right or wrong, black or white, good or bad. People whose "way of knowing" is dualistic are passive learners, dependent on external authorities to instruct them in truth and falsehood. (2) The position of *multiplicity* recognizes that many issues are matters of taste or personal preference rather than issues of right or wrong. People in this position carve out some mental space for personal opinions, accepting external authorities only up to a point. (3) The position of *relativism subordinate* consciously cultivates an analytical approach to knowledge. People in this position insist on supporting evidence, at least in academic areas, for the things they take as true. (4) The position of *full relativism* maintains that truth is relative in all areas of life, that the meaning of any event depends on the context of that event. Thus knowledge is constructed, not imparted by external authorities; it is contextual, not absolute; and it is changeable, not fixed (Perry, 1970).

When Belenky and her colleagues interviewed a wide spectrum of women over a five-year period, they uncovered five epistemological perspectives, similar to but subtly differing from Perry's categories: (1) In the position of *silence,* women experience themselves as mindless and voiceless and subject to the whims of external authority. They are incapable of knowing anything. (2) In the position of *received knowledge,* women conceive of themselves as capable of receiving or even reproducing knowledge from the all-knowing external authorities, but not capable of recreating knowledge on their own. (3) In the position of *subjective knowledge,* women reject external authorities and conceive of truth or knowledge as something personal, private, and subjectively known or intuited. (4) In the position of *procedural knowledge,* women invest in learning and in applying objective procedures for obtaining and communicating knowledge. (5) In the position of *con-*

89

structed knowledge, women experience themselves as creators of knowledge, and they value both subjective and objective strategies for knowing (Belenky et al., 1986).

Most germane to this study is the large group of men and women in the epistemological category labeled *basic dualism* or *received knowledge.* These people rely exclusively on external authority figures to instruct them in "truth." It is inconceivable to them that, apart from such authorities, ordinary people can arrive at truth. Received knowers also categorize life in dualisms with no gray areas, no gradations of truth. In terms of set theory, they operate within a bounded set; they focus on the boundaries of their belief system and are clear about what lies inside and outside those boundaries (Hiebert, 1978). Women who are received knowers are often able to articulate well what they have been taught, but they cannot allow themselves to question the teaching itself. Thus, when Christian authority figures (from Bill Gothard to Elisabeth Elliot to John Piper and Wayne Grudem) proclaim that asymmetrical marital structures in which the husband is in the dominant position of leadership and the wife assumes the posture of submission, received knowers accept that teaching with no epistemological category available to them for questioning it.

Sociology of Religion

The second source of insight into the question of women's experience of hierarchical marriage comes from the discipline of the sociology of religion. Received knowers cannot question the teaching of hierarchy because it is legitimated by a sacred or cosmic frame of reference. Wheaton College president Duane Litfin articulates this ascriptive worldview:

> The Bible presents a world view . . . based on the assumption that a sovereign, personal God designed an ordered universe to function in a particular way, and the finest achievement of the creature is to discover that design and fulfill it. At its essential level this design is not open to change or redefinition. . . . Feminists find the biblical vision of a divinely ordained male/female hierarchy galling. . . . They have embraced a profoundly unbib-

lical—indeed anti-biblical—ideology and are pressing it on the church. (1979, pp. 267, 268, 271)

In the ascriptive worldview, men and women are assigned separate spheres within which distinctive roles have been assigned cosmic significance. This doctrine of separate spheres received its most dichotomous definition in the early nineteenth century. "Male" and "female" came to symbolize mutually exclusive oppositions expounded in every organ of the press and pulpit throughout the Victorian period.

The doctrine of separate spheres, called the "Cult of True Womanhood" by historian Barbara Welter (1976), justified ideologically separated roles for men and women. Welter characterized Victorian womanhood by four primary attributes: piety, purity, submission, and domesticity. A woman's piety keeps her in her proper sphere, the home. Her purity must be maintained at all costs, for without it, a woman is no woman at all. A woman's submission is the most feminine of all her virtues. It is the order fixed in heaven itself, and to tamper with it is to tamper with the order of the universe. A woman's domesticity places her by her own fireside, where she is to dispense comfort and cheer to husband and children. A woman's happiness depends on fulfilling her pious, pure, submissive, and domestic nature by remaining at home. In the nineteenth century, it was commonly believed that the differences between male and female were total and innate. These were fixed in heaven. If a woman were a "true woman," she expected a life of self-sacrifice, because this was God's will. This nineteenth-century definition of the feminine nature and role has, with some change of rhetoric, passed down to the end of the twentieth century substantively unchanged because the teaching has been legitimated by the sacred frame of reference of God-ordained hierarchy. Beverly LaHaye gives a modern version of the teaching:

> Submission is God's design for woman. Christ's example teaches that true submission is neither reluctant nor grudging, nor is it a result of imposed authority; it is rather an act of worship to God when it is a chosen, deliberate, voluntary response to a husband. . . . God's design is that the husband be in charge. . . . Oh, that we could just grasp the attitude in the heart of Jesus—the

willingness to be humbled, to be obedient unto death, and to be submissive. It is the principle of losing oneself to find oneself. As the woman humbles herself (dies to self) and submits to her husband (serves him), she begins to find herself within that relationship. A servant is one who gets excited about making somebody else successful. . . . You can live fully by dying to yourself and submitting to your husband. . . . The wife who truly loves her husband will make his happiness her primary goal. (1976, pp. 71–74)

The "promise" for women is both a carrot and a stick: It includes the assurance of fulfillment for compliance, but it also carries penalties in both this world and in the world to come for those who fail to follow the teaching. John R. Rice, writing half a century ago, put it this way: "The crime wave that plagues America is part and parcel of the rebellion against authority in which every woman who does not submit to her husband has a part" (1941, p. 36). A more contemporary work, the Danvers Statement, concludes with this warning: "We are convinced that a denial or neglect of these principles [of asymmetrical relationships in marriage] will lead to increasingly destructive consequences in our families, our churches, and the culture at large" (Piper & Grudem, 1991, p. 471).

The carrot-and-stick double message of divinely ascribed marital roles for women based on mutually exclusive natures provides a theodicy of social order. While the "carrot" is the promise of a rich return in exchange for a woman's self-surrender, the "stick" enforcing this submission is the threat of both personal sorrow and the total breakdown of society. Thus, while the promulgation of ascriptive gender roles often begins with beguiling promises, it is firmly rooted in a theodicy of the social order that provides men with a divinely sanctioned rationale for their power-over position, and gives women a way of making sense out of their experience of life when the promise is not fulfilled. Women are urged to accept their subordinate role both because God will compensate them in life after death to balance out the deficits of their present position (Stark & Bainbridge, 1985), and because failure to do so has disastrous consequences for the entire society. Such theodicies maintain the institutional order.

Sociology of Self

The socialization provided by the theodicy of social order is often partial. When evangelical women in hierarchical marriages talk about their lives, it soon becomes evident that not all of them buy into the hierarchical paradigm uncritically. Sociologist Arlie Hochschild (1983) employs this useful metaphor: All women in traditional marriages must bow; some bow from the heart, others learn to bow from the waist while standing upright inside.

Erving Goffman (1961) distinguishes between the primary and secondary adjustments individuals make to any institutional order. Carrying out required activities to an institution constitutes a primary adjustment. A secondary adjustment consists of keeping back a part of the self from the grasp of an institution. The primary adjustment depicts the official definition of roles, attitudes, and acceptable behaviors. The secondary adjustment puts distance between the self and the prescribed role. Some women adjust to hierarchy by becoming true believers. They internalize the "unit" notion of marriage, seeing themselves as appendages to their spouses. In the process, they often surrender all sense of personal identity. Other women adjust to hierarchy by creating distance or space between the "real self" and the role they are required to play. This is often done in a wide variety of creative ways, but it usually feels false, as a betrayal of one's personal integrity.

Primary Adjustments

When women enter traditional marriages, they place themselves in relationships Robert Connell labels as having "a strong power imbalance" (1987, p. 123). This calls for primary adjustments to their positions of subordination and dependency in the relationship.

1. *The primary adjustment of economic dependency.* According to Blumstein and Schwartz:

Money establishes the balance of power in relationships. . . . The amount of money a person earns—in comparison with a partner's income—establishes relative power. . . . In marriage, adher-

93

ence to the male-provider philosophy grants greater power to husbands. (1983, pp. 53, 56)

The consequences of this are clear for most married women. Sorensen and McLanahan note:

> Married women's economic dependency is one of the central mechanisms by which women's subordinate position in society is maintained. Power differentials between husbands and wives are directly related to differences in contributions to family income. . . . Economic dependency is always associated with the risk of losing the particular source of income on which the dependency is based. (1987, pp. 661–662)

When women marry, in most cases they bargain away their independence in exchange for the higher income level a man is able to provide. But with that bargain comes vulnerability: What if the marriage ends in divorce? Women must do whatever it takes to maintain the marriage so that their economic vulnerability will not be activated. To help them with this ongoing maintenance project, a host of Christian seminars, workshops, books, tapes, and retreats offer women tactical instructions for keeping the sizzle going long after the fire has gone out. These same resources are designed to help women with their second primary adjustment.

2. *The primary adjustment to a subordinate role in the relationship.* Gene Getz makes it clear that a woman's submission is not a fingers-crossed-behind-the-back accommodation: "For the wife to submit to her husband as the church submits to Christ means total dedication" (1972, p. 28). Sociologist Ralph Turner examines the appeal of this kind of self-surrender:

> From the poet Francis Thompson, writing in religious terms, to the psychoanalyst Erich Fromm, students of human nature have understood the appeal of self-surrender. For Thompson, the errant soul flees the Hound of Heaven in desperation until in abject surrender, he discovers the fulfillment of his deepest desires. . . . But implicit in self-discovery through self-surrender is the assumption that one has been absorbed into a caring, gratifying entity, both powerful and dependable. . . . *The discovery of self in love for another is made real by the reciprocated love,*

94

the dependability of the relationship, and the new opportunities for gratification that come from the relationship [italics added]. (1976, p. 1005)

What makes it possible for a woman to discover herself in love for another? It comes with the presence of three things: (1) the reciprocated love, (2) the dependability of the relationship, and (3) the new opportunities for gratification that come from the relationship. These make self-discovery real. The question is whether most women—Christian and otherwise—experience the three contingencies Turner set up for this rich return on self-surrender.

3. The primary adjustment to an institutional view of the self. Around 1970, our culture experienced a major shift in the way the self was viewed. Until the early 1970s, the "real" self was an *institutional* self, defined by sociologist Robert Park: "The role we are striving to live up to—this . . . is our truer self, the self we would like to be" (1927). This institutional view of the self was characterized by (1) setting high standards for fulfilling our duty, (2) seeing the "self" as something to be achieved or attained, not as something to be discovered, (3) being fully in control of all our faculties and behaviors, and (4) giving error-free, polished performances at all times (Turner, 1976, pp. 989–1016).

After 1970, social scientists began asking questions about this institutional self. More and more people were slipping the institutional anchor in exchange for an *impulse* anchor for the self. As Turner explains:

To one person . . . the true self is recognized . . . in the pursuit of institutionalized goals, and not in the satisfaction of impulses outside the institutional frameworks. To another person, the outburst of desire is recognized as an indication that the real self is breaking out. (1976, p. 991)

The role of duty and submissiveness in marriage is an institutional anchor. For people with this institutional anchor, the discovery of the self is found in self-mastery and in altruism. It turns out that these are the personal goals that serve women best in making a successful primary adjustment to a June Cleaver type of marriage. In the past, this institutional anchor was assumed to be the only option women had. It was not acceptable for women to slip out of that anchor. But after 1970, more and more people moved from an institutional, duty-bound anchor for the self to an impulse anchor. Increasingly the institutional anchor was seen as a role people put on the way one puts on a shirt; the real self was hidden behind the role and showed itself only on impulse. Yet hierarchical marriage requires an institutional locus of the self.

Secondary Adjustments

Women who are identified as "received knowers" and who have made a total primary adjustment to submission and to an institutional locus of the self are the most likely candidates for overcommitment or overattachment to their role. Some of these women never make secondary adjustments in marriage. They learn to manage their emotions about the gap between the promise and the reality in such a way that they do not consciously need to put distance between their role and the self. But the vast majority of women *do* make secondary adjustments.

Ralph Turner (1976) suggested that the appeal of self-surrender was based on the rich return of reciprocated love, dependability of the relationship, and new opportunities for gratification that come from the relationship. He went on to state that *if reciprocation does not occur, neither does the vital sense of the real self*. People then revert to secondary adjustments, which are a way of saying, "I'm a person too. I'm not just part of the furniture."

When individuals employ secondary adjustments in marriage, it is a way of staking out some selfhood, some personal autonomy. Erving Goffman (1961) notes that secondary adjustments come in two forms: disruptive and contained. A disruptive secondary adjustment is one in which a woman intends to abandon the institution of marriage or radically alter its structure. In contrast, a contained secondary adjustment is a gesture that does not introduce pressure for radical change, but does signal to the woman herself that she is creating some space between herself and the marital role of *wife*.

1. *Disruptive secondary adjustments.* Belenky and her colleagues (1986) observed that:

96

Society teaches women to put their trust in men as defenders, [as] suppliers of the economic necessities, [as the] interpreters of the public will, and [as] liaisons with the larger community. Women learn that men hold the power and in society's eyes have the ultimate authority. (pp. 57–58)

But for many women in their study the male authority in their personal lives was not stable. Their sense of disappointment and outrage was pervasive. Belenky and her colleagues found that "it was only after some crisis of trust in male authority in their daily lives, coupled with some confirmatory experience that they, too, could know something for sure, that women . . . could take steps to change their fate and 'walk away from the past'" (Belenky, et al., 1986, p. 58). These women moved from the category of "received knowers" to a new category, that of "subjective knowers." They reached a point of saying that they could not trust what they had been told by external male authorities. They could only trust what they could know in their own gut. In the five-year Belenky research project, more than half the women in this category had recently taken steps to end relationships with lovers or husbands, to reject any further obligations to family members, and to live away on their own: "The claims of others, for years so salient for them, are often suddenly disregarded when the women begin to assert their own authority and autonomy" (1986, p. 77). Furthermore, in the Belenky study, women's stories of loss of trust in male authority were most often linked to sexual harassment and abuse.

Sociologist Talcott Parsons (1947) observed that the role of an adult woman contains sufficient strain and insecurity to produce emotional instability. Many Christians would agree that it is neurotic behavior indeed when a woman walks away from her marriage and hitchhikes to San Francisco to become a hooker. Yet such an event has a trigger. Unquestionably the "feminine role," as Parsons put it, places crucial strains on wives. In a high percentage of cases there has been physical, sexual, or emotional abuse.

2. *Contained secondary adjustments.* The range of contained adjustments is as wide as women are creative in erecting these

97

subtle barriers between the self and the role to which they have made primary adjustments in marriage.

People carry out primary adjustments whenever they participate in prescribed activities *with the prescribed spirit.* Any time they carry out prescribed activities in unprescribed ways or for unprescribed purposes, they detach themselves a bit from their official role. A secondary adjustment is anything people do to stand apart from the role imputed to them by society. This is *defiance within compliance.* This is bowing from the waist while standing tall in the heart. It is to comply and defy at the same time.

Contained secondary adjustments come in many forms. All of them represent ways women deal with their need for some sense of personal identity in the midst of carrying out the primary adjustments required by their subordinate position. The secondary adjustment may be as simple as a glare behind the offender's back. It may be the use of hostile humor, irony, sarcasm, or griping. Sometimes it is "unauthorized role distance" whereby a woman creates some private space. Some women use an attitude of stiffness, dignity, and coolness or "utter self-possession" to create that personal ledge. For others, stashing away mad money against an emergency creates the ledge. Passive aggression wears a hundred faces. It can be chronic lateness, unfulfilled good intentions, sloppy grooming, obesity, or low sexual responsiveness. In any form, it is a secondary adjustment putting distance between the self and the role. Impulse shopping also serves the same purpose.

Surface acting is another form of a contained secondary adjustment. In terms of Stanislavski's Method Acting, sociologist Hochschild distinguishes between "deep acting" and "surface acting." In surface acting, "the body, not the soul, is the main tool of the trade" (Hochschild, 1983, p. 37). Deep acting, on the other hand, brings the soul on stage. It is possible to surface-act as a secondary adjustment. It is a way of saying, "This is the self you want. You get what you want, but I know it's not the real me." However, if a woman chooses to surface-act, two things occur: First, she pays lip service to the primary adjustment; second, she knows that the role does not reveal the true self.

What goes on in a marital relationship that makes secondary adjustments necessary in the first place? Hochschild notes that "when one person has higher status than another, it becomes acceptable to both parties for the bottom dog to contribute more to the relationship than the top dog" (1983, pp. 84–85). This overturns the appeal of self-surrender that Turner (1976) wrote about. When there is *not* the expected reciprocated love, dependability in the relationship, or new opportunities for gratification in the relationship, the bottom dog either manages her emotions about the lack, finds secondary adjustments to distance herself from the role, or decides to walk away from the past.

Clearly, a woman's "way of knowing" determines what options are open to her in her definition of self and its relation to her marital role. Whether or not a woman can use secondary adjustments to ward off the role-engulfment of submission as defined by LaHaye (1976) is governed by her epistemological position. A received knower whose external authorities use the divine sanction of submission to legitimate hierarchical marital structures may have no resources to protect the self from absorption into the marital role. This is alienation that substitutes a false unity of the self for a true self, a "unity" in which ambivalences are removed and contingencies become certainties—the only comfortable position for the received knower. Goffman (1961) concludes that both compliance and rebellion are required to have a complete self: It is *against* something that the self can emerge. Yet a received knower who has embraced this false unity of the self cannot allow herself to experience the conflict inherent in "compliance with defiance." Self and role are fused together (Berger, 1969).

The essence of all alienation, according to Berger, is the imposition of a fictitious inexorability on the humanly constructed social world. The inexorable cannot be challenged. Roles take on the quality of immortality. Women who have internalized an ascriptive understanding of marital roles cannot risk tampering with such structures—to do so is to throw the universe out of kilter. Max Weber observed that "the sacred is the uniquely unalterable" (1922, 1963, p. 9). When hierarchical roles are stamped *sacred*, they are also stamped *unalterable*. What would otherwise be merely a contingency of human existence becomes a manifestation of universal law.

Yet wider cultural forces encourage some conservative evangelical women to question this legitimation. Economic factors have led to the dramatic rise of dual-career couples within conservative Christian churches on a par with national averages. As such women become wage earners outside their homes, their perceptions of themselves and their marital status have undergone some significant changes. In many cases, these women have begun to question the primary adjustments they had previously made to their position of subordination (Janeway, 1975). This trend has frequently led to inner turmoil and ultimately to efforts at realigning the spousal relationship. Supposedly enduring marital ties are being disrupted by women's increased self-awareness. This disruption calls for an evaluation of the effect of hierarchy on women's experience of marriage.

One assumption underlying this paper is that current generalized anxiety about traditional gender roles has been significantly heightened by women's changing self-perceptions and their entry into the labor force. This has altered the balance of power between income producer (husband as sole provider) and income processor (wife as caretaker); women have become income producers and have often insisted on shared responsibility in income processing (domestic activity). The resulting threat to the traditional balance of power creates such anxiety that a reiteration of the sacred legitimation of hierarchical order is called up to thwart potential moves toward more flexible gender roles and shared power. Which way individual women choose to go is often a function of the degree of fusion of self and role—that is, how much of the self is allowed to exist outside the prescribed role (Goffman, 1961; Hochschild, 1983).

Myth-Making and Myth-Unmaking

The myth is that all is well in Cleaverville, that the family unit in a traditional marriage is happy. In 1975, a *Redbook* survey reported that of all married women, those in traditional Christian marriages were the happiest. Yet even evangelical clergy have increasingly felt the sting of rising divorce rates. In an undocumented report, a small but well-known evangelical denomination recently announced that in the course of a year, they lost one clergy couple per week to divorce. Did the *Redbook* survey miss something about Christian marriages?

In a recent study conducted by the author, all the presently or previously married women on the staff of an evangelical Christian organization were asked open-ended questions about their expectations and experience of marriage. All the women who responded are committed Christian women. Seventy-five percent of the respondents are presently married; 19 percent are divorced; 6 percent are widowed. The women ranged in age between twenty-nine and sixty-three, with a median age of forty-six. The divorced women in the sample ranged in age between forty-five and sixty-three; they had been married between fifteen and thirty years with a mean of twenty-two years. These were not women with short-term commitments to marriage.

The first survey interview question asked the women to list up to five reasons it is advantageous for a woman to marry. The second question asked each woman to evaluate her own marital experience, past or present, in response to the advantages she listed as her answer to the first question. Seventy-five percent of the women listed "companionship" as an important advantage women gain when they marry. Yet when the women looked at their own experience, less than 20 percent rated their own marriages as highly successful in the area of companionship. To the contrary, their comments included statements like these:

"Companionship is very deficient and lacking."

"Companionship is poor—we have incompatible interests."

"Sometimes married people can be lonelier than singles, because if the mate doesn't or isn't able to provide the needed companionship, married women are *very limited* in their options and alternatives in filling this need."

"Companionship—this has been possibly the biggest disappointment for me personally as I chose to marry someone with very different interests than mine. . . . Hence the companionship relationship in my marriage has been disappointing, frustrating, hurtful, at times abusive—emotionally and mentally, not physically."

The third question in the survey asked about the disadvantages women experience when they marry. The most often mentioned disadvantages included these:

"Loss of potential for growth and development of talents."
"All-consuming responsibility for others (spouse and children)."
"Loss of one's own vision for ministry."
"Loss of independence, freedom to 'do my own thing.'"
"Time is no longer my own."
"Loss of freedom to make my own decisions."

How did these women rate their own experience of marriage on this question? One woman wrote:

I used to be artistic and actively involved in expressing myself artistically as well as musically—more *before* marriage. My husband was overbearing, selfish, critical, and controlling. I let him have his way while I served as laundry lady, cook, maid, and submissive, compliant doormat. He "increased" professionally, socially, financially, etc., while I "decreased"—becoming bitter and angry.

Another wrote:

My failure in marriage affected me in these ways: It almost completely destroyed my faith in God, self-confidence hit rock-bottom, no financial income for a while—difficulty in finding a job after not working for fifteen years (two children at home), loss of friends, loneliness, and total despair.

Other comments included,

"All I do is work and do childcare. Have to fight depression, fight to be innovative and pursue anything creative."
"I struggle to find time to do what I want to do and I feel guilty and selfish for wanting time to myself."
"Sometimes I feel 'controlled' or restricted in independence and freedom, which sometimes makes me depressed. . . . My identity is rather confused—as a single I felt whole, but as a married I feel like half a person and it's hard to know my identity."

The fifth survey question asked each woman how her job in the Christian organization affected her marriage. Because most staff women in that organization are in "jobs" and not "careers," few found their work particularly satisfying. Some said they would prefer to be full-time homemakers. With only a few exceptions, these women are in clerical positions. Their feelings about their work corroborated wider research findings that when women's work is not fulfilling, they prefer homemaking. In contrast, one woman with two master's degrees wrote:

> If I were not married, I would have stayed in the . . . work I was in before; probably would have moved around a little more. After marriage, my focus shifted from a highly satisfying but precarious *vocation* to a more dependable, less interesting *career*. My marriage has kept me employed in a position that is stable, but no longer satisfying. I have been stifled. I cannot advance by taking a job that would require moving because my husband will not move.

Additional questions in the survey asked women about the resources to which they turned in adjusting to the demands of marriage. Most women listed their relationship to God, prayer, Bible reading, and Christian friends as primary sources. A few used professional counselors to help them. In response to the question about ways their Christian faith and the church have helped or hindered their adjustment, more than half of the women indicated that the church had been a hindrance. In some cases, it was merely ineffective. Other women indicted the church more forcefully. In contrast, most of these women found their personal Christian faith a strong support.

Of the women in this study, a few decided to walk away from marriage. Most of the women stayed in their relationships, working hard either to manage their emotions about what they lacked or to adopt secondary adjustments to help them cope. The reality is that relatively few women—Christian and non-Christian alike— are genuinely happy in their marriages. That gap between the promise and the reality jars them almost daily.

Samuel Huntington (1981) has supplied a macrosociological analysis of political response that has ramifications for the study of women's experience of hierarchical marriage. Working with the perception of the gap between the promise of the American constitution and the reality of people's experience of it, he produced the following table:

	Perception of Gap	
Intensity of Belief in Ideals	Clear	Unclear
High	Moralism (eliminate gap)	Hypocrisy (deny gap)
Low	Cynicism (tolerate gap)	Complacency (ignore gap)

Top right table quadrant: In most role strain, people feel uncomfortable without knowing why. Their perception of the gap between promise and reality is unclear. If, at the same time, they believe intensely in the role as a social construct, they will deny the strain. If the discomfort they feel is vague, they discount it as unreal.

Bottom right table quadrant: If they only casually accept the role as authoritative in their lives, they will probably choose to ignore the gap. It is likely that the role is not high in their hierarchy of salience if intensity of belief in it is low. They become complacent.

Bottom left table quadrant: When the perception of the gap between promise and reality is clear, however, the responses are very different. If the person sees the gap clearly but has a low intensity of belief in the social construct, it usually leads to cynicism about the role. The person tolerates the gap and puts enough distance between the self and the role to handle the strain.

Top left table quadrant: If, at the same time the person sees the gap clearly she also believes intensely in the role as a social construct, that becomes a prod to reduce the gap between the ideal and the reality. This usually puts several actions in motion:

The person begins to question the authority behind the social construct: "Who says so? How can I be sure that person is right?"

Moral passion develops. The person takes the ideal seriously and asks, "Why isn't this my experience? What needs to change?" The urgency to recapture the ideal grows.

Questioning the authority behind the social construct turns to attacking the institution.

When taken to this point, the person begins experimenting with alternatives and also begins questioning all social conventions.

It is precisely people who take the Scriptures seriously and have a clear vision of the gap between the biblical ideal and their experience who initiate movements like Christians for Biblical Equality. This moral passion fuels social change. But the crisis in marital experience today is not always resolved with moral passion. More often, the perception of the gap is unclear and some men and women deny its existence, while others only casually accept the role as authoritative in their lives because their belief in it is weak. For others who clearly discern the gap between the promise and the reality, their belief in the ideal is so weak that they use an arsenal of secondary adjustments to distance the self from the imputed role.

The question is how should the church respond to this gap created by what it promises women and what women experience in hierarchical marriage? Is it enough to reinforce the theodicy legitimizing asymmetrical marital relations? Ought its response focus on telling women to knuckle under because it is their Christian duty to do so? More and more women are moving from an institutional view of the self to an impulse view of the self. Even Christian women are walking away from their past. In the process, they often also walk away from God and the church. We need to do better in the future than we've done in the past in understanding and helping women in such crises.

6

No Church to Call Home

Shirley Gillett

When I was a little girl, I was told that women were supposed to keep silent in the church. And they did. They were not allowed to speak. They were not allowed to read even the announcements. They could not pray aloud. They could not ask questions. Their voices were effectively smothered. If a man had led a life of complete debauchery, if he had killed so many people he could not remember the number, if he had raped and degraded women, if he had indulged himself, not caring whom he hurt—all he had to do was confess Christ and the next day he could be preaching in the church to the glowing introductions of Christian leaders. But the women he had raped and brutalized would have been told to keep silent. Their stories would never be told. It was the perfect system to assure the continued abuse of women.

I have sat in church pews and listened to wife beaters and rapists speak freely while their victims were silent. I have listened to a man who sexually assaulted me tell people how to live the Christian life while I stared at the wall and tried to keep breathing. But I am not alone. My experiences are not as unique as I would wish.

I was blessed with wonderful, loving parents who greatly reflected God's love and provided a happy home life. They introduced me to Jesus and the power of faith and prayer.

Sadly, though, the lessons the church and society taught me regarding my gender left indelible scars. Despite all the talk about "different" ministries for women, as opposed to "inferior" ones, it was pretty obvious to me, even as a young child, who was important to God. No one who says that men should do all the speaking, run things, and make all the decisions should really expect women not to get the message of their inferiority. I remember as a little girl crying myself to sleep at night, wondering why God didn't love me as much as a little boy.

In the area of sexuality, both adults and Sunday school papers alike taught that men had powerful sexual urges that once roused, could not be controlled. It was a woman's job to control them. In fact, it was a woman's *fault* if they were not controlled. I often wondered why it was that men who couldn't control their own bodies got to control everything else.

I also learned that the only status women were accorded in society was that regarding their youth and beauty, or their childbearing. There was some talk in the church about the status accorded godly older women, but since they couldn't preach or teach and since no one seemed to consult them about anything, it didn't appear to me to be anything more than words. Watching beauty contests and looking at magazines, I soon learned to hate my body, my face, and my future. I starved myself all day only to gorge myself at night and dream of massive plastic surgery.

When I was sexually assaulted by an older male church member, he told me what the Sunday school papers had told me: "It was all your fault that I couldn't control myself." When a woman is raped or otherwise assaulted, the first question is generally about her behavior rather than that of her attacker. What was she wearing? Why did she go to his apartment? What was she doing out at night alone? Why did she marry such a creep in the first place? Even when a woman cannot think of anything she could have done differently, the nagging feeling that it is somehow her fault seldom leaves. The resulting low self-esteem often leaves her open to further abuse.

That incident confirmed for me my worthlessness. It didn't occur to me to tell anyone. If he denied it, whom would they believe?

Men were considered powerful and important. They preached. They taught. Their words were considered worth something. Women's words were worth nothing.

I became severely depressed. I cried a lot of the time. I began to notice how left out I felt in the church. I cringed every time I heard someone say that a woman brought an attack on herself. And I noticed that I heard that quite often. I also heard both men and women talk about how women "made up" stories of rape to cover their own indiscretions. I never spoke to anyone in the church about the things that happened to me. I realized it was not a place I could feel safe. It was not a place I could call home. I gradually drifted away. I made up excuses for not going to church. I crawled inside myself. I still prayed. I still believed. Somehow, I was sure that Jesus would not have treated me that way.

Proposals to Help Abused Women in the Church

Healing has not been an easy process. It was years after the last incident of violence that it even began. The following list of proposals is offered for churches to adopt if they wish to keep abused women from leaving the church and if they wish to attract women outside the church who have not seen the church as a place of help and healing. All of these changes were proposed by survivors who have left the church because of their experiences and by survivors who have never approached the church because of their negative contacts with Christians, Christian literature and broadcasts, or because of abuse by a church leader. Many of the women are Christians; many are not. Yet all of these women share a deep spiritual longing. Some of the Christian women hope desperately that they will some day find a church where they can feel safe instead of being further victimized. Some of the women have never belonged to any religious organization but know that they have a deep void, a spiritual self that needs filling.

Use Female Imagery When Referring to God

For many survivors, relating to a male image of God is impossible. Depictions of God as a loving Father wanting a close relationship with his children may be comforting to those who have had loving earthly fathers, but for women whose fathers approached them looking for close relationships that involved pain and humiliation, these depictions are both terrifying and distancing.

Fortunately, the Bible contains a number of female images of God which can be used to balance those of a male (Deut. 32:11, 18; Ps. 131:2–3; Isa. 42:14; 49:15; 66:9–13; Hosea 13:8; Luke 15:8–10). Many other images of God, such as those of Creator, Friend, or Rock are gender-neutral and open to interpretation by the listener.

Confront the Inequality in Male-Female Relationships

One thing I discovered early on was that the survivors who had made the most progress in their healing were those who had come to see their abuse not simply as a personal tragedy, but as part of a systematic injustice. As they made the connection between women's devalued and powerless status in society and their own devalued and powerless status at the hands of their abuser, in the justice system, and in the eyes of society, they began to understand why beauty contests often made them feel like so many slabs of meat, and why speakers and writers who used only words like "mankind" and "he" to refer to both genders made them feel left out and invisible. Once they had made these connections, they could break free from the destructive patterns engendered by their abuse and begin to envisage a radically different and healthier way for men and women to relate.

Unfortunately, the evangelical church for the most part tries to obscure the fact that these connections exist. Some try to say that although women may be silenced, not allowed to preach, hear God spoken of at church services as male, and see the podium filled with male authority figures, that is no reason for them to feel second class. They try to say that although the man should make all final decisions in a marriage and the wife should be the one following and submitting, there is no reason to believe that this dominance in spiritual matters leads to dominance in other forms. They may grant you that it could possibly do so with a husband who was not a Christian, but certainly not in a Christian marriage. This idyllic assumption, however, has no basis in fact.

Inequality at one level of a relationship leads to inequality at others. As sociologist Robert Brym points out:

Sexual assault in general is encouraged by a lesson most of us still learn at home, in school, and in the mass media—that it is natural and right for men to dominate women . . . in the paid work world, in the household, in government, and in all other spheres of life men still tend to command substantially more power than women, which is to say that they have a greater capacity to influence and control others. Men typically have more authority than women too, which means that their greater power is generally considered valid or acceptable. Daily patterns of gender domination, viewed as legitimate by most people, can and do spill over into the realm of sex. From this point of view, most sexual assault is simply an expression of male authority by other means. . . . Sexual assault and other forms of woman abuse are rooted in the structure of social relations between men and women. It follows that while policies to punish and reha-bilitate rapists and other woman abusers are desirable, the prob-lem of woman abuse cannot be solved comprehensively unless power and authority between men and women are more evenly distributed in society and unless our culture comes to reflect that redistribution. (1993, pp. 6–7)

Although some evangelical Christian magazines and books have begun to deal with the subject of incest, rape, and wife beating, few are willing to confront the basic inequality of male-female relationships that is at the root of all forms of woman abuse. A typical response regarding incest is that "These fathers abuse their God-given roles as leaders of their families" (Sanford, 1994, p. 30). Unfortunately, it is this very role that sets up the basic inequal-ity between men and women, thus encouraging abuse, discourag-ing disclosure, and turning survivors away from a church that had a hand in their abuse.

Rethink the Way in Which the Church Treats Women's Sexuality

An Ann Landers column (1994) supported a man wishing to marry a virgin by telling him that he should not marry a woman whose hymen was not totally intact or he would always consider that he had settled for "damaged goods." The column even suggested sending a potential mate for a medical exam to confirm this. A number of evangelical books on the market also tell young men not to even consider marrying a woman unless she is a virgin. Although some of them suggest the same strategy to young women, there is no physical equivalent of the "intact hymen" ever suggested for males.

This concept of virginity equaling an intact hymen encourages legions of raped and incestuously assaulted women to view themselves as damaged goods. A woman who has been raped is no more "impure" than a woman who has been stabbed in the arm. A weapon has been used violently against her. The fact that that weapon is part of a man's body may be held as a mark against him, but a woman cannot be made impure by an act which is committed against her.

Knowing that they will be viewed as damaged goods, as somehow complicit in their attack if they admit to having been raped or sexually assaulted, most women keep silent. This encourages their assailants to continue the abuse of other victims and prevents women who have been attacked from ever healing. If a woman has never told her husband about the attack, she will never feel truly loved by him, wondering, "If he knew, would he think less of me?" Until survivors of rape and other forms of sexual assault are seen as victims of violence and treated with the same concern and nonjudgmental attitude reserved for victims of other violent crimes, these crimes will continue to be underreported, abusers will be free to abuse again, and survivors will never heal.

Since women generally have been viewed as responsible for the sexual crimes committed against them, it is not surprising that the church has tended to portray prostitutes as sinful, oversexed women who lure "good" men into illicit sex. The facts that most prostitutes loathe sex, that most are in desperate economic circumstances, and that the great majority are survivors of atrocious sexual abuse are largely ignored.

Behind the tough exterior that many prostitutes erect, I have found vulnerable, hurting women who learned as little girls to devalue themselves as they were devalued by their abusers. The little girl inside is still waiting for someone to tell her she is worth something, to tell her she did not "cause" grown men to assault and degrade her. Yet the woman she has grown into lives in a society that allows almost any sexually violent act or perversion to be committed against her because, supposedly, she has "chosen" this lifestyle. Prostitutes are viewed as disposable women, with even their murders largely ignored. And sadly, the evangelical church has most often stood as their enemy instead of as their friend and protector.

I do not think it is insignificant that the author of Hebrews—who in chapter eleven lists only a few of the great men and women of the faith and who says that time would fail to tell of Gideon, David, Samuel, and others—does not fail to tell of that great woman of faith "the harlot Rahab." God does not view prostitutes as disposable women; neither should we.

Women's sexuality cannot be discussed without giving attention to the large number of sexual crimes committed against women and to the long-term effects these crimes have on a woman's life and sexual functioning.

Have More Women in Leadership Positions

One of the reasons for this is practical. If an abused woman comes to the church, it is often very difficult for her to go to men for counseling and advice. When women are readily visible in positions of authority, it will be easier for her to come forward. As one abused woman said, "Am I supposed to tell a man all the stuff this guy did to me? It's hard enough to talk about it to another woman, but at least she'll know how I feel."

Another reason to have women leaders is the effect it has on women's sense of worth. If a church shows that it values women's thoughts, words, and leadership abilities, then it sends a strong signal to abused women whose own sense of self-worth is generally at low ebb that they, as women, are valued by the church and by God. If they see that women are encouraged to speak publicly in the church, they will not fear being silenced and will be more likely to believe that their voices will be heard.

Support Feminism and Women's Equality

Webster's Tenth New Collegiate Dictionary defines feminism as "(1) the theory of the political, economic, and social equality of the sexes; (2) organized activity on behalf of women's rights and interests." Yet even some Christians who support the above definitions find themselves unable to say that they support feminism. It probably has something to do with the way in which the media portrays feminists. It may have something to do with certain proposals put forward by individual feminists or feminist groups. But why should that be a problem? Christians don't mind defining themselves as Christians despite the fact that they disagree with others who so define themselves. The broad sweep of those calling themselves "Christian" covers, among others, Greek Orthodox, conservative Catholics, high Anglicans, charismatic Pentecostals, Jehovah's Witnesses, Mormons, and a group now springing up in North America that advocates capital punishment for adulterers, homosexuals, and incorrigible youth. One does not have to agree with everything that each of these groups believes (in fact it would be impossible to do so since their beliefs differ from each other) in order to identify oneself as a Christian.

The same is true of feminism. A recent banner headline on *Ms.* magazine (September/October 1993) read, "No, Feminists *Don't* All Think Alike," and nothing could be truer. Identifying yourself in support of feminism means that you believe in the equality, worth, and dignity of all women, just as defining yourself as a Christian means marking yourself as a follower of Christ. It does not mean that you must stop disagreeing with positions taken by individual feminists or advocated by particular groups any more than it means as a Christian you must stop speaking out against misinformation or damaging proposals put forward by others who call themselves Christian.

Many survivors I spoke with had their first (and often their only) experience of being believed, valued, and comforted from feminists. Often, reading feminist books or magazines opened their eyes to the realization that they were not alone and that they were not at fault. It took one young woman thirteen years to tell her mother about being raped. When asked why she could tell her mother now and not before, she responded, "Well, now she's become a feminist." That change made her feel that, finally, it was safe to open up.

When Jesus was teaching on this earth, it is worth noting that he loved, forgave, and championed the weak, the abused, and the social outcasts. Most of his verbal attacks were reserved for the rich and the powerful, whether in religious, political, or economic circles. When the Pharisees beratingly asked why Jesus ate with the outcasts, he replied, "Because people who are well don't need a doctor! It's the sick people who do! . . . Now go away and learn the meaning of this verse of Scripture, 'It isn't your sacrifices and your gifts I want—I want you to be merciful'" (Matt. 9:12–13 TLB).

Unfortunately, in most of the sermons I have heard and in most of the evangelical Christian magazines and books I have read, the emphasis has been reversed. There were plenty of attacks on the "selfish" women who sought equal rights, but no attacks on the selfish men who retained privilege. When there was any mention of abused women, homeless people, or other outcasts, it was often followed by a quick condemnation of them as part of a snidely labeled "victim subculture," or at best followed with the simple admonition to "give a bit more food to the hungry," or to tell Christian men not to beat up on their wives or sexually molest their daughters. There was no insistence on radical change, no call for a closer look at the religious, political, and social structures that have fostered these abuses.

If we are really interested in using the Bible to stop abuse instead of to encourage it, then we have to reverse this trend. If we are really interested in stopping abuse, we must return to following Jesus' example. Jesus was not afraid to confront the Pharisees; we must not be afraid to confront church leaders and laypeople. We must not say that we will wait until they get around to accepting equality. Women are hurting. Women are dying. Women are being turned away from Christ. Women are being attacked in Christian homes by Christian men. For too long we have been like the Pharisees, straining at gnats while swallowing camels. It is time we used the spirit of the law to guide us in our interpretation of Scripture. It is time we took the outcasts, the bruised and broken women, into our arms and into our hearts. It is time the church stopped being a place of hurting and became a place of healing.

PART 2

TO HEAL

7

Some Biblical Reflections on Justice, Rape, and an Insensitive Society

Craig S. Keener

Various sociological, psychological, and theological approaches to abuse are vital in seeking solutions to the crises facing people whose pain is often neglected by our society. In addition, an examination of biblical texts addressing abuse can provide insights both to encourage Christian victims of abuse and to call the Christian community as a whole to a more concerted and vocal stand against abuse.

The Bible is practical—more practical than many of its defenders often realize. It does us little good to call ourselves Bible believers if we do not care to obey the teachings on compassion and justice in the Bible we claim to believe.

I am trying to understand some of the pain and feelings of worthlessness that motivate some abusive men, but I do not know what motivates the cruelty of alleged Christians to pronounce judgment on broken people who have done them no wrong. When Desirée Washington accused Mike Tyson of having raped her, the Bible study at our church was split down the middle on the question of whether rape victims might sometimes share some of the guilt for the rape. That the president of our National Baptist Convention took Mike Tyson's side complicated matters further.

The Bible teaches that rape and divorce are crimes, but also that like murder, theft, and adultery, these crimes can involve an innocent victim; it also teaches that rape by definition *always* includes such a victim. Yet some church people are as out of touch with the Bible as they are with the reality of the pain around them. The prophets denounced the injustice abounding in their lands, and we must denounce it today—wherever that injustice manifests itself. It may be injustice in the failure of our judicial and educational systems and, yes, even our churches, which permits entire neighborhoods to be terrorized by murder, theft, and abuse. It may be injustice that manifests itself in the trivialization of sins by many liberal churches and the condemnation or neglect of sin's victims by many conservative churches.

As we turn to a discussion of the biblical issue of rape, then, I need to warn you that this is not a dispassionate paper but a discussion that is fueled by pain that I have witnessed among people who are dear to me. Nevertheless, I believe this paper accurately reflects the biblical witness concerning rape, a witness that speaks to the pain and rage of God over the abuse of precious people he has formed in his image for eternal fellowship with himself.

A Conspiracy of Society and Church

What motivated me to focus on the issue of rape in particular was the concern of a minister in my Old Testament class when we were discussing Amnon's rape of Tamar. She told me about an anonymous young woman in her congregation about to enter college, who had saved herself for her future husband. She was raped by two men and, beyond the trauma of the rape, began to question whether she was still a virgin. Her grades began to drop and other aspects of her life began to fall apart. Like Tamar, David's daughter, she felt that she had been defiled for life and felt like giving up.

Her pain reflected both the insensitivity of our society and the insensitivity of much of the church. Our society opposes rape insofar as it is one act of violence, but is incapable of understanding how deeply the scars of violation burn beyond the immediate physical pain involved. Some societies could offer a more sensitive appraisal. When Prince Shechem raped Dinah, Jacob's daughter, Dinah's brothers killed Shechem and declared, "Should he have treated our sister like a prostitute?" (Gen. 34:31 NIV)—that is, like a person one may use sexually without committing one's life to that person as a partner of equal human dignity. Our society has trivialized the horror of rape in part because it has also devalued the sanctity of human sexuality; sex is considered ethical so long as one does not pay a fee for it. It does not matter whether one respects the other person's dignity enough to commit one's life to the person or simply uses the person's body to gratify one's own desires. This is what Cornel West laments as the "market morality" of "the American way of life" by which our entertainment media reduce people to mere "objects of personal pleasure" (1993, p. 17).

A society that readily condones emotional seduction, that negligently considers it immoral to offer sexual novices moral advice (yet looks askance at unwed mothers as a tax burden), that views "safe" sex as partial protection from viruses and pregnancy, but ignores the relational dimensions of sexual intimacy, will also likely trivialize physical rape.

Society's sexual ethics are not alone in contributing to the isolation of rape victims. In extolling virginity, the church has usually failed to mention the Bible's explicit exception for an innocent party raped against her will, leaving victims feeling unclean instead of embraced by those who should be defending them. Silence is an inadequate response to oppression, whether that oppression is slavery, murder, pornographic exploitation, marital betrayal, or rape; those who have been wounded need to feel God's love through God's church.

Some friends close to me were raped either before I knew them or since I met them. Two young Christian women I know who were raped gave up the ideal of virginity and abandoned Christian sexual values altogether. One has since returned to Christianity, and she lamented to me that if she had just known that God was not rejecting her for what had happened to her, she never would have turned her back on biblical sexual teachings to begin with. I first collected the following biblical insights to share with one rape victim questioning her moral status. I encouraged her to believe that she retained her virginity in God's sight, and I share these insights now in the hope that they may encourage others who have experienced similar pain.

My thesis is that *rape victims do not lose their moral virginity.* Not only must we recognize that they are innocent in the sight of God—for they are not morally responsible for an act to which they did not consent—but we must also recognize that the God of justice is actively on their side in this situation. God does not view our sexuality from a purely physiological perspective (otherwise a woman could lose her virginity if her hymen ruptured while riding a horse, and a man could lose his through a nocturnal emission), but from a moral and relational standpoint.

A Biblical Perspective on Relationships

Before one can examine the biblical perspective on rape, one must examine the biblical perspective on proper covenant relationships as the appropriate context for sexual intimacy. Our society treats rape too lightly in part because we treat sexuality too lightly; some view an invasion of one's body as no more significant than any other invasion of privacy (like the burglar I found in my apartment a few months ago). Society particularly trivializes rape when the woman was on a date with a man she thought she could trust, as if betrayed trust reflects a flaw in the victim rather than in her assailant.

The Bible places great value on sexual autonomy, by which I mean a person surrendering this most intimate possession only voluntarily and to one other person whom he or she can trust for life. In this context, the rapist's perversion of an act that should be the ultimate act of love and commitment into an act of violence and control is analogous to Judas's sinister kiss. By perverting a normal sign of affection for one's teacher into a betrayal for death, Judas turned a kiss into the ultimate act of treachery. Old Testament law prescribed for breaches of sexual fidelity the same penalties it prescribed for murder (Deut. 22:20–24), and compared the violation of rape to the violation of murder (Deut. 22:26). Old Testament narratives likewise list the sufferings of rape victims alongside those slaughtered in war (Isa. 13:15–16).

Because the Bible makes a lifelong covenant commitment the prerequisite for sexual intimacy, the biblical perspective on sexuality is rooted in the biblical perspective on all human relationships; they are to be based on mutual commitment and sacrifice. This is what God intended for the special relationship of wife and husband in marriage, except on an even higher level. Even though one's relatives were called one's "flesh" (Gen. 29:14), God calls a man to leave his parents and be joined to his wife (not a near relative), so that he becomes "one flesh" with her (Gen. 2:23–24). God's intention for husband and wife is thus unity of the highest kind, superseding even the deepest of previous family ties. Because marriage is based on such a deep commitment, marriage partners should be able to be intimate with one another without fear of being betrayed.

God never intended for such relationships to be a power play; that was introduced into the world by sin. When God says, "It is not good for the man to be alone. I will make a helper suitable for him" (Gen. 2:18 NIV), the Hebrew term used for "helper" does not refer to a servant; indeed, the term is usually used in the Old Testament for God, our ultimate helper. The image in Genesis 2 is that man was not complete enough on his own; he needed the strength of woman, and they together would become one flesh. God meant men and women to have a beautiful relationship of committed intimacy without betrayal and selfishness.

Sin introduced conflict into the relationship. As God told Eve after the fall, "with pain you will give birth to children. Your desire will be for your husband, and he will rule over you" (Gen. 3:16 NIV). When we compare Genesis 4:7, which uses the same Hebrew figure of speech, it becomes clear that Eve's punishment in Genesis 3 was not a divine decree subordinating women, as some people think. Rather, the punishment was conflict with her husband, with the husband enforcing his rule over the wife because he was stronger.

Like divorce, however, this conflict was never God's original purpose (Matt. 19:3–8). Toil (Gen. 3:17–19), labor pains (3:16), and death (3:19) were all results of the fall, but none of them was good, and we are called to work *against* them. Human sin introduced conflict into marital relationships, but God wants his followers to have marriages that reflect the original ideal in the garden—

"one flesh." Relationships have become distorted through sin in this world, but those who are living under God's rule can model a different kind of lifestyle. As people of his kingdom, we can all learn to model the lifestyle of the world to come.

A Biblical Perspective on Sexuality

The ultimate commitment that can be made between two persons is the lifelong commitment to be husband and wife. Although many kinds of intimacy can be shared among friends (such as that between David and Jonathan), God reserved one unique kind of intimacy for the marriage relationship, to keep it special—sexual intimacy. That ancient Israel conceived of sexuality in terms of committed intimacy is suggested even by the Hebrew term they used for the act of marriage: "The man knew his wife Eve, and she conceived and bore Cain" (Gen. 4:1 NRSV). Further, God demanded not only faithfulness to one's spouse after marriage, but also faithfulness in advance to one's future spouse before marriage.

God gave Israel many laws to ensure that this perspective was maintained, even though it contrasted starkly with the behavior of some of the surrounding nations. The nations around Israel did uphold marriage and punish adultery, but many also practiced ritual prostitution (sex with prostitutes in their temples) and told stories of gods who freely impregnated whatever mortals they chose (typically by rape or deception). In contrast, God exemplified fidelity to the marriage covenant by his special faithfulness to Israel.

The Old Testament law, being a civil law, did allow some concessions to human sinfulness (ultimately abolished by Jesus), since it was thought better to regulate certain unjust acts by civil law than to lose control of them altogether. For instance, God did not directly forbid polygamy, divorce, blood-avengers, or certain kinds of servitude, though God regulated them and enacted principles that would ultimately challenge the right of such institutions to exist. Other practices, however, *were* explicitly forbidden even under Old Testament civil law, such as premarital sex, adultery, murder, and rape. It is important for the modern reader inclined toward ethnocentrism to keep in mind that the biblical laws permitting concessions to sinful structures addressed a cultural situation very different from our own, where the best available solution was sometimes less than what we would consider ideal. Yet in addressing its culture, the text presupposes some ethical criteria that, as I have mentioned, exceed the concessions; I here advocate as transcultural not the cultural situations, but the principles by which the text addresses them.

Our culture takes interpersonal factors in human bonding—especially in marriage and the relationship that leads to it—far less seriously than ancient Israel and many other societies have. In many societies, marriage includes a monetary transaction—the dowry or the bride-price (money brought by the wife from her father's house to protect her financially, or money paid as barter to the bride's father to symbolically repay the father for raising the groom's future wife). In some societies, even cohabitation does not mean a couple is married unless there is also a transaction between families (e.g., laws of Eshnunna 27–28). For all the chauvinism of "primitive" societies, such cultures often respect both parties as individuals from diverse backgrounds and offer more rules protecting the parties economically and socially in event of marital failure than we do.

Because sexual activity was reserved for marriage, the only *cheap* sex one could have in such cultures was with a prostitute. Then, as today, prostitutes were often without other means of support for themselves or their children; in the Roman period, many or most were slaves. We rightly contend that prostitutes sell themselves too cheaply, that men are exploiting human beings by using them for a small price; yet many men and women in our society charge even less to be exploited. Biblical ethics urge men and women not to give themselves away in sexual intimacy to anyone not willing to pay the ultimate price for it: the commitment of his or her whole life.

Although other biblical passages such as Proverbs 5:15–20 and Genesis 38–39 do address the importance of the husband's faithfulness, Deuteronomy 22 addresses particularly the ancient Near Eastern legal issue of the wife's fidelity (without minimizing the husband's). These particular laws probably especially address the woman because she was the one whose virginity could be tested in the manner this text depicts. To ensure that a woman waited for her future spouse, the text lays down strict laws. A woman who was supposed to be a virgin and whose hymen had not been ruptured some other way could be executed if she were found not to be a virgin—that is, if she had had premarital sex but tried to get married as a virgin anyway (Deut. 22:15, 20–21). We lack evidence that ancient Israel ever actually carried out this law, but the purpose of including it was to deter sexual immorality (22:21). The penalty for having engaged in sex with someone other than one's future spouse (22:23–24)—even before one knew whom one's future spouse was—was the same as the penalty for adultery after marriage (22:22). This is because sexual immorality before marriage was viewed as adultery in advance—adultery against one's *future* spouse. This was treated more severely than mere theft—as severely, in fact, as murder—because adultery involved the stealing of a person's most precious possession: the faithfulness of one's spouse and the ability to trust him or her.

If the man had falsely accused the woman of not being a virgin, he was publicly beaten and paid a fine for shaming her. He also forfeited the possibility of ever divorcing her (22:18–19). This final penalty may sound more cruel to the wife than to the husband; why would she want to stay with a man who had treated her so unjustly? But two answers to this objection must be offered. First, unjust as it may have been, men controlled ancient societies, and women would be hard-pressed to find support if they were unmarried (Ruth 2:2, 17–23); this text's arrangement provided the woman permanent financial security. Second, and more important, the arrangement discouraged the practice of falsely accusing a wife when a man wished to be rid of her; if he ended the marriage, he had to grant her a certificate (freeing her to remarry) and return her dowry (Deut. 24:1).

Paul reiterates the importance of sexual fidelity in the New Testament. When we are joined with someone sexually, an intimate bond is formed; this is a precious bond, not to be thrown around cheaply without the intimacy that accompanies it (1 Cor. 6:16). Someone who has sex outside of marriage sins against not only God, but against his or her own body (6:18), which was meant for better things—for faithfulness to God (6:19–20) and for faithfulness to one's spouse (7:4).

The Bible speaks of marital and premarital fidelity as a matter of justice in interpersonal relationships, and many cultures' wisdom gleaned from human experience seems to support the biblical perspective. All traditional cultures form marriage structures (although the nature of marriage varies from one culture to the next); most societies regard adultery negatively, and many also regard premarital sex and sometimes divorce as destabilizing forces; many cultures impose sanctions against those who violate these cultural codes. Our culture's experiment with antitraditional sexual ethics has ultimately confirmed the wisdom of many traditional societies; in the meantime, our intelligentsia's experiment has left many broken lives in its wake.

Yet our society's growing recognition of the value of faithfulness in relationships derives not only from general social observations but also from the basic character of human nature. When we make ourselves vulnerable to others (or are born in that relation to them) and they betray us, that is unethical. This is true whether the betrayal is merely gossiping about a secret we confided in them or exploiting our sexuality for their own passions, without any intention of commitment. To invite someone to become so intimate that we admit them into union with our own bodies is perhaps the ultimate vulnerability; to learn that they wanted the goods without so much as an enduring friendship is probably the ultimate betrayal. No matter how common such betrayal becomes, it remains agonizing to its victims.

Intimacy only flourishes in the context of trust, and trust only flourishes in the context of commitment, which nurtures unconditional love. Betrayal can severely damage its victims' capacity for trust, hence the victim's capacity for intimacy; betrayal easily clones itself as novices to love are instructed in its ways. If our society treats the sexual relationship so lightly and ignores its emotional repercussions, is it any wonder that we are less horrified and enraged by rape than we should be?

The Meaning of Rape

As strictly as Israelite law forbade sexual relations with someone to whom one was not married, it was careful to point out that rape was a different, special case. In the biblical perspective, rape was not an act determined by mutual sinful consent, like adultery or sexual promiscuity; rape was a sin imposed by one person on another, like murder or theft. The rape victim had no choice in her situation.

If an engaged woman was raped, the man who raped her was put to death for committing adultery against her impending marriage union (Deut. 22:25, cf. Eshnunna 26). She, however, was not to be punished, for as the Bible explicitly says, "there is no sin in the girl worthy of death, for just as a man rises against his neighbor and murders him, so is this case" (22:26 NASB). In fact, if no one else was present as a witness of her innocence but she was clearly violated, biblical law assumes her innocence without requiring witnesses (22:27); she does not bear the burden of proof to argue that she did not consent. This was a society where sexual fidelity was highly prized. If the couple definitely had intercourse, the man was guilty either way, but if the woman *might* have been innocent, her innocence must be assumed.

One drawback of ancient Israelites' usual chastity, however, is that most men choosing a wife for the first time wanted a woman who had never had intercourse before, and this *could* pose a problem for a virgin who had been raped. She had lost future proof of her virginity, and some men would have been tempted to view her as other than a virgin in a society where most potential spouses were virgins. Since she could prove the circumstances under which her hymen had been ruptured, she would not be subject to shame or penalties after marriage (Deut. 22:17). It would still have been somewhat harder (though not impossible) for her to find a husband, just as it was for widows and divorcées. The man who had raped her had thus potentially deprived her of her future hopes, including financial security in a society where men controlled all sufficient means of economic production.

To protect the woman placed in this situation, two options were provided in the cases when the man was not executed (i.e., if the woman were not already betrothed or married). Either the rapist had to marry her and support her financially all her life, or (and this is assumed here as self-evident, but is explicitly stated in Exod. 22:17), her father as legal guardian (unmarried women were usually minors in that society) could exercise the right of refusal on her behalf and demand instead sufficient monetary payment to cover her dowry. If the Exodus text refers to a traditional dowry, it means the money she would take into a marriage with her to keep her financially secure if something happened to the marriage; at any rate, in that culture the money would probably ensure her a new husband. What is most significant for our point is that Exodus 22:17 calls it a dowry "equal to the bride-price for virgins"; she was violated against her will and therefore must be treated as a virgin would be.

The consequence of such a law would be to discourage rape. It sent a message to the man: Sex is an act of covenantal intimacy only proper in the context of a committed relationship. If you are going to have sex with someone, you must be prepared to support her for the rest of your life. If you force her against her will, you must not only be ready to support her, but also to do without the benefit of ever having her affections—to be ready for her and her father to exercise the right of refusal. This apparently kept rape a rare occurrence in ancient Israel.

Our culture is different from ancient Israel, and I am neither suggesting that we execute rapists nor go back to an economy where only men get paid for their work. I am suggesting, however, that the Bible leaves no doubt as to how strongly God feels about rape. Modern laws may not offer sufficient vindication for a rape victim or demand sufficient restitution from her assailant, but the Bible leaves no question concerning whose side *God* is on—an encouragement many Christian rape victims today desperately need.

A Case of Rape

Israel never viewed rape lightly; as rare as rape was in ancient Israel, brothers of rape victims sometimes felt that the act should be avenged by the rapist's death. In Genesis 34, Shechem, a local Canaanite prince, raped Dinah, the daughter of Jacob; two of her brothers responded by not only killing Shechem, but also every male in his city to prevent retaliation for killing him. Although their vengeance went too far, as Jacob pointed out in Genesis 49:7 (perhaps because it got him in trouble with his neighbors—Gen.

34:30), it illustrates the strong feelings some of Israel's forebears had against rape.

The Bible provides a more detailed story of rape itself, in this case acquaintance rape, with regard to the family of King David. His eldest son, Amnon, heir to his throne by birthright, conceived a passion for his half sister Tamar (2 Sam. 13:1–2). A friend helped Amnon plot against Tamar, who never suspected his motives for wanting to see her (13:3–10). Once he revealed his motives and asked for intercourse, she pleaded with him: If they engaged in premarital sex, she would forfeit her evidence of virginity and would thus be unable to marry later; better that Amnon should ask for her hand in marriage (13:11–13). But Amnon performed his will on her by brute force (13:14), and once he had finished, he lost all interest in her (13:15).

If Tamar was like most Israelite girls her age (probably in her young teens), one of her fondest dreams was of a happy marriage. Amnon had apparently ruined her dreams and potentially ruined her life in a single act of his own self-gratification (13:16); afterward he wanted nothing to do with her (13:17). In Tamar's case, it appears that she was so discouraged that she gave up on intimacy altogether (13:20); Amnon had ruined her life.

David was angry (13:21), but the text does not suggest that he severely punished Amnon for his act. It is thus not altogether surprising that Tamar's brother Absalom, perhaps second in line for the throne anyway, decided to avenge his sister by having Amnon killed (13:28–29). Absalom turned out to be as bad as Amnon, but Amnon's sin was the catalyst that allowed Absalom's own evil to surface. The biblical narrative indicates that all this trouble in David's household reflected judgment for David's sin with Bathsheba (12:10–12). In other words, this biblical account is so horrifying precisely because it was meant to be. In this case, unlike those of Deuteronomy 22 and Genesis 34, the sufferings *were* divine judgment, but even in this case they were *not* judgment on Tamar. The narrative portrays Tamar as innocent, her trust savagely betrayed.

Many Jewish teachers in the time of Jesus blamed men's lust on the way women dressed or acted, but Jesus placed the blame for lust squarely on the man who did it (Matt. 5:28; see Keener, 1991, pp. 16–19). Nowhere in the Bible is *any* guilt assigned to a rape victim, nor does anyone question whether she might have done something to have invited it. Anyone who attributes to the rapist anything less than *all* the blame is making up his or her own ideas, not reflecting those of the Bible.

God Is on the Rape Victim's Side

In the Bible, God always defended the oppressed, enforced justice, and commanded his people to do the same. Sometimes judgment does not come at once; sometimes it is delayed till the day of judgment—when it will be most severe. But *God clearly promises vindication for those who have suffered unjustly.* Judgment is not only God's punishment of the wicked; it is his way of vindicating those who have been mistreated (Deut. 32:43; 2 Kings 9:7; Ps. 79:10; Rev. 6:10; 16:6; 19:2). Our sanitized society may think notions of divine vengeance are primitive, but the Bible's warnings resonate with the anguish of the oppressed as promises of hope. The New Testament teaches that the penalty God has decreed for those who exploit others sexually is eternal damnation (1 Cor. 6:9–10; Rev. 21:8; 22:15). While the New Testament also offers forgiveness for all who repent of any sin, it offers forgiveness only to the genuinely repentant, and the mercy transgressors can receive from God still does not diminish God's justice on behalf of those they oppressed. According to biblical teaching, when Jesus died on the cross, God was not ignoring justice; God was punishing Jesus in our place. That is the greatest act of avenging justice on our behalf possible, because only Jesus was innocent enough to be an adequate sacrifice for all the sins of this world, including our own.

Rape is traumatic and usually has long-term emotional consequences, but churches must publicly declare clearly that God is working *for* and not against the person's healing. The church must then confirm that faith by providing unfailing emotional support and whatever other resources the wounded among us need. The pain a rape victim can carry around inside her can affect her future relationships if that pain is not resolved productively. For example, Tamar was completely innocent, and her words to Amnon indicate that she had longed for marriage, but Amnon ruined her hopes and her marriage prospects. Rape victims were no more required to remain single than widows or virgins were, and Tamar even had an advantage that few marriageable virgins in Israel did: She was the king's daughter, and that would make any man who married her the king's son-in-law. There would have been hundreds of virgin men in Israel eager for her hand, but Tamar chose to avoid intimacy. She did not consent to the rape, but unlike many rape victims, she did consent to a life of failing to come to terms with what had happened to her.

It is not wrong for the rape victim to seek justice or to cry out to God for vindication; no court in this land takes rape as seriously as God does. But the Bible also offers a deeper hope to victims of rape and other major traumas: If they continue to cultivate their relationship with God, *God can turn their pain into healing for themselves and for others.* What others have wounded, God and time can put back together. We must let the victims of rape and other crimes know that God is on their side, and that we are on their side too. Like God, we must walk through their pain with them, that our love and compassion may reflect in some small way the infinite love and compassion God feels toward his daughters and sons violated by others' spite, selfishness, or insensitivity.

Depression in Abused Women

M. Gay Hubbard

bused women are subjected to chronic threats to their physical and emotional sense of safety. In tragic numbers, these women suffer the trauma of physical violence, as well as chronic verbal and emotional assaults upon their competence, self-worth, and value. It is scarcely surprising to find that with rare exception, women experiencing such life events also suffer from depression.

What is surprising, however, is how little is known about depression in abused women. Common wisdom would suggest that victimization in interpersonal relationships is likely to increase the risk of serious depression. Therapists and counselors report that women who are victims of interpersonal violence demonstrate many of the characteristics associated with a primary diagnosis of depression—hopelessness, helplessness, negative self-esteem, a limited range of emotional response, high levels of self-criticism, self-defeating strategies of life management, and difficulties in forming and retaining intimate relationships (McGrath, Keita, Strickland, & Russo, 1990).

A major study of women and depression was recently completed by the American Psychological Association (APA). In its 1990 final report, the APA Task Force on Women and Depression (McGrath et al., 1990) noted that formal research inquiring directly into possible links between interpersonal victimization and depression in women is just beginning. The task force recommended that top priority be given to mental health research that looks at the effects of interpersonal violence, particularly as it relates to depression and associated disorders for women. The task force also concluded that the current knowledge base regarding the psychological impact of interpersonal violence upon women victims remains meager. Even more disheartening is the task force's assertion that what *is* known has not been incorporated into either education, training, or effective patterns of prevention and treatment (McGrath et al., 1990).

It is unfortunate that the 1990 Task Force on Women and Depression omitted entirely any consideration of women's religious faith and practice as relevant to the study of women's strengths and problems. It appears probable that unacknowledged bias rather than lack of clinical significance underlies the omission of this factor in studies of women's psychological health (Hendricks, 1984; Hubbard, 1992).

At the current time, depression is a fact of life for an astonishingly large number of women. At the time of the 1990 APA report, there were at least seven million women in the United States suffering from a diagnosable depression; evidence indicated that most of these women would go untreated. Many of this vast number of depressed women were women who had been or were currently being physically and emotionally abused. The final report concluded:

> The rate of sexual and physical abuse of females is much higher than previously suspected and is a major factor in women's depression. One study estimated that 37% of women have a significant experience of physical or sexual abuse before the age of 21. Several Task Force members felt these figures were an underestimate and the real numbers may be as high as 50%. More research is strongly needed in the area of violence against women and consequent depression. Depressive symptoms may be long-standing effects of posttraumatic stress syndrome for many women. (McGrath et al., 1990, p. xii)

132

There is no indication that the rates of depression or victimization of women have substantially decreased since 1990. Consequently, the situation in 1994 was seven million or more depressed women, with the depression of perhaps as many as half these women associated with past or present ongoing abuse (Finkelhor & Yilo, 1985; Koss, 1990; Russell, 1986; Walker, 1984). Without question, large numbers of these women are in the church; some certainly are in our own local congregations and are known to us by name.

It has long been known that women experience depression at a rate approximately twice that of men. This is one of the most consistent findings regarding women and depression, and occurs in many cultures, countries, and ethnic groups. The reason for this consistent gender difference is not fully understood. However, as the appalling rates of victimization for women and young girls has become more apparent (Koss, 1990; McGrath et al., 1990), it appears probable that the differential rates of depression for women and men may be attributable in part to the increased incidence of interpersonal violence experienced by women.

Characteristics of Depression

The word *depression* can be confusing since it is used both as a general and as a technical term. In a general sense, the word *depression* is used to describe normal emotional reactions of grief and discouragement that come in response to ordinary, but unwelcome, events of life. For example, moving (with an associated loss of friends and support systems), divorce, loss of a job, death of a close friend or family member, failure to achieve a promotion—events such as these evoke emotional distress and a sense of melancholy in almost everyone. However, these feelings are transitory, and as the tension and difficulty in an individual's circumstances ease, the person begins to "snap out of it," as friends and family frequently observe. This disturbance of mood is a normal response to life's painful events during which an individual experiences *temporary* feelings of sadness, grief, discouragement, and loss of hope. While unpleasant and emotionally painful, this transitory experience is not depression in the technical, clinical sense in which the term is used by mental health professionals.

How can clinical depression be distinguished from the normal life response of feeling discouraged or "blue"? Symptoms of clinical depression include:

Persistent sad, anxious, and/or "empty" mood

Persistent feelings of hopelessness, pessimism

Persistent feelings of guilt, worthlessness, helplessness

Loss of interest or pleasure in activities once experienced with enjoyment

Insomnia, chronic early-morning awakening, or chronic over-sleeping

Appetite and/or weight loss, or overeating and weight gain

Decreased energy, fatigue, a chronic sense of being (and feeling) "slowed down"

Thoughts of death or suicide, suicide plans, suicide attempts

Restlessness, irritability

Difficulty concentrating, remembering, making decisions

Persistent physical symptoms that do not respond to treatment, such as headaches, digestive disorders, chronic pain

If four or more of these symptoms occur continually for more than two weeks, the American Psychiatric Association (1993) recommends that professional help should be sought.

In many cases, family, friends, and coworkers must be assertive and persistent in helping the depressed person to get help. Sometimes victims of depression feel so exhausted and have such feelings of despair and hopelessness that they will not make an appointment for professional help, and may even refuse to go to an appointment that has been set up by family or a concerned friend. Depressed individuals often respond to efforts to help by saying things such as, "I just don't feel like talking to anybody. Besides, it wouldn't do any good." Seeking to help a depressed individual can be a frustrating experience. Persistence can pay off, however, and in the case of individuals struggling with recurring thoughts of death or suicide, persistence by friends and family can save a life.

Abused Women and Depression

Attempting to help an abused woman who is experiencing depression poses some additional and special problems. The woman may seek to hide her depression or deny the seriousness of her despair, both because she fears that nothing can be done and because she fears drawing attention to the trauma and danger of her relational world. She fears that if she acknowledges her depression, it is the first step on the slippery slope of acknowledging the reality of the abuse with which she lives. She may fear also that any action by others on her behalf such as taking her to a physician or therapist may evoke greater violence and result in still greater isolation from potential sources of help. She may need to "keep" her depression as a source of protection. She may be in an emotional position in which she needs to say to herself, "My situation really isn't bad. I just feel awful because I'm depressed." Intervention is not simple or easy.

In seeking to become more aware of individuals who may be experiencing serious depression, it is important to keep in mind that depression is heterogeneous—that is, it occurs in a variety of forms. Not all depressed people demonstrate their depression with the same set of behaviors; not all depressed people are depressed with equal severity. Just as abused women are abused in different ways, they express depression in different ways and levels of severity.

Varieties of Depression

Major depression is a condition in which the individual experiences a combination of symptoms (see symptom list above) with such intensity that the individual's ability to work, sleep, eat, and manage life activities is seriously impaired. *Dysthymia* is not disabling, but involves long-term, chronic symptoms (see list above) that the individual experiences at a sufficiently high level that prevent the person from feeling "on top of the world" or functioning at full capacity (Weissman, Leaf, Bruce, & Florio, 1988). People

135

with dysthymia can still function, but they do so sadly, slowly, with little or no sense of positive anticipation in their lives, and little experience of satisfaction in their achievements. They often give the impression of being unsure they'll make it through the day, while hoping that tomorrow will not come.

A much rarer form of depression is called *bipolar* or *manic-depressive illness.* This form of depression involves cycles of mood changes between depression and elation or mania. Most often the mood switches are gradual, but in some cases they may appear to be dramatic and rapid. In the depressive portion of the cycle, the individual demonstrates symptoms of depression. In the manic portion of the cycle, the individual demonstrates markedly increased energy, increased talking, grandiose notions, inappropriate elation, and poor judgment, often acting in ways that are potentially destructive (such as unwise, impulsive sexual encounters, reckless spending, and similar behaviors).

Subtypes of depression are not mutually exclusive. Overlap of two types (a major depression, for example, that is found to be superimposed on a dysthymic disorder) is referred to as a double depression. Physically and emotionally abused women are often dysthymic. Outbursts of physical and emotional violence can trigger an episode of major depression. Abused women are at high risk of double depression because of the cyclic nature of the battering process whether the violence is physical, emotional, or both.

Causes of Depression

Causes of depression are complex and usually incorporate a number of factors. Some factors are primarily physical—genetic and/or biological factors such as an imbalance of neurotransmitters (serotonin or norepinephrine, for example). Some factors are primarily social or psychological—life events such as a serious loss, chronic illness, a difficult relationship, or chronic high levels of stress, anger, or fear. Any of these factors alone or in combination can trigger depression. It is not difficult to see why women who are victimized, who experience physical trauma, and who live daily with fear, anger, and hopelessness become seriously depressed.

When emotionally and physically abused women become depressed, the depression they experience can then in turn exacerbate their sense of helplessness and further incapacitate their ability to deal with the dangerous circumstances of their lives. If left undiagnosed and untreated, the depression of abused women contributes substantially to the prison in which they feel condemned to live out their lives.

Treatment of Depression

The good news is that despite the gravity of the condition, depression is one of the most treatable mental illnesses. Nearly all depressed people who receive treatment see at least some substantial relief from their symptoms. Antidepressant medications, psychotherapy, or the two in combination generally relieve the major symptoms of depression in twelve to sixteen weeks. When an abused woman who is depressed receives successful treatment for her depression, she often is able to begin to think more clearly about the situation she is in and to identify realistically the options available to her.

For those seeking to assist abused women, it is particularly important to remember that depression is persistent and recurrent. It does not simply dissipate with time and, in a high number of cases, will reoccur at a later time after initial symptoms have been successfully treated. Because the abused woman may continue to live with ongoing trauma, response to treatment may be slowed; the abused woman may then view the persistence of symptoms as evidence of her inability to change her circumstances. In the event that treatment eventually leads to significant remission of symptoms, but then the symptoms reoccur at a later time, the abused woman may again view this as evidence of her helplessness and incompetence. Her thinking may be, "See, even with medicine I can't change things—there's no chance for me to make things better. Things may change for a little while, but they never *really* change." In order for the abused woman to deal more effectively with negative self-defeating thinking, it is important that she (and friends and family) understand that depression is persistent and symptoms can reoccur even after initial successful treatment. It is essential in such circumstances to insist that further treatment be undertaken.

The complexity of depression and the high possibility of complicated contributing factors make it essential that depressed victims have a complete evaluation by a competent professional. The woman may be emotionally resistant to such evaluation for reasons suggested earlier. Additionally, she may have no money and may have been forbidden to seek mental health services of any kind, particularly those of a psychiatrist. The woman's sense of fear, of shame, and her lack of financial resources often serve as formidable barriers to receiving outside help. Frequently, pastors and church staff can play a crucial role in enabling the woman to secure evaluation and treatment of the depression, which combines with abuse to keep the woman immobilized.

Other Problems Linked to Depression

Depression is often linked with other problems such as alcoholism or other substance abuses, eating disorders, or anxiety disorders. It can also be related to reaction to some commonly prescribed medications or other physical problems. There is increasing concern that in cases of severe physical trauma, the abused woman may have depression related to minor or moderate closed head injuries, which have been undetected because of the victim's failure to seek medical care, or because of the absence of overt signs of neurological distress (McGrath et al., 1990; see also Kwentus, Hart, Peck, & Kornstein, 1985; van der Kolk, 1988). There is also a relation between chronic sexual abuse and lethality of suicide attempt (Rosenthal, 1986).

Marital Role

Unhappily married women experience substantially more depressive symptoms than either happily married or unhappily married men (Aneshensel, 1986). D. C. Jack (1987) reported that the clinically depressed married women she interviewed described themselves as "isolated and lonely with relationships of inequality and emotional distance" (p. 165). Weissman's (1987) analysis of the ECA data on marital status and risk of depression showed that an unhappy marriage is a reliable predictor of depression and constitutes a grave risk to a woman's mental health. In unhappy marriages, women were three times as likely as men to be depressed, and almost half of all women in unhappy marriages were significantly depressed. Current studies (McGrath et al., 1990) strongly indicate that women are at higher risk for depression when they experience persistent strains in their ongoing relationships (see also Kandel, Davies, & Ravels, 1985).

Employment Role

Women who have the most complete role configurations (function as wife, parent, and worker) generally experience fewer depressive symptoms (Kandel et al., 1985). However, the relationship between employment and mental health of a wife is not simple and appears to be related significantly to the husband's participation in child care (Kessler & McRae, 1982). If employment outside the home is consistent with the preference and values of both husband and wife, and the husband participates in child care, employment increases the mental health of wives (Ross, Mirowsky, & Huber, 1983). Ross and Mirowsky (1988) found that children increased depression level for women not employed outside the home, but that employed mothers with sole responsibility for child care had extremely high depression levels. Mothers of young children are highly vulnerable to depression; the more children in the house the greater amount of depression reported (McGrath et al., 1990).

Aneshensel's research (1986) explored the joint interactive effects of strain from marital and employment roles on women's experience of depression. She found employed wives with a combination of low marital strain and low employment strain to be the least depressed; she found nonemployed wives with high marital strain to be the most depressed group. These women were depressed at a level nearly five times greater than the group of happily married, happily employed women.

Clearly, there are many factors which interact to affect women's mental health and level of depression. Abused women certainly experience high levels of marital unhappiness. They often experience social isolation and frequently have sole responsibility for care of children who also need to be protected from abuse. These women suffer from low self-esteem and stressful life events. A great number of those factors known to increase vulnerability to depression are chronically, consistently present in the lives of abused women.

Whatever else we may or may not know, empirical evidence strongly supports what we have intuitively surmised: Women are significantly affected emotionally by the quality of interpersonal relationships they have; consequently, physical and emotional abuse place a woman at grave risk for severe depression and other associated disorders (McGrath et al., 1990). Sticks and stones do indeed break bones, but, contrary to the old nursery rhyme, words also have a frightening capacity to wound and to depress.

Difficulties in Diagnosing Depression

A number of factors make it difficult to estimate accurately the number of physically and emotionally abused women within this current population of seven million (and more) depressed women.

First, crime statistics are collected in a way that does not permit accurate identification of the nature or frequency of acts of interpersonal violence against women (McGrath et al., 1990). Additionally, mental health records are collected in ways that ignore, confuse, and confound various aspects of an abused woman's experience so that it is impossible to secure consistent reporting of rates and types of depression.

For example, if an abused woman becomes a psychiatric patient, her history of victimization is likely to be ignored. If it is noted, it is likely to be incorporated as support for a diagnosis of personality disorder; exploration for symptomatology of depression is not likely to occur (Bryer, Nelson, Miller, & Krol, 1987). Put bluntly, there is evidence of a diagnostic bias which makes it probable that a woman who reports a history of victimization in a psychiatric setting is more likely to be viewed by the mental health professional interviewing her as a woman who has something wrong with her personality, rather than being viewed as a woman who has had something terrible happen to her, and is, consequently, and sensibly, seriously depressed. Depression in many of these women is associated with post-traumatic stress disorder (McGrath et al., 1990).

The general diagnostic disorder is further muddled by the fact that abused women often withhold history of their victimization from professionals as well as from friends and acquaintances. Abused women feel deep shame; they thus anticipate quite accurately that as victims they are likely to be blamed for the pain and injury they have experienced—often by the very professional they have sought out for help. If an abused woman consults a pastor, he may well suggest that it is her lack of submission that provoked the brutal beating she received (Alsdurf & Alsdurf, 1989). If she consults a mental health professional, he or she may imply that the woman's unconscious desire to be punished was the primary catalyst that elicited the man's violent response.

To further complicate the diagnostic problem, in those instances when a woman's depression is properly identified, the mental health professional often fails to inquire into the woman's life history in a way that permits the woman to share her story of victimization. As a result, the depression and the victimization never appear together in the professional report as pieces of the same puzzle.

Many depressed women are in the health care system, but few are in the *mental* health care system. These women commonly make multiple visits to a nonpsychiatric physician for symptomatic complaints which neither the woman nor her physician identify as aspects of depression. Consequently, few of these women receive therapy or antidepressants; they are more likely to be given a mild tranquilizer. The depression (and all too often, the associated abuse) therefore go unrecognized, untreated, and unreported (Weissman, 1987).

Primary care physicians tend to prescribe antianxiety drugs rather than antidepressants for depressed women (McGrath et al., 1990). Therapists and counselors who have worked with physically and emotionally abused women have numerous stories of clients who came to them for therapy having been medically diagnosed as suffering from one or both of the never-fail explanations for women's emotional pain: The woman is suffering from hormonal difficulties (the infamous PMS or the controversial DSM-

III-R diagnosis of late luteal phase dysphoric disorder), or she is experiencing high levels of stress. In such cases, the woman often has been given some form of estrogen-progestin treatment or has been placed on antianxiety medication by a physician who has not identified the presence and gravity of the woman's depression or considered the possibility of interpersonal violence the woman may be currently experiencing.

We know that the woman who is the victim of interpersonal violence is, in the majority of instances, also suffering from depression. We know that we may fail to identify this depression because the woman may hide the depression, regarding it as telltale evidence of her abuse. We may also fail to identify her depression because we fail to recognize depression as such and do not fully realize the serious consequences of the condition. Additionally, we may fail to respond to the woman's depression because, unknowingly, we have adopted an explanation of the woman's depression that diminishes the gravity of her condition and reflects stereotypical beliefs about women that have come to us through both the culture and the church.

Beliefs about Women Related to Depression

False Beliefs

Common beliefs about women have included a distorted concept of female masochism that suggests women tolerate abuse because inwardly they couple pain and pleasure. This idea underlies comments such as, "She asked for it," or, "She must like it or she wouldn't have stayed." Another explanation of women's inner world is the idea of "learned helplessness." This concept suggests that women have an impaired sense of instrumentality, and therefore respond passively in abusive relationships because they have learned to see themselves as helpless to act in a way that would change things. Another common idea (with debts to both Freud and attachment theory) explains the behavior and depression of abused women by attributing the woman's failure to separate from a problematic love relationship to her dependency and overreliance upon attachment to the male for her identity and self-esteem.

Responsibility for interpersonal violence is sometimes assigned to women globally. The infamous women's movement is blamed for encouraging women to be too angry, too strong, too competitive, too independent; in so doing, women have produced men whose loss of power and decreased sense of self-esteem is now expressed in rage.

Whatever the theoretical (or theological) explanations of women's victimization in interpersonal violence, the explanations commonly revolve around two themes: (1) women themselves have made the violence happen, and (2) women's failure to respond properly to male anger that they themselves have created is the *real* cause of the pain and injury they have suffered.

Women have been told many contradictory things—that interpersonal violence would not have occurred if they had only loved more, or if they had only loved less; that there would have been no abuse if they had only been more dependent and submissive, or if they had only been stronger and less dependent. Whatever the content of the specific criticism, however, the refrain was always the same: If only the woman had been different, the problem wouldn't have occurred, or the problem would have vanished like a puff of wind, and the woman wouldn't have been hurt. The message to the abused woman has been that the whole thing is her fault, and her depression is the logical outcome of her improper actions and attitudes. One woman said, "I was told to jump through all these hoops and keep him happy. When things got so bad I had to leave, they told me I just hadn't jumped high enough or fast enough. Don't they know that when you're broken you can't jump at all?"

In order to avoid the practice of blaming the victim it is necessary for us to ask ourselves two very different questions: In an abusive relationship, what are the goals the woman herself is trying to achieve? How does *she* explain her experience? We have been slow to understand that in dealing with women who are victims of interpersonal violence, we must learn to hear and understand the woman's experience as *she* constructs it (Kaplan, 1986), rather than as *we* may theoretically presume it to be.

A Different View

Recent study of women's development has focused on the ways in which relationships shape women's sense of self and moral development (Chodorow, 1978; Gilligan, 1982; Jordan, Kaplan, Miller, Stiver, & Surrey, 1991; Miller, 1984, 1986; Surrey, 1985). We must seek to understand the experience of the emotionally and physically abused woman (including her depression) in terms of the sense of self and moral imperative that frame the meaning *she* assigns her experience, and that underlie *her* construction of her goals.

This developmental approach gives a quite different understanding of the abused woman's experience than do earlier theories of feminine masochism, learned helplessness, and dependency. And this understanding also gives some sobering insight into the ways rigid, fundamentalistic uses of biblical passages regarding women's roles and responsibilities have tended to legitimize and/or excuse abuse and add to the problem of the low self-esteem suffered by Christian women (Neff, 1991).

The work of Miller (1986), Gilligan (1982), and others have provided strong support for the hypothesis that women's orientation to relationships forms the central component of their identities. The sense of self that women experience is "self-in-relation," to use the phrase coined by the Stone Center studies (Jordan et al., 1991). It is a self that defines itself and develops in the context of relationship, a self that achieves identity and growth in connection with others.

If this is indeed the case, then women's experience of emotional and physical abuse and their experience of depression may significantly differ from the experiences of men (Jack, 1991). Given a relational sense of self, women may persevere in the face of pain and abuse because to lose the relationship is to lose something of the self; defense of the relationship holds a higher moral imperative than defense of the individual. This concept demonstrates the ethic of "caring as the highest good" (Gilligan, 1987, 1988).

Depressed and abused women *can* serve as reliable reporters of their experience, despite the traditional academic distrust of self-reporting (Jack, 1991). When we listen to these women's reflections about themselves, we can hear the beliefs that shape the worth they assign themselves and the meaning they assign their actions. In listening to their stories, we can see where some of the paths into their depression began.

Some abused women begin with the belief that they are the cause of the man's behavior. A self-help book that teaches this idea is entitled *The Fulfilled Woman* (Beardsley & Spry, 1975). The authors caution, "Remember, your husband's actions are probably a result of *your* [italics added] wrong attitudes" (pp. 26–27).

A recent client expressed this idea. Clara had been badly burned as a child, and carried terrible memories of this early trauma. In her late teens, she married a man who soon began to demonstrate increasingly abusive behavior—verbally and physically. On one occasion, he deliberately burned her with his cigarette, seeking to coerce her into a sexual act that was personally repugnant to her. When Clara sensed my strong but unspoken response as she told me her story, she paused, then said apologetically, "Well, I know that it's really my fault. If I were a better wife, he wouldn't want to hurt me."

Abused women often believe that they cannot say no, that their husbands have a God-given right to use their bodies and to control every aspect of their lives. In *You Can Be the Wife of a Happy Husband* (Cooper, 1974), the author begins the chapter "Follow the Leader" by declaring that "Stability for both home and nation depends on recognizing the man as the head of the family" (p. 61). In support of this idea, she cites Ephesians 5:22–23 as paraphrased in the Living Bible:

You wives must submit to your husbands' leadership in the same way you submit to the Lord. For a husband is in charge of his wife in the same way Christ is in charge of His body the Church . . . so you wives must willingly obey your husband in everything, just as the Church obeys Christ. (pp. 61–62)

Cooper goes on to add, "When you are having doubts as to how to respond to your husband, remember . . . just as the church is totally dependent on Jesus Christ, so you as a wife are to be totally dependent on your husband. In this atmosphere, you are protected and fulfilled" (pp. 64–65). To further emphasize her point, the author states, "You are rebellious to Christ's leadership to the same degree that you rebel against your husband's leadership" (p. 76).

While Cooper attempts to avoid teaching the concept of submission as passivity, she nonetheless concludes: "Being submissive does not mean saying nothing; it means *putting yourself completely at the disposal of the person who is over you"* [italics added] (p. 67).

If indeed women do engage the self in relationships at the developmental level that Miller (1986), Gilligan (1982), and others have suggested, application of Scripture in the way illustrated above acts in effect as a command from God for the woman to sacrifice her essential self to the will and pleasure of the male, regardless of the destruction that results for the woman. The woman is taught that her highest moral obligation is the preservation of the relationship and the satisfaction of the man.

Beginning with a developmentally based desire to create an intimate, lasting relationship, the woman first gives up her power and responsibility to choose, then invests her "self-in-relation" in the welfare of the man who is named to her as the representative of God in the relationship. Submission (as unto Christ) becomes the silencing of the self (Jack, 1991) as the service owed to God. Depression echoes the stillness of these women who have lost their voices and can no longer speak for the self that has been abandoned. Jack (1991) noted: "The women silence themselves, not because they are dependent and passive, but because they value relationship" (p. 137). And for the woman who has been taught that such loss of self in the service of the male is service to God, the silencing of the self is a moral act, a sacrifice required in the preservation of relationship both with the man and God.

Pointing out that their husbands are acting in selfish, hurtful ways does little to help those depressed, abused women who have learned—however erroneously—that God commands them to serve the male as God's representative in the relationship. We must recognize the double bind in which these women find themselves. If they withdraw from the relationship, they will have violated their own moral imperative that forbids them to care for themselves at the cost of the relationship; if they stay in the relationship, acting to silence and abandon the self, they find themselves alone, walled away from intimacy and connection in the darkness of their depression.

Help for these women must begin *not* by asking them to abandon their developmental reality of "self-in-relation," nor to violate their moral commitment to a life lived in connection to others and in obedience to God's Word. We must begin by helping these women examine their understanding of God's character and his directions to women as members of the family of God. We must build clearer understanding of exegetical and scientific information that will lead to the building of healthier, egalitarian relationships between men and women everywhere, but most particularly within the church and the community of faith.

Pastoral Care for Abused Women

Joan Burgess Winfrey

The words of Psalm 55 express the anguish of one who has been the recipient of domestic violence. Surely the words of the psalm could aptly portray the grief of one whose body is betrayed by physical abuse; yet they might also express the betrayal of one whose personhood and spirit are violated by a member of the clergy (Fortune, 1991), a helper who should bring healing, care, and nurturance, but whose words increase the grief and shame of the abused.

> My heart is in anguish within me,
> the terrors of death have fallen upon me.
> Fear and trembling come upon me,
> and horror overwhelms me.
> And I say, "O that I had wings like a dove!
> I would fly away and be at rest;
> truly, I would flee far away;
> I would lodge in the wilderness;
> I would hurry to find a shelter for myself
> from the raging wind and tempest."

It is not enemies who taunt me—
  I could bear that;
it is not adversaries who deal insolently with me—
  I could hide from them.
But it is you, my equal,
  my companion, my familiar friend,
with whom I kept pleasant company;
  we walked in the house of God with the throng.

Psalm 55:4–8, 12–13 NRSV, italics added

Glaz and Moessner (1991) eloquently speak to the issue of the response of clergy to the unique needs and life experience of women. Women, they believe, have for centuries experienced inner struggles with religious systems and theological questions that have seemed incongruent and distant from their own realities. The authors relate a true story that serves as a sad example of the possible long-term outcome of a pastor's lack of skill and knowledge in the life of one woman. Her story depicts what they term a "failed moment" in pastoral care (p. 1).

June, a mother for the first time, had had a harrowing delivery: she nearly died in childbirth. Exhausted and frightened, she lay awake in her hospital bed unable to close her eyes. She was glad that the birthing process was finished, but the baby, she felt, had nearly killed her. When her pastor arrived, five hours had passed since the ordeal.

She could not bring herself to describe her feelings: the pastor, aware that she had been near death, did not inquire. Instead, after introductory talk, the pastor repeated how grateful to God she should be for the wonderful new life that had been entrusted to her. June felt even worse after the visit because one major part of her experience had not been acknowledged: the baby's threat to her own life.

June did not establish a non-ambivalent relationship with her infant. In therapy years later, she concluded that the emotions formed at the birth sealed inside by the pastor's oblivious remarks were a significant factor in her lack of bonding with her child. Because she could not bring herself to share her feeling, she felt victimized, increasingly guilty, and cornered as the mother of this child. The outcome of this, she surmised, was a troubled adolescent. . . .

Can a thirty-minute pastoral visit have such reverberations for a mother when the unspoken cry of her plight is missed or ignored? June thought so. (Glaz & Moessner, 1991, pp. 1–2)

June, as far as we know, was not an abused woman, but we must ask the question, What are some of the variables that might account for this pastor's missed opportunity for bringing comfort and healing to June's situation? Lonnie Collins Pratt, wife of an abusive evangelist, recounts her own shocking encounter with her pastor in the story "The Lost Coin" (1992). Hospitalized as the result of a severe beating from her husband, she relates the words spoken to her by the minister, who leaned over her bed and told her, "All things work together for your good. This is the cross God has called you to bear. Think of how glorious it will be when you see your husband conforming to what God wants for him. It will happen if you just continue to love him. . . . the devil is after him, but we aren't going to let old slewfoot have him, are we?" (p. 17). Words can be used to impart empathic understanding or to distance us from human experience.

Other authors (Alsdurf & Alsdurf, 1989; Garma, 1991) have related similar tragic accounts of failed moments in pastoral care. What are the theological, social, psychological, and historical factors that inform the attitudes and behaviors of pastors, fostering the frightful ignorance and, at times, complicity that characterize inadequate or damaging pastoral care for women? It is instructive to trace certain trends in pastoral theology in order to gain insight into this question.

Historical Perspectives on Pastoral Care

Directions and practices in pastoral care have been shaped in cultural/historical contexts. Clebsch and Jaekle (1964) identify eight major epochs in the history of pastoral care that characterize the social realities and Christian thought of each historical era. During the era of persecutions in the fourth century, for example, pastoral care emphasized the reconciling of persons to God and the codification of major sins. Medieval Christendom brought an elaborate sacramental system and an interest in the healing of various maladies. During the Enlightenment, pastoral care focused on the sustaining of personal morality in a world that no longer relied on God or religion for explanations of truth and reality.

Clebsch and Jaekle (1964) identify in modern Christian thought the impact of "the appearance of modern personhood—self starting, self examining, capable of living serially in many dimensions and moods" (p. vii). They go on to say, "It is just this new personhood that has become the baffling, versatile object of attention for the secular healing arts as well as for the contemporary practice of pastoral caring" (p. 6). Modern pastoral care, the authors acknowledge, has developed under the tutelage of psychological theories. Campbell (1981) remarks, however, that a contemporary sense of confusion about the nature of Christian caring exists and a rediscovery of pastoral care and its biblical/theological roots is needed. Recognizing the value of psychological insights, Campbell nevertheless calls for a reclaiming of the best of the Christian theological heritage, including the rich metaphors and symbols that have shaped the meaning of caregiving.

Psychological theory has reformed and redirected pastoral care in many valuable, positive ways. But pastoral attitudes about the value and role of women have also been misinformed by psychology. In large measure, psychological research and writing prior to the 1960s tended to conceptualize masculinity and femininity as bipolar opposites. Human development theories have used male development as a standard and characterized female development as different from and therefore inferior to male norms. Hence gender-biased psychological assumptions are pervasive in pastoral care literature. We now have much-needed critiques on the theories of Erikson, Kohlberg, Freud, and others whose ideas represent male psychological bias (Belenky, Clinchy, Goldberger, & Tarule, 1986; Gilligan, 1982; Jordan, Kaplan, Miller, Stiver, & Surrey, 1991; Miller, 1986). "Pastoral care has been uncritical in the appropriation of psychology. . . . The perspective of women's experiences— thinking about being human from a woman's vantage point— allows us to reexamine both the ancient Christian message of God's redemptive love and care for all people and psychology's basic assumptions" (Glaz & Moessner, 1991, p. 11).

Alsdurf and Alsdurf (1989), Clarke (1986), Leehan (1989), and Glaz and Moessner (1991) have identified patriarchy and sexism and their impact on social institutions—including the family and

151

the church—as major contributing factors in pastoral theology. Pagelow (1981) suggests that as a starting point for a theory about wife abuse, we must recognize the patriarchal and hierarchical foundations of social systems. A "broad range of internalized beliefs" affirm the rightness of this social structure order (Pagelow, 1981, p. 16). This traditional ideology, Pagelow states, "is a set of beliefs and attitudes that is a fundamental part of the way persons evaluate life and circumstances. . . . Traditional ideology is the configuration of all the conservative wisdom passed down through the ages as the 'inherent' natural order of things" (pp. 23–24).

Unfortunately, the "conservative wisdom of the ages" and "the natural order of things" include the subordination and devaluing of women and the subsequent tendencies for male pastors to respond to abuse victims in a mistrustful or condemning manner, and to minimize the evil and horror of the violence. Clarke (1986) states that "Male oriented theologies, religious beliefs, and church practices, derived from sexist interpretations of certain biblical passages tend to foster violence against women" (p. 9).

JoAnn M. Garma (1991) has this to say:

> The church has a long history of projecting external dictums on the woman, especially the battered woman. The worldview taught by the church subjugates the woman to the authority and control of the man through the patriarchal language of its Scripture, ritual, hymns, and theology. The woman's God is *Father*, her Redeemer is *Son*, and her priest or pastor, who theologizes, teaches, and preaches about her God and Redeemer is usually a man. The woman is taught to believe that the patriarchal ideologies come from God and are therefore true. The dominant language and symbols of the church give the woman little with which to identify; if she is a battered woman committed to the male ideology of the Christian faith, she has even less with which to build her self-esteem. (p. 133)

Scharfenberg (1980) states that pastoral care has suffered from the "ever-persistent conviction" that dialogue, if it is legitimately pastoral, must involve proclamation of the gospel and appearing and speaking in the name of God (p. 3). Dialogue in this sense is designed to capture the person rather than set the person free. An autocratic stance is assured by the pastor who appears and speaks in the name of God. Thus the reciprocity of dialogue is something to be overcome in the interest of bringing proclamation to bear. The pastor has, in effect, been sent on patrol. Decade after decade, nice-sounding theological prescriptions were formulated for what was supposed to take place in pastoral care. The concrete human need is addressed through the inevitable advice to pray. Scharfenberg quotes the German theologian Hans Asmussen:

> However softly and smoothly the dialogue begins, it will at some point experience a break initiated by the pastor. Then it will receive a new beginning, which the pastor will determine. The pastor will prefer to terminate the discussion rather than give up control of the dialogue, because he comes not as a private individual but as the bearer of an office. When I relinquish the leadership of a dialogue, I become unfaithful to my Lord. (p. 6)

Paul Tournier (1964) expresses pity for people in hospitals who are visited by certain pious chaplains who derive considerable satisfaction from talking with great fervor, even using the patient's illness as a point of persuasion. They never think of listening, but are enjoying themselves, oblivious to their own exercise of domination in this unequal battle.

Tournier (1964) addresses the great schism in our lives that is evidenced in two streams—the despiritualization of the world and the "disincarnation" of the church. The church has turned inward; it talks of theology, psychology, and other abstractions, but cannot or will not assist people in their place of need and in their real difficulties. Tournier states, "Their hands are clean, but they have no hands" (p. 160). Surely the blatant indifference of today's Christian leaders to the staggering incidence of domestic violence stands as a shameful parallel to Tournier's diagnosis.

Dualism has an added edge for women. Mind/body dualism has tended to equate femaleness with the body, with nature, and with the earth. Maleness has been equated with the spiritual, the intellectual, and the cultural. That which is corporeal and natural is regarded as inferior to that which is spiritual and cultural. Van Leeuwen (1990) frames this line of thinking in a "nature versus culture" context. In our fallen state, human pride finds greater value in that which is built, shaped, and refined by human effort (culture) above that which is part of natural existence. Because women bear and nurture children, their realities are shaped, to a great extent, out of bodily experience, while males are freer to pursue art, politics, technology, and other aspects of culture. Van Leeuwen points out, however, that most New Testament metaphors that symbolize life in Christ are drawn not from war, politics, or art, but rather from birth, body, life, nurturance, and servanthood. Views of women's inferiority cannot be supported biblically.

Women's bodies are also commonly viewed as sources of sinfulness; therefore, denigration of the body and bodily experience is equated with pursuit of spirituality. An important aspect of human experience is, therefore, disenfranchised. Spiritual and psychological wholeness are not attainable for women who cannot view their own bodies as sacred temples of God. An incarnational view of human existence rejects the notion that the body is less valuable than the spirit. Ramsay (1991) states that "the radical assertion that God came among us in human flesh (incarnation) contradicts cultural dualisms that divide spirit and body" (p. 117). James Nelson (1983) suggests, "we either experience God's presence in our bodies or not at all" (p. 18). The symbolism of the body offers the most profound of all spiritual insights.

The Psychology of Women and Pastoral Care

Many changes have occurred in the way women think about themselves, their own lives, and their relationship to God over the past three decades. The second wave of the feminist movement has focused inquiry on female experiences and needs; additionally, women have sought to reshape their faith in concert with these new understandings. Pastoral theology and pastoral care must move from an outdated, male-oriented perspective and allow female views to influence new approaches. Pastoral care for both genders will be enriched in this process. Pastoral theology as a theological discipline that is incarnational at its base can profit from female psychology.

Carol Gilligan (1982) attempts to establish a separate mode of reasoning moral problems in women. She argues that women, because of their value for connectedness and reconciliation, attempt to resolve social and moral dilemmas in ways that will not threaten relationships. Men, by contrast, value separateness and tend to invoke abstract principles in forming moral judgments.

Nancy Chodorow (1978) examines the idea that gender identity proceeds differently for males and females because women, almost universally, are largely responsible for early child care. Girls experience themselves as like their mother, and their gender identity is, consequently, fused with the process of attachment and affiliation. Boys, in identifying themselves as male, must experience themselves as opposite from the mother, therefore male gender identity involves separation and individuation. Male gender identity is threatened by intimacy, while female gender identity is threatened by separation. A basis for empathy, then, is built into the female's primary definition of self. Thus, relationship and issues of dependency are experienced differently by the sexes.

Betty Friedan (1986) speaks to the need for affirmation of the differences between men and women, believing that true equality of the sexes is possible only in this context. Her call to absorb women's issues into the fabric of the needs of all of society, including family, government, and economics, provides the essential thesis of the book.

Belenky and colleagues (1986) provide one of the most comprehensive and perhaps one of the most useful models for understanding female experience. The authors describe five different perspectives of epistemological categories from which women view reality and form conclusions about knowledge and truth. The development of voice and self-concept are woven together with the stages of knowing, which are developmentally determined. The authors attempt to show "how women struggle to claim the power of their own minds" (p. 3). They believe that the use of male experience to define human experience has resulted in stereotyping and devaluation of interdependence, intimacy, nurturance, and contextual thought.

Feminist revision and addition to developmental theory offers a fertile medium for more valid approaches in pastoral care for women. Theories such as that of Belenky and colleagues (1986) can help pastoral caregivers enter into female experience. Belenky and her coworkers have identified five major categories (or ways of knowing) used by women to process an experience such as abuse. These five ways are:

1. *Silence*—A position in which women experience themselves as mindless and voiceless and subject to the whims of external authority. Women in this position have often been severely repressed or abused.

2. *Received Knowledge*—A perspective from which women conceive of themselves as receiving, even reproducing, knowledge from the all-knowing external authorities, but are not capable of creating knowledge on their own. Women in this stage listen to others. They rely on experts, viewing ideas as right or wrong.

3. *Subjective Knowledge*—A perspective from which truth and knowledge are conceived of as "personal, private, and subjectively known or intuited" (Belenky et al., 1986, p. 54). The self is in the process of becoming.

4. *Procedural Knowledge*—A position in which women are invested in learning and applying objective procedures for obtaining and communicating knowledge. Critical thinking and the voice of reason are developing.

5. *Constructed Knowledge*—A position in which women view all knowledge as contextual, experience themselves as creators of knowledge, and value both subjective and objective strategies for knowing. Feeling and thinking are integrated. The process of self-reclamation is occurring and ambiguity can be tolerated.

New Directions in Pastoral Care

Personhood Revisited

Various dimensions of personhood are explored by Carrol A. Wise (1966). Hinkle (1989) devotes considerable critique to Wise's concept of optimal personhood, which places "high priority on the traits of autonomy, privacy, awareness, and uniqueness" (p. 151). A strong emphasis on self-reliance is found. Hinkle challenges Wise's definition of optimal personhood on the basis that it is inconsistent with personhood concepts from other cultures and with female identity formation. Hinkle raises questions: If pastoral care is to be directed toward self-development, what kind of self is to be developed in a given culture? What are the implications of the gospel for such diverse definitions of the self? The revision of Wise's optimal personhood must include themes of mutuality and relationship.

Additionally, Hinkle appropriates the concept of "interpathy" as he discusses the texture of new approaches in pastoral care:

> Interpathy is an intentional cognitive envisioning and effective experiencing of another's thoughts and feelings, even though the thoughts and feelings arise from another process of knowing and the feelings spring from another basis of assumptions. In interpathic caring, the process of "feeling with" and "thinking with" another requires that one enter the other's world of assumptions, beliefs and values and temporarily take them as one's own. . . . In the interpathic approach, relationship and communication are preserved, but the process of taking into account other views of personhood and other views of the world is added. Pentecost is added to Incarnation. (p. 161)

The Wounded Healer

Perhaps the fullest, most splendid metaphor of pastoral care, and the one which offers the greatest significance for pastoral care of abused women is that of the "wounded healer" (Nouwen, 1972). Campbell (1981) describes the wounded healer caregiver as one who enters into the pain and loss of others through personal vulnerability. Christ is the Wounded Healer who restored the broken world to God. Campbell quotes from Colossians: "Through him God chose to reconcile the whole universe to himself, making peace through the shedding of his blood upon the cross—to reconcile all things, whether on earth or in heaven, through him alone" (Col. 1:20 NEB).

The sufferings and wounds of Jesus are more than a legal payment for sin. They are the symbols of his wounded love that carry the power to heal. But wounds have healing power only when they are seen. Those who deny or hide their own woundedness cannot be of help to others who are wounded. Wounds open up a bond of grief, allowing the caregiver to bring genuine consolation.

Four Dimensions: A Model of Pastoral Care for Abused Women

Clebsch and Jaekle (1964) have defined pastoral care in the following way: "The ministry of the care of souls, or pastoral care, consists of helping acts, done by representative Christian persons directed toward the healing, sustaining, guiding, and reconciling of troubled persons, whose troubles arise in the context of ultimate meanings and concerns" (p. 1). These four dimensions of pastoral care suggested by Clebsch and Jaekle offer a useful basis for defining the personal needs of the abused person and the functions of the pastoral helper in the recovery and growth process. The helper need not always be the pastor; the role of the pastor here is, in part, to mobilize the resources of the Christian community. The dimensions are viewed as sequential, cyclical, and simultaneous.

Healing

The healing dimension reflects needs that exist early in the helping relationship. The helper must establish a climate of acceptance through the acts of "interpathy." He or she must enter into the abused person's world through deep and active listening, while displaying genuine sorrow for existing wounds. Trust is established through the demonstration of grace and *agape* love. Though the healing process will continue throughout the recovery, the pastoral caregiver will begin the restoration of personhood, honoring the uniqueness and dignity of the abused woman. Nurturance, support, and connection will help move her from a position of silence; dialogue which comes out of love, compassion, and grace will assist her in recapturing inner dialogue and self-voice.

Sustaining

The sustaining dimension may resemble a pastoral counseling component in the recovery cycle. The abused woman needs the opportunity to recognize, to own, and to explore the many psychological repercussions of her experience. If she has been in an abusive environment for a long period of time, this process cannot be truncated through superficial advice. The psychological experience of shame is deeply debilitating: "Shame is the inner sense of being completely diminished or insufficient as a person. It is the self judging the self" (Fossum & Mason, 1986, p. 5). Women who have been abused will also have deep, pervasive anger—anger toward the abuser, the self, and probably God. The caregiver must be willing to allow the venting of anger, and avoid the typical Christian response that the anger itself is wrong. Using the stage theory of Belenky and coworkers (1986), we might expect the sustaining function to involve patience on the part of the caregiver. The abused woman will need input from loving, caring external advisors, but she may also be in a place of setting aside or bracketing previously held beliefs about male authority and male-oriented theology. Her position of "subjective knowledge" may feel threatening to the caregiver who cannot recognize this important inner search for the self.

Guiding

The guiding function involves many practical, decision-making actions. For the woman in a dangerous situation, this could include locating a shelter or other safe place. Utilizing church and community resources is a part of this phase. Support groups and dialogue with other abused women are important pieces of the recovery process. The abused woman must move away from passivity, dependence, and learned helplessness. She must develop or regain inner confidence in her own ability to make changes and plans for her life. "Procedural knowing" for her will involve understanding God's truth in the context of her present reality. She must learn to value her own inner voice, her sense of reality, and the validity of her own life experiences in evaluating alternative courses of action. Decisions about remaining in her home, remaining in her marriage, and relating to the perpetrator must be internally congruent, outwardly sound, and biblically faithful.

Reconciling

The biblical definition of reconciling means "no longer enemies." This function will include the rebuilding of bridges. Self-reclamation or "constructed knowing" is a precursor to forgiveness in its deeper sense. Forgiveness, as addressed by Allender (1990), is bold love. "'Forgiveness' based on 'forgetfulness' is a Christian version of frontal lobotomy" (p. 15). "The sweet fragrance of forgiveness is the energy that propels the damaged [person] toward the freedom of love" (p. 219). Bold love includes the willingness to confront. It is not an absence of anger but may indeed be "holy hatred" (p. 222). It does not minimize evil, but neither does it seek revenge.

Reconciliation is a means to optimal personhood. It begins and ends with the cross of Christ; the abused one must ultimately reimage God as the Wounded Healer who reconciles all things. Psalm 91 is a beautiful expression of this truth:

> You who live in the shelter of the Most High,
>   who abide in the shadow of the Almighty,
> will say to the LORD, "My refuge and my fortress;
>   my God, in whom I trust."
> For he will deliver you from the snare of the fowler
>   and from the deadly pestilence;
> he will cover you with his pinions,
>   and under his wings you will find refuge;
>   his faithfulness is a shield and buckler.
> You will not fear the terror of the night,
>   or the arrow that flies by day,
> or the pestilence that strikes in darkness,
>   or the destruction that wastes at noonday.
>
> Those who love me, I will deliver;
>   I will protect those who know my name.
> When they call to me, I will answer them;
>   I will be with them in trouble,
>   I will rescue them and honor them.
> With long life I will satisfy them,
>   and show them my salvation.
>
> Psalm 91:1–6, 14–16 NRSV

10

Creating Healing Environments for Abuse Survivors

Mary Nella Bruce

n the mid 1980s, I was co-pastoring with my husband a small
inner-city church on the south side of Chicago. The new converts coming into the church were often homeless, abused,
drug addicted, with children in gangs. We were overwhelmed
with the problems. Our parsonage had become a twenty-four-
hour emergency room or shelter for those in need of a safe place.
We were looking for answers to problems we had never dealt with
before. All attempts to get help from the city were fruitless; the
systems were on overload. Our denomination was without urban
resources. We were on our own.

At the same time, I began to study the stories of women evangelicals in the nineteenth century who led the great social movements of their day and changed their world. Much of their work
was in the urban areas. They aggressively tackled the inhuman
conditions so many families endured through poverty and abusive
home situations. Alma White and Rachel Wilde Peterson went
into the slums of Denver in the nineteenth century and reached
out to the poor with the gospel and missions of mercy. Rachel

Wilde Peterson went into the worst districts of Denver to win prostitutes to the Lord. Mission accomplished, she would return with her reformed prostitutes on the back of a wagon pulled by horses. The newly won converts would play the upright piano, sing hymns, and preach to their old pals. Rachel helped these women rebuild their lives by providing mission refuge housing for them to get a new start in life.

I was soon to discover through my research at local archives and historical libraries that Rachel Wilde Peterson and Alma White were only the tip of the iceberg. The evangelical women of the 1800s who addressed the issues destroying society numbered in the thousands. Here were the models for ministry in our pastoral work on the south side of the city. We began to pray for a refuge house for the homeless and abused women with children who were overwhelming our ability to provide for each crisis. Our city ministry took a new turn as we were encouraged by the aggressive, caring Christianity our foresisters in the faith modeled for us. Following is the story of how our church became a healing community for abused and homeless women with children. We learned that the church is the most powerful force in the world today. Our problem is that we seldom act on the power we have in Jesus' name to make a difference. The stories of the female evangelical leaders a hundred years ago who cared enough to build refuge houses for homeless and abused women and children empowered us to do the same.

Margie's Story

I was also receiving a very practical hands-on education. The first teacher God sent to instruct me was a woman by the name of Margie. I met Margie when a person I did not know called the parsonage looking for help. She said she had heard that our church would help people in crisis and could we please come and get the young woman she had discovered that morning sleeping in her building. When I asked about the circumstances, she told me she had heard thumping noises early in the morning on her stairwell. When she inspected the noise, she discovered a two-year-old boy at the foot of her stairs. The two-year-old belonged to a homeless mother living in the attic crawl space. The mother had gotten drunk and fallen asleep, and her child had fallen down the stairs. Margie (the homeless woman) also had a five-year-old daughter. Later Margie told me about being a Christian several years ago, but said she always hooked up with the wrong men. They abused her, got her pregnant, and threw her out. She had turned to alcohol. The streets were now home because her mother couldn't take the drinking, and Margie didn't want to give up her kids. She loved those children very much. Her greatest fear was that the authorities were going to take away her children. She knew that she needed help to get a home for them, but she was not going to trade a roof for abuse any longer.

I spent eight solid hours trying to find help for Margie. My last call, right before five in the evening, was to the Department of Human Services. They told me that it was too late to help her because what beds might have been available had all gone that morning. And they were just speaking of emergency overnight beds.

My education was just beginning. I learned a lot that day. I learned that a woman in crisis has very few options. The shelter system is so overloaded that a woman has little opportunity to find housing and refuge in an emergency situation. In the city of Chicago, over six thousand women and children are turned away daily from refuge houses and emergency shelters. Most women are homeless due to abusive situations they are fleeing.

At these shelters the residents must leave by eight in the morning. Human Services recommended that I take Margie and her children to the police. It didn't seem like an option—the church going to the police for help with a homeless woman. Reluctantly, I drove over to the address given me to pick up Margie and her children. I fixed up a bedroll for everyone in our office off the kitchen—the only available space. They stayed for six days. Margie needed help with her alcohol abuse, a healing environment to work through her abuse issues, and a way to make a life for herself and her children.

In trying to meet all these needs, I discovered that in the greater Chicago area, there were only two hospitals that would take in addicts without insurance, five detox centers (always full with a waiting list), and two halfway houses for transition back to independent living. In none of these situations was there a place for her and her children to be together.

It took me six days to work out an option—a Christian foster home for the children until Margie got on her feet. Over breakfast, I told Margie of the plans that had been made. She asked if the arrangements meant that she would have to give up her children. I assured her it was only temporary and she could visit them whenever she wanted to. It was in everyone's best interest. One tear fell. She excused herself and said she had to walk her daughter to school. She left with her little boy in her arms, holding her daughter's hand. I never saw Margie again. In my office were all her belongings and clothes in garbage bags.

That was when I asked God to use me to help other Margies. If I could make a difference for homeless and abused women, I would create a safe refuge where they could come and live with their children. I never wanted to tell another mother that I had to separate her from her children in order to help her.

Another Margie

The next abused woman who came in to our church's life was also named Margie. She had been raised by her parents in the same neighborhood where our church was located. Her father had worked at the steel mills. He would leave work every night, as most of the mill employees did, with a stop at one of the many corner bars on his way home. The men who worked for Margie's father at the mill had a great deal of respect for him, and he was well liked. Like so many others, his private life was far removed from his public life.

Margie's father would walk in the door each night and terrorize his family. His wife would hurry to reheat the dinner. If he didn't like the food or it wasn't hot enough, he would turn the whole table upside down and beat his wife. More than once, the seven daughters saw their mother stabbed and beaten by a drunken and enraged father. Margie's father would make all the girls come down and clean up the mess he had made and bandage their mother.

Needless to say, the father's return home every night sent the girls running to their bedrooms. His rage and lust knew no bounds. Every daughter was either molested or attempts had been made to molest them. The youngest daughter told me of how she would run and hide in the darkened closet when her father came home. She would crawl into the corner of the closet and try to make herself into a small black dot. She felt that if she could become the smallest speck in the closet that he would not find her. But he did.

For years Margie and her sisters lived in this terror. Their father did not allow them to spend money on clothes or school supplies. He made a very good living at the mill, but very little of it was seen by his family. When the winters were harsh, the girls did not go to school because they had no winter coats or boots. By the time each of them reached the age of thirteen, their father pushed them into marriage and out of the house. Education was seen as useless for girls, hence the investment in winter clothes for school was viewed as a waste of money.

The family witnessed the death of their favorite uncle one day. He was gunned down by a friend of their father's in front of their eyes. His sin? This uncle had stood up to their father and told him never to abuse his wife and daughters again. Not long after this incident, the father left with another woman and the family went on welfare to survive. The abuse was over.

Margie's story was not unique. We were to discover that she was one of the 80 percent of the women in our congregation who were molested by the men in their family! And this statistic included the older women. Margie's husband was no different from her father. They survived on her welfare payments because her husband rarely worked. When Margie's husband was killed in a gang war, her landlord evicted her because he didn't trust women alone to pay the rent. This was ludicrous, since Margie's husband did very little to support the family. It was at this point in Margie's life that I met her.

She was homeless and open to hearing about the love of Jesus and turning her life over to his care. I saw her go from hopelessness and despair to joy and hope for the future. Her circumstances had not changed, but Margie had. We labored in vain for three months to find her an apartment. No landlord was willing to rent to her even though the church was willing to stand behind her financially. All landlords know that a welfare mom living on a four-hundred-dollar monthly cash grant from the government cannot afford housing.

Although the church was small and very poor, we knew we had to continue to provide a safe refuge for Margie and her children. My husband, David, visited the local bank and asked for help to buy a home. David spoke to the bank president and reminded him that as a local institution, the bank had an obligation to be part of the solution to the community problem of abuse and homelessness. The president agreed. The church was guaranteed a 100 percent loan, which meant no money down. That is exactly what we had—no money down; so an agreement was struck. Margie and her children moved into a two-apartment home, the Jubilee House, so named in honor of the new lease on life the home offered her and another homeless family in the church who moved in on the first floor.

Margie's Sisters

Margie had six sisters, and all but one lived in abusive situations. Here are some of their stories along with the healing solution God called us to extend.

Gladys

Gladys had lived with the same man for eight years. She had four children by him. In addition to her children, Gladys discovered one night that Reuben also had another family—a younger woman with two children. Reuben was an alcoholic and an abuser of cocaine. In their early years, he beat Gladys violently but had stopped the beatings due to threats from Gladys's family. However, the treatment had worsened in some respects. Reuben brought girlfriends home to party with him and sent Gladys and the children into the bedroom during these times. Gladys had no education, nor had she ever worked. She felt trapped and did not know how to leave. She received welfare assistance, but it was not enough to rent an apartment, pay utilities, buy clothes, and purchase other necessities for a household.

Gladys's story stumped us for a long time. We were learning firsthand why so many women trade abuse for a roof. There are no other options. Gladys's life demonstrates dramatically how a life without options leaves women suffocated by their own hopelessness. Gladys became a strong Christian, but as her faith grew, so did her frustration over the often vile conditions in which she and the children were forced to live. We knew we had to do more than "God bless" her and send her on her way. We made it a matter of intense prayer.

Eddy

Eddy, another sister, was married to a man who shot up cocaine and was an alcoholic. Eddy herself was an alcoholic. They had two teenage children who ran the streets of south Chicago and were failing in school. One of the latest incidents was when the father, Carmello, locked the boys out of the house on a below-zero night while he and some other men shot up cocaine. Eddy was at a bar. The boys found her and asked her for help to get into the house. She ran all the way home. This was the last straw for her. Carmello often spent all his paycheck on drugs, and when that wasn't enough, he sold Eddy's jewelry, stereo, and anything else he needed to support his habit. That night, Eddy tried to kill Carmello. Several people from the church community went over to intervene. After this incident, Eddy finally came to Bible study and decided to follow Jesus.

I decided it was time to reach Carmello with the same good news. From all the reports I had heard, I knew the transformation Jesus offered was the only answer for him. I was warned that he was violent and would not spend more than two seconds telling me to get out. But I also knew it was one visit I couldn't avoid.

Carmello and Eddy lived on one of the worst drug streets in south Chicago. Their apartment was in the rear and seemed to be almost underground. The doorway was so low I almost had to crawl up to look down. I could see through the curtain that Carmello was sitting alone in the living room watching television. With a trembling hand, I knocked on the door. He was so shocked by my presence that he didn't even greet me. He called Eddy, who introduced me as her pastor. She then excused herself so we could talk.

167

He tripped over himself trying to get the X-rated show on the television turned off. He showed me a lot of respect out of deference for the church. I wanted to laugh at my fears, now banished. How close I had come to letting my fear of his violence keep me away!

I told Carmello that I had come because I believed that Jesus Christ was the only answer to his problems. I knew that drug abuse and violence go hand in hand and I understood the terrible struggle to do the right thing when your body craves a destructive force. I asked him if he had ever gone to church or if he knew anything about Jesus.

Carmello shared the most amazing story with me. He had been in church all his life, growing up in Puerto Rico. His family were devoted Pentecostal Christians. He was the only lost sheep. He knew that his family in Puerto Rico prayed for him; he said he didn't want to beat Eddy and the boys, but he couldn't seem to stop his drug use and violence. We talked a long while that night, and at the end of the evening, Carmello bowed his head and prayed his own prayer of confession and supplication that Jesus would come into his life and make him a new man. Carmello promised me he would come to church that Sunday and begin a home group with others. I assured him he would feel at home in the small group as everyone was either struggling with being violent or a victim of abuse. It was a safe place.

That evening was more than I expected. I left exhilarated by our conversation and broken at the end by his touching prayer for help and a new life. But did I expect to see Carmello in church Sunday? I did not. Imagine my surprise when he showed up for Sunday worship. I will never forget that moment. He was ready to be saved from himself; he just needed the invitation. I learned a lesson that day. I have tried never to fear someone's violence and abusiveness. I believe that many men who are violent *do* want to stop. The only real hope they have is the transforming new life Jesus offers. I also learned that the church has the mission to create safe places for people to change. Carmello felt safe in that time we had together and continues to be drawn to the safety of the church community for his healing.

The church has the answer to breaking the pattern of male violence in society today. The church has the *only* answer. Violence is a way of life for many men; it is no different now than it was in the ancient world of Paul. That is why Paul spends time encouraging men to be good husbands and fathers by behaving in a loving manner toward their family. The mandate is clear: The church needs to bring men to a saving knowledge of the gentle Lamb of God and to disciple converts in the ways of the Christ who taught us to turn the other cheek, to love others as ourselves, and to give our lives in selfless service to others. But Paul had a great deal to say about male violence. I think the church today would better serve its members if it would deal honestly with the issues of male violence in our culture by looking at these exhortations for enlightenment. Many of these passages are neglected and passed over for the more culturally acceptable verses on wifely submission. The emphasis that Scripture makes is on *mutual submission.*

When the woman's submission is addressed over and above male violence, the unspoken (and sometimes spoken) message is clear: Women are responsible for the violence done to them. Many women who are beaten at home look to the church for help. Most of the women who were coming to our Bible study groups had been told by their priest or Protestant clergy member not to provoke the man to violence, to stay home and be dutiful wives, and that God would honor their submission. The main issue is then not addressed—the violence of the man.

Carmello's hope for conversion lies in the church being the redeeming, healing community Jesus calls us to be. Carmello continues today in the church. The road has not been easy. He has fallen many times, but the church has always been there for him when he was ready to pick up and try again. Lifelong habits are not easily broken, and God's grace, patience, and mercy need to be extended to the errant one if lifelong change is going to happen. Transformation changes both the sojourner and the companion for the journey; as we grow through patient loving-kindness, we are called to extend mercy to others in their struggle for freedom from sin.

Marissa

Another sister of Margie is Marissa. Marissa had come to a home Bible study and found Jesus. She was living with a drug dealer and had two sons by him. She was unhappy with his dealing drugs, but he refused to change. One night she found out he had been living a double life and had another family on the north side of the city— a wife and three teenage children. When Marissa confronted Carlos with her new information, Carlos got drunk and decided to kill her. Carlos indeed had another family across town, and in a similar confrontation he had shot this woman in the face, but she had survived.

On the fateful night that Marissa found out about Carlos's other family, he brandished a weapon in her face also. She managed to flee out the back door and called me from a neighbor's home. She was hysterical and asked me to please hurry and come get her. She would wait for me in the alley. I called another woman in the church and her husband to go with me. It was two in the morning, and the neighborhood was not safe at two in the afternoon, let alone in the early morning hours. We drove over to the house to find police cars in the street. We were told Marissa was upstairs and her husband was in jail. Evidently, a neighbor had called the police, and they came to the house.

Usually the police will ask the man to leave and can give no other protection unless the wife has been shot or beaten. When the police tried to talk to Carlos, he became violent and they arrested him. As Carlos was dragged down the street, shoeless and shirtless, he still yelled out threats of murder right in front of the police. They told us that they could only hold him three hours. That would be the time he needed to make bail, and then there was nothing they could do but release him. They suggested that Marissa leave the house since his threats against her were definitely real. We got two vans and quickly loaded everything in her house into the vans. She wanted as much as she could take, because she believed he would destroy what was left. As we carried her household items, furniture, and clothes down the stairs, the drug dealer friends of Carlos circled us like buzzards ready for the prey. They drove around and around the block. We tried to ignore their presence, but we were very aware of the guns they carried. Our main objective was to get Marissa out before Carlos got out of jail. We did it, but it was close . . . and scary.

The problem then became what to do with Marissa. Carlos would expect her to go to her sisters' homes, so we decided to take her back to the parsonage. She and the children stayed with us for one week. It was an interesting week. Carlos eventually discovered that Marissa was in our care. He learned that if he wanted his family back, he would have to deal with the pastors. My husband met with Carlos at a local restaurant. The threats were gone. He was sober and desperate. This is a crucial time for the woman. At this point the abuser becomes very conciliatory and agrees to do anything to get her back. Then the cycle of violence begins again. We were determined not to let that happen if it was within our power.

David's meeting with Carlos went well. Carlos seemed to be sincere about changing his life. David told him that Marissa was now a Christian, and as a Christian, the church was standing with her in her commitment to lead a new life. If Carlos wanted Marissa back, he was going to have to prove himself by giving up drug dealing, making things right with his other family, giving his savings account to Marissa so she could establish a home for her children, finding a job, and seeking spiritual help. Carlos balked at giving Marissa his savings (thirteen thousand dollars) but objected to nothing else. David spent some time with him about what it meant to be a Christian and asked Carlos if he objected to Marissa's new lifestyle. Carlos insisted he had no problem with the church but wanted to attend Catholic mass with Marissa, not a Protestant church. *Any* church attendance was welcome!

The church took a stand. The members showed solidarity with Marissa and her suffering and stood against evil and violence. Carlos was impressed with the show of strength, and the people committed to help Marissa with her new life. Carlos, much to everyone's surprise, stuck by the terms of the agreement. Eventually, he and Marissa married. Their marriage was in the Catholic church, and while Carlos did not approve, Marissa also worshiped with us. Carlos's other family was told about Marissa and their two sons. Over time, this woman and her children became good friends with Marissa and her sons; they also had become Christians. Carlos wavered only once from his agreement with the church to do right by Marissa. But after three years (and another child), Carlos decided he needed more money and was going to start dealing drugs again. Marissa pleaded with him not to jeopardize the life God had given them, but to no avail; his mind was made up. The next day he was killed in an auto accident on his way home from work.

The Answer to Our Prayers

Marissa, Gladys, Eddy, and others God brought our way made us realize that the church needed more than a Band-Aid approach to the emergency situations. We wanted to provide more than a living-room floor for a shelter. We envisioned a refuge house for abused women similar to the ones that the Christian women in the 1800s established to help women in crisis. After the Jubilee House, we had just enough faith to believe that God would help us create such an environment.

The WellSpring House became the answer to that prayer. The WellSpring was a six-unit apartment building. Each unit had two bedrooms and a large living area. In deciding what kind of home environment we wanted to create for women in crisis, we visited shelters in the city of Chicago and other cities. One of the first things I noticed was the overemphasis on rules and demands placed on mothers. They were punished for the most trivial of offenses. Three demerits and they were out of the building. It appeared to us that demanding attendance at meals and all house meetings was a heavy burden for mothers seeking work, housing, welfare assistance, and schooling. Other shelters are ruthless and abusive in their demands, and bed checks in the middle of the night by male guards can be traumatizing to women who see their abusers around every corner. The shelter system is so abusive in some cases (if not most) that women often return to the abuser to escape the dehumanizing conditions of the shelter.

My discussions with a nun in Kansas City, Missouri, crystallized our thinking into a plan for a better environment. She told us if she had it to do over again, she would create a healing environment where each woman had her own apartment and set her own goals for independence. After what we had seen in the shelter system, we determined to follow this advice. Independence was a natural setting for living; rows of cots did not allow for privacy. Privacy was something abusers often deny their victims. Women would be allowed to come and go as they needed. Weekly house meetings would occur on Saturday mornings so as not to disrupt anyone's schedule during the week. Each woman would establish her own goals for independence; the director's job then would be to facilitate these goals by keeping each resident on track and sharing resources with her. Every family could live in their apartment for a maximum of two years. This would give them the time they needed to rebuild their lives through schooling, job training, and emotional and spiritual renewal. Many women who live in abusive situations are not allowed to have their own money, friends, or a life of their own. Their every moment is often taken up with having to keep an abusive partner happy. Since the companions of violence are often drug and alcohol addiction, women are responsible to raise the children and maintain the household on their own. Our goals for a healing environment for abused women meant privacy, empowerment through goal setting, accountability through interaction with other residents and the director, and an environment conducive to spiritual and emotional healing.

The WellSpring program has been in effect for six years now. It is encouraging to see women healed, their dignity restored, with hope for the future. Three years ago, we opened up another apartment building on the north side of Chicago that houses nineteen families. The Leland House allows women to rebuild their lives over a two-year period in a healing Christian environment.

The Jubilee House and the WellSpring House helped us grow in our faith as a local church. We could see in visible and dramatic ways the results of our standing with the oppressed, abused, widows, and orphans. We heeded the words of James, "Religion that is pure and undefiled before God, the Father, is this: to care for orphans and widows in their distress, and to keep oneself unstained by the world" (James 1:27 NRSV), and we discovered that when you set yourself on the side of the weak, God makes you strong.

We discovered that when the church really *is* the church, then there are no limits to how God will help it stand for the fatherless and orphans among us. Suburban churches joined with us to finance and rehab the buildings we were able to buy. Rural churches also participated: Farmers with extra time in the winter built bunkbeds, women sewed quilts, children gave toys, and many drove in from Iowa and South Dakota to build and paint. The rural churches became so energized by their new mission that they began to take some of our gang kids at the church out to the farms to plant seed and work with the animals. An amazing sight—an Iowa farm family and members of the Chicago gang world "walking the beans" together. The result was so stunning that we opened up a youth farm in rural South Dakota under the auspices of a sister church. Young men seeking a life outside of the violence found hope in rural America for a new life.

Our little church became a catalyst for healing and transformation, not only for the victims of violence and abuse who found haven in our refuge houses, but for members of the church who needed to know that they are part of the most powerful force on earth—the healing church of Jesus Christ.

11

Competent Christian Intervention with Men Who Batter

Steven R. Fleming

S ince it has become an ecclesial concern, the focus in Christian literature on domestic violence has been primarily on the injustices done to the victims of violence. Of course, this emphasis is justified. Victims of violence should always be of primary concern. However, the violent abuser may be dealt an injustice as well, characteristically very different from the injustices experienced by victims. Ironically, as the church fails to meet the needs of the abused wife, it also fails the abuser by reinforcing his grip of power in an abusive situation. The church is meant to be a bastion for hurting people, not only for the victim, but for the abuser as well. He is also a wounded person in need of help. Without an astute understanding of his needs and the issues behind his violence, the congregation is more likely to harm him by enabling him to continue violence than to help him by holding him accountable for his behavior. Conversely, the local church has the potential of being a significant agent for change and a source of healing in the abuser's life.

Some may be wondering why the issue of husband abuse is not included in this work. In my experience, I have found, as have other practitioners, that the vast majority of domestic violence is directed from husband to wife. I acknowledge, as do others, that violence often goes both ways. But researchers Gelles and Straus note that the motivation is generally different. They found that female violence was in self-defense, as a response to violence by their husbands (Gelles & Straus, 1988). Generally, when men are violent, it is as an act of coercion or control to establish power (Straus, Gelles, & Steinmetz, 1980).

Abusers come from all socioeconomic levels, all religions, all races, and all cultures (Sonkin, Martin, & Walker, 1985). In fact, abusers are unrecognizable to the average observer. Pioneering researcher Lenore Walker found some common characteristics among abusers in her early work. She found that the typical perpetrator has low self-esteem. He holds to traditional ideas of family roles, particularly that the husband is the supreme leader of the home. He maintains power and control as autocrat of the home. He may believe men are superior to women. The man who batters tends to blame others for his own behavior—including his violence. He may be excessively possessive and jealous of his wife. Obsessed with the threat of losing her, he may check on her periodically throughout the day or demand a minute-by-minute account of her day. He may be suspicious that she is having an affair and may harass her for this alleged impropriety. Victims commonly complain of a Dr. Jekyll and Mr. Hyde personality. At one point the abuser can be very charming—one reason why his partner was initially attracted to him—then suddenly an alter ego takes control that exhibits explosive rage (Walker, 1984).

Lindsey, McBride, and Platt (1993a) describe this phenomenon as the maintenance of a facade. The abuser presents a personality to the public world that is charming and attractive. This persona began to develop when the abuser attempted to survive as a child. At that time, the abuser developed and used roles that reduced punishment and gained acceptance from the adults in his life. Today, instead of presenting his real and vulnerable self to those close to him, he has found a "safer" way of interacting. In fact, he may not even be aware of the real person behind the facade, so extensive is this aspect of his personality (Lindsey et al., 1993a).

The batterer is also known to minimize, deny, and blame his partner for the abuse. Minimization is characterized by diminishing the violence and its effects. "She bruises easily," and, "I just tried to keep her from hitting me," are typical examples. Denial can take the form of distorting the situation, excluding details, or blatant refusal to acknowledge the violence and take responsibility for it. Usually more severe acts of violence are not "remembered." Some batterers claim they have blackouts and cannot remember when they get extremely angry. In many ways, this response is natural, much like that of the little boy caught with his hand in the cookie jar. Any shameful act brings with it the temptation to save face. This is not only to save the abuser's public face, but also to protect what fragile self-esteem he may have. Understandably, the more fragile he is, the stronger the denial will be.

Another common trait of the male batterer is a deep need to control his external world. To him, being in control is equivalent to being in charge of his environment (control equals dominance). Self-control is not considered in this scenario. As a result, the perpetrator resorts to efforts directed toward dominating others through aggression and violence to gain feelings of well-being.

Another research team, Hamburger and Hastings (1986), has done much to quantify personality traits of men who batter. Their studies, as well as the clinical observations of others, demonstrate that abusers tend to exhibit considerable psychopathology within their basic personalities. In their research they found that only 12 percent of abusers studied did *not* demonstrate any discernible psychopathology of personality. They have systematized three constellations of personality characteristics among men who batter. An abuser can display significant evidence for one or more of the following groups of characteristics. One constellation showed a person who is withdrawn, moody, and hypersensitive to "slights" by others. He is volatile, generally unstable (borderline characteristics), and overreactive. He may be calm one moment and very angry the next. He tends to be depressed.

The second group of characteristics describes a man who is self-centered, rigid regarding values, uses others, and feels entitled to be treated well by others according to *his* standards. Refusal by others to respond as he desires may result in aggression. He is happy with himself, has lots of energy, and may have alcoholic tendencies and drug problems. Clinically this constellation of characteristics is close to the narcissistic and antisocial personality disorders. These men use thinking processes that enable them to continue their violence. They reason, "I won't get caught. If I do get caught, the consequences will not be serious. If there are consequences, I can talk my way out of them" (Lindsey et al., 1993a). If this man loses his partner, he will move on to find another. This group seems to be the most common of the three types. Nearly one half of the men fell within this constellation.

Finally, the third constellation is similar to the clinical diagnosis of dependent and compulsive personality. This man is generally tense and rigid, and behaves with weakness and passivity. He usually exhibits low self-esteem and a strong need for a significant other. Generally, he is mildly depressed; he may think, "As long as she is with me I am okay." He is obsessed with her and may threaten suicide to manipulate her into staying.

When any or all of these three profiles are combined in one person, the instability and volatility are magnified. Nearly half of the men in this study demonstrated two to three of the profiles combined (Hamburger & Hastings, 1986). The significance of this research is extensive. It indicates that domestic violence involves something deeper than merely learned behavior. In clinical psychology it is generally understood that a person possessing such pathology of personality requires intense long-term therapy to achieve significant results. These men may be able to stop the physical violence, but handicaps of character may perpetuate other forms of abuse in interpersonal relationships.

The reader may ask, "How could a Christian be a wife abuser?" Simply because we who belong to Christ are sinners saved by grace. Christians come from various backgrounds, some that contribute to this problem more readily than others. Even the apostle Paul, after many years of discipleship and ministry, found himself falling into sin (see Romans 7). The question that naturally follows is, "How does the Christian who batters differ from the non-Christian abuser?" The difference is primarily in the way he talks. Instead of justifying his abuse by saying he was provoked, he is more likely to say, "She is not submissive enough." This assertion is the language that hooks other Christians and keeps them from questioning him.

Roots of Violence

How can someone be violent to the person he is supposed to love the most? To adequately understand and intervene, one must know the roots of violence. The first thing that must be clear is that the cause of domestic violence is the man committing the act. Violence is a choice and is always the choice of the one committing the act. The abuser is always responsible for his behavior. This is the most important message the perpetrator must learn. Otherwise he will never take responsibility for the violence. The choices the abuser makes may, however, be influenced by certain factors or roots. Based on social exchange theory, merely lowering the rewards and raising the consequences for violence should make a difference. When he finds that violence is no longer rewarding, he may seek alternative behaviors.

Social attitudes also exert their influence on domestic violence. There is a prevalent attitude that under some circumstances it is appropriate to be violent with one's mate. A survey from the late 1980s revealed that one out of three husbands and one of four wives felt that slapping one another is somewhat necessary, normal, and good. Seventy percent of those surveyed felt that slapping a twelve-year-old child was necessary, normal, and good (Gelles & Straus, 1988). Social attitudes are also reflected in and influenced by the media. Movies commonly portray domestic violence without consequences. It has been humorized on television shows such as *The Honeymooners* when Jackie Gleason threatens to hit his wife to the moon.

Many men who drink and are violent blame it on the alcohol. Indeed, nearly half of all couples who experience violence report alcohol involvement. This apparent relationship between alcohol and violence does not necessarily indicate a causal relationship however. Research is demonstrating something different—that alcohol is used as an *excuse* for abusive behavior. A study of different cultures by anthropologists seems to confirm this. If alcohol has a disinhibiting physiological effect, then drinking would bring about violence in all cultures. The anthropologists did not find this to be true. In some societies people became violent, but in others passivity and withdrawal were more typical. It was concluded that drunken behavior is typically a learned behavior. "In our society, as well as in others, individuals learn that they will not be held responsible for their drunken behavior" (Gelles & Straus, 1988, p. 45).

Moreover, the family in which the abuser was raised may play a role in the genesis of his violent behavior. When parents are abusive to each other, they model violence as a viable way of resolving conflict. Likewise, many abusers have been abused and neglected as young children. Such experiences are the foundation of personality disorders mentioned previously (Hamburger & Hastings, 1986).

While growing up, boys are socialized not to be "sissies." The expression of vulnerable feelings by boys is discouraged, even punished. Boys learn that anger is the only acceptable emotion when things go wrong. Sonkin and his colleagues conclude:

> Boys are not only taught to be dominant and aggressive, they are taught to avoid behavior that could in any way be construed as womanly. . . . In this conditioning process, however, *the message is anti-woman* [italics added], boys learn to glorify masculinity and despise all things female. (Sonkin, Martin, & Walker, 1985, p. 22)

This leads to a polarization of genders as adults.

The Role of the Church

Where does the church fit into this picture? Is it possible for the church to be a place of healing and accountability for the abuser, or is it doomed to either condemn or collude with the abuser? Should the church side with the abuser or the victim? Remaining neutral is the same as colluding with the perpetrator because it preserves the status quo.

The biblical mandate is to side with the oppressed—the victim. Jesus said, "Whatever you did for one of the least of these . . . you did for me" (Matt. 25:40 NIV). Throughout the Bible there is a mandate to care for the downtrodden, and women play that role in the abusive situation.

How can the church care for the abuser when it sides with the victim? When we understand the situation from the victim's perspective, we may prevent ourselves from being influenced by the perpetrator's wiles. It is the reality check that keeps those who are in contact with the batterer from being pulled into his distorted view of the situation. The people around him must remember the abuse and understand that the abuser's main concern is to keep or get his wife back. He will manipulate church leaders and members into fulfilling this objective. Unfortunately, manipulative people generally accomplish their objectives. Those unfamiliar with the abuser's ways may succumb to his persistence and become convinced that he has changed. Verbally gifted abusers can convince people that they are the true victims of an unjust separation from their partners. At this point the true victim becomes the "sinner," because through the separation she is prolonging her husband's agony.

On the other hand, if people do not succumb to the abuser's wiles, he might feel betrayed when church leaders disagree with his perspective. But the only way he will change is if others do not tolerate his behavior or join with him in his rationalizations. This perspective is much like the "tough love" approach that has become popular in other contexts.

From the pulpit in most evangelical churches, one can hear preached that homosexuality and abortion are destroying the American family. I would contend that the true nemesis of the family is domestic violence (including wife abuse and child abuse). It is probably the most devastating social problem in America, because it is at the root of many others including crime, drugs, gangs, and teenage pregnancy. Church leaders can be part of the problem or choose to be part of the solution. To be part of the solution, leaders can preach about domestic violence from the pulpit. If done with care and sensitivity, this will raise awareness of the problem and let the perpetrator sitting in the pew know that violence is immoral and will not be tolerated.

Colorado pastor Bob Wahl states that there are several hindrances to appropriate pastoral intervention in the local church (Wahl, 1990). The first is lack of training. There has not been much energy and time spent thinking through this problem as being of primary importance in many churches.

A survey team has concluded, "We have yet to talk to a woman who felt that she had received much aid from a clergyman" (Stacy & Shupe, 1983, p. 105). This conclusion came after gathering extensive histories from 542 abused women. James and Phyllis Alsdurf published a clergy survey in 1989, finding that only 8 percent of clergy claimed they felt wife abuse occurs often. Eighty percent of the same pastors said they had encountered domestic violence in their ministry. Sixty percent of pastors had encountered the problem in the previous six months. One of three pastors questioned the reliability of the victim's report in regard to who is responsible for the abuse. The victim was held responsible even though research shows that the victim is more likely to take responsibility for the violence than the abuser. Gelles and Straus (1988) found that wife abuse had occurred in one of seven families of those surveyed in the previous year. Thus the preacher can be sure that when he stands before an average-sized congregation of one hundred or more people, he or she is most likely speaking to at least one family faced with wife abuse. Yet the evidence points to tragic ignorance and minimization of the problem by congregation leaders.

The second hurdle for pastors to overcome is a deep commitment to the indissolubility of marriage. So deep is this commitment for some pastors that they encourage women to risk their lives for the sake of the marriage. This strategy fails to confront the abuser and hold him accountable. Very often, the threat of losing his wife and family is the only thing that will bring the perpetrator to true responsibility and repentance. If this is true, then in many cases the only thing that will motivate the abuser to change is the threat of divorce. Ironically, this threat is the only thing that may save the relationship. The crisis that is created by the threat of divorce is an open door for change. It has been said a crisis is actually a crossroads in disguise. If the abuser is not challenged adequately, the destructive cycle of violence may continue until the family is in ruin.

It has been argued from Scripture that Jesus allowed for divorce only in the case of adultery (Matt. 19:9). Gary Llaboe (1985) argues convincingly that the Greek word written by Matthew here *(porneia)* contains a broader meaning than adultery. Other Greek words are used more specifically for adultery. Indeed, there are occasions where the word is not used for adultery. Llaboe defines the word used here as "a general act of immorality entailing a violation of one's partner related to aspects of the marriage which are necessary for complete and full intimacy" (p. 131). The exception for marital indissolubility, therefore, is expanded to immoral violations that disrupt "God's intended intimacy to the degree that it can no longer be continued or restored" (p. 131). Divorce should not be the first alternative and is not God's preferred solution. "However, after legitimate and sincere attempts to restore the situation have been made, dissolution of the relationship is viable for cases of *porneia* (immorality)" (p. 134). In the case of domestic violence, if the husband's behavior fails to change or he has committed violence that has permanently devastated the relationship, the victim should be free to divorce.

The church-attending victim who initiates divorce generally is denigrated and held responsible for it. But when the wife threatens divorce or separation and the husband does not respond with a sincere effort to reconcile, it is justified. The effort to reconcile must include confession (taking full responsibility for the violence without minimizing, denying, or blaming) and repentance (seeking professional help that results in permanent replacement of old behaviors and attitudes that lead to violence with new and healthy ones). If the abuser fails in this process, he is the one who passively chooses to divorce. His wife is merely carrying out the act that he has sanctioned.

It is granted that God "hates" divorce. One of the verses quoted most frequently on the matter is Malachi 2:16. However, those who speak out against divorce fail to read on. In the same verse God declares, "And I hate a man's covering himself with violence" (NIV). God considers both divorce and violence as evil. It may be argued that at times violence can outweigh divorce as an evil, therefore justifying divorce as an act. Divorce may be more desirable for the abused wife, but what about the children? A review of research and literature on the effects of wife abuse has found that children of discordant families compared to children of relatively peaceful broken homes are at significantly greater risk of experiencing adjustment difficulties (Jaffe, Wolfe, & Wilson, 1990).

One can conclude that divorce at times may be the lesser of two evils in a fallen world. Divorce may be the just answer to an unjust situation. Just war may be called for when injustice challenges;

likewise, a just divorce may be the appropriate response for the emotional and physical sake of the weaker and abused party. "As killing is sometimes allowable with fear and trembling, as in just war, so divorce may sometimes be permissibly done accompanied by mourning and repentance" argues Christian ethicist Allen Verhey (Alsdurf & Alsdurf, 1988, p. 121).

Another hindrance to appropriate intervention in regard to the perpetrator is that church leaders fail to have an adequate counter to the "headship" argument when used by the abuser as a justification for wife abuse. The attitude adopted regarding this concept can profoundly affect the approach made toward batterers. If a leader believes headship of the husband has a connotation of lord and master, his intervention will reflect this interpretation, with the resulting tendency to blame the victim for the violence, hence colluding with the husband's abusive behavior.

Usually an abuser uses the passage from Ephesians 5, "Wives submit to your husbands as to the Lord" (v. 22 NIV), to support his belief in the subservience of wives. Indeed, the traditional view is that the apostle Paul is setting a precedent for male authority and female subjection in marriage. But in the context of the rest of the passage (vv. 25–33), this view does not stand. Grant Martin argues this point eloquently.

> Paul uses the example of Christ's self-sacrificing action on behalf of the church. This action defines the meaning of headship. The example does not mean that the husband should become a Lord and Master like Christ. The purpose of the comparison is to show headship becoming a means of responsibility and initiative—responsibility to act in love and initiative to act in service. As Christ gave himself in love and humbled himself, so husbands are to take the initiative in building an atmosphere of loving, self sacrificing service. (Martin, 1987, pp. 118–119)

The response of the pastor/counselor to the abuser who externalizes his responsibility should be: "Let's look at *your* behavior. What have *you* been doing to love your wife, to lay your life down so that she can become all that she is meant to be?" Servanthood is the example Christ models for husbands. In response to externalizing and blaming, Jesus said that we must take the log out of our own eyes before we can help our neighbor with the speck in his/her eye. The abuser must be encouraged to look at his *own* sin.

Hierarchicalism in the home is at the core of abusive behavior. There would be no need for abuse if the desire for power and control did not exist. Paul Jewett argues:

There are husbands who do not drink, who earn piles of money, who evidence no pangs of jealousy and who seem to suffer no sense of insecurity yet still lay violent hands on their wives.

When we ask why this is so, we are driven back to more universal considerations, one of which has to do with Christian theology. I refer to sexual hierarchy, the view that the man is over the woman and the woman subordinate to the man, especially in husband-wife relationships. (Jewett, 1982, p. 9)

Hierarchy is the window of opportunity for husbands to use coercion and abuse to gain selfish ends. Because of our selfish nature, the more unaccountable power one has, the more likely that person will be corrupted. One-sided accountability and submission is the foundation of all abusive relationships. The balance of power (mutual submission) is essential for healthy relationships.

Research seems to confirm this. Straus and his colleagues (1980) found through a representative survey that 20 percent of homes in which the husband/father dominated the household had experienced domestic violence in the previous year. In comparison, less than 2 percent of democratic homes in which power was shared among family members experienced domestic violence. They suggest that domestic violence is used by husbands as a means of establishing and maintaining authority in the household (Straus et al., 1980).

The attitude within the church must be that wife abuse is immoral and will not be tolerated. If the local congregation fulfills this objective, it can be part of a system of accountability that forces the abuser to look for appropriate alternative behaviors that lead to harmonious relationships.

Amend (a counseling agency in Colorado for abusive men) has implemented a model of intervention called "containment" that works when all the components do their part (Lindsey, McBride,

& Platt, 1993b). It begins with a batterer who escapes conse-quences for his violence and uses all the resources he can to con-trol (or contain) his wife. He takes advantage of those who would intervene. For example, the victim may call the police after a bat-tering incident. The police arrive and talk to the perpetrator. He convinces them that the argument was two-sided—she said some words that provoked him. The police leave without making an arrest, telling him to take a walk. If the police had understood that abusers commonly use provocation as an excuse for their violence, the outcome might have been different. Instead, the abuser has tightened the wall of containment around his wife. She will be more reluctant to notify the police at the next occur-rence because they were not helpful and her attempt to appeal for help led to further abuse.

The abuser can use the church for the same end. Congregation members may see him as a very nice and charming man—this is the facade that he presents to the public world. When the wife tells a church leader of the abuse, that person may have difficulty believing her because the abuser is known to be so nice. The church leader is already colluding with the abuser, and the abuser's objective of control is being met with outside help. If church members and leaders were educated regarding the char-acteristics of wife abusers, it would probably be more difficult for the abuser to use them in controlling his wife. Instead, they could become part of a system of accountability called the "wall of con-tainment," a system in which the abuser finds it increasingly dif-ficult to continue his abusing behavior. The victim may also begin to feel more empowered as her husband is contained. Ideally, con-tainment will engage all relationships and institutions in the abuser's life to build an impenetrable wall around him, reducing the rewards of his violence and motivating him to look for alter-native solutions.

If the wall of containment fails in any section—including that belonging to the church—the abuser's prognosis for change is reduced. Unfortunately, more often than not the local church has failed the abuser by failing to hold him accountable for his behav-ior. Those in the community who wish to contain the abuser find themselves frustrated many times by Christians and their failure to help in the containment process.

The Role of Therapy

Pastors and church members do not have the time, energy, or skills to focus on treatment in their intervention with the abuser. It is a daunting task. One pastor concedes that his role is to be a support person and to provide pastoral care as the abuser and his wife get outside help. Church members will find themselves needing to refer the abuser and his wife to competent therapists (Wahl, 1990). It is crucial that the counselors are trained and experienced in domestic violence treatment. Safety is a vital issue here.

When looking for a referral, beware of the counselor who uses couple therapy to treat violence. This is not safe as long as the threat of violence exists. Violence is not a couple issue. Responsibility for violent acts is purely the abuser's. Couple therapy tends to spread the responsibility around. The message the victim receives is that she is partly responsible for the husband's behavior. It is also difficult for the victim to be frank in a couple session; even if she is, she is at risk for further abuse.

Traditional individual therapy is generally not the most effective way of addressing abuse either. Therapy that is nondirective fails to confront the abuser's behavior. He can maintain a facade and have it reinforced because of this. A therapist who is attempting a "therapeutic alliance" with the abuser may find himself/herself buying into the abuser's rationalizations. Therapy that is working primarily on the emotional level may exacerbate violence and reinforce denial (blaming current violence on childhood victimization). Once violent behavior has stopped and coping skills regarding anger are in place, individual therapy can be very helpful.

The treatment of choice for most domestic violence therapists is group therapy. This has been found to be an effective modality for confronting denial and blame. In a group that is working properly, the members confront each other when this is happening. The confrontations of group members are much more powerful than those of the therapist because the group members are peers. Groups create a safe micro-society where new behaviors and mores are tried on for size. Group members find new and rewarding behaviors they were never aware of before. Groups also serve as a safety buffer for the therapist who often runs across an angry client when doing his job. Outcome studies have shown that

187

group therapy is significantly effective in reducing violent behavior (Dutton, 1986).

The goal of eradicating violence cannot be met if at least two things do not change regarding the abuser. First of all, he must take responsibility for his behavior, meaning he must acknowledge the violence without leaving out details. Denial can be confronted by pointing out inconsistencies as the perpetrator tells his story. Inconsistencies with the police report (if available) and the victim's story can be pointed out as well. Research indicates that the police report and the victim's account of the incident are generally more accurate than the perpetrator's story (Claes & Rosenthal, 1990).

Another common method of saving face is blaming. In this case, the abuser may accept the inappropriateness, but then deny responsibility. His behavior, he feels, is excused because of provocation (or alcohol, or something else). An abuser understandably uses denial, minimization, and blame to protect himself. There is a tendency to feel all good or all bad about himself. To confront this misjudgment, the message to him should be that no one is completely evil. The abusive behavior is only *part* of his life. It does not necessarily make him an utterly evil person.

The second crucial item that the abuser must face is power and control. He must be willing to give up the need to control his external environment and replace this with a sense of personal control and empowerment. At first the abuser resists, thinking the expectation is to allow himself to be abused. Soon, however, he learns that there are alternative ways to avoid feeling powerless rather than using coercion.

Consequences for continued abuse and other major infractions of group rules must be applied without exception. The therapist conspires with the abuser when he fails to be consistent. The role at this point is much like loving parents who do not withhold discipline because they see the long-term benefits. Overidentifying with the client undermines needed objectivity. If the victim reports another offense, she must be encouraged to call the police. The abuser may need to be terminated from the program or put back to the beginning. If it is deemed that therapy is not helping the client, more stringent consequences such as jail time may be suggested to the authorities. This approach is not meant to be punitive, but the price of violence must be raised higher than its rewards.

The therapeutic goal for group process is to create a safe environment where new behaviors and feelings can be tried and discussed without embarrassment. Social workers Nosko and Wallace argue that this is more important to achieve than merely teaching the men new skills; in fact, it is the "central vehicle empowering cognitive behavioral interventions" (1988, p. 39). The group in this model serves as a "micro-society with its own set of curative norms and values" (Nosko & Wallace, 1988, p. 38). The safe environment of acceptance reduces the need for distortions and defenses that prevent the abuser from changing. This "subculture" provides a model for group members to follow, relearning and redefining the masculine role (Nosko & Wallace, 1988). As a result, the men begin to experience and express new emotions. Whereas anger was the only acceptable feeling in the old role, the new role brings experiences of sadness, isolation, fear, worry, hurt, and other feelings that broaden their emotional selves. In this environment, they learn that their anger has been in reaction to or defense of these more primary and threatening feelings. "Cognitive and behavioral interventions complete this process by providing the necessary interpersonal skills to express anger in a nonviolent way when it does arise" (Nosko & Wallace, 1988, p. 42).

The Amend model I have worked with asserts that one to five years of therapy is necessary to bring about lasting change for the abuser. The issue of abuse is not only learned, but, as discussed previously, it involves deeper character issues having their roots in childhood neglect and abuse. In general, the deeper the wounds, the greater the duration of therapy must be. During check-in I encourage group members to say what they are feeling right then. This is usually awkward for newcomers, so they are given a list of feeling words to choose from. This encourages clients to begin labeling feelings, a precursor to assertive communication. Group rules must be clear and repeated frequently.

The first lessons that should be learned are some basic skills for anger control. "Time-out" is an excellent tool for controlling anger. When a client is aware of various signs of anger—physical (such as rapid heartbeat or sweaty palms), behavioral (clenched fists, pacing, and others), and psychological (negative thoughts such as,

"That witch!")—this indicates a need for time-out. It is important for these men to be sensitized to these signs because anger awareness is usually lacking. When a husband takes a time-out, he should tell his wife what he is doing and leave without further words. It is important that he avoid bars, driving, and hitting objects to vent anger. Time-out should be for only one hour. During time-out, he may vent feelings by performing a nondestructive physical activity (walking, exercising). The next step is to think about what he feels and prefers to see happen. This serves as material for later communication.

Anger journals are also an excellent method for controlling anger and developing a deeper awareness of feelings (Sonkin & Durphy, 1989). They provide a systematic opportunity to analyze thoughts, feelings, and behaviors related to anger. Sonkin and Durphy's journal addresses several critical behaviors such as stuffing (ignoring feelings of frustration that will build), escalating (bringing anger intensity up), and directing (appropriate communication of concerns).

Another method for reducing anger addresses self-talk, or mental dialogue. Negative self-talk focuses on other persons and the "wrongs" they have committed ("That witch, she has no right . . ."). This thought pattern escalates the intensity of feeling and may lead to abuse. Positive self-talk focuses on the self ("What do I need right now? What am I feeling?") and tends to de-escalate the emotional intensity, enabling rational behavior. These tools should be sufficient in the short-term to suspend violence, while deeper issues are addressed.

It is also helpful for clients to go through Domestic Violence 101. Covered in this course are the cycle of violence, categories of violence (physical, psychological, property, and sexual abuse), and roots of domestic violence (power and control, family of origin, male socialization, and sex role stereotyping). Men adhering to the traditional Christian perspective may be resistant to viewing family roles in a different light. Anything else may be considered liberal, feminist, and worldly. It is advisable to avoid theological arguments, however, especially over the meaning of "headship." Instead, appeal to the rewards of intimacy, unity, and trust. This can be achieved through mutuality (Eph. 5:21–33).

Long-term anger management involves learning how feelings are related to perceptions. Attached to an event ("Dinner is late") is an interpretation ("She is doing this to get even"), followed by an emotional reaction (anger). The way the event is interpreted has an impact on the feeling response. If the husband were to find out that one of the children had an emergency that day, his reaction would be significantly different. Abusers tend to interpret events in the worst light, exacerbating anger. Withholding judgment until all the facts are in will decrease the negative reactions.

The abuser's life is often characterized by chaos. Credit problems, outstanding traffic tickets, alcoholism, and other problems abound. His life has become unmanageable. This chaos serves a purpose, however. It is a decoy from deeper problems in the client's life. Therapy is an opportunity to find a new, more realistic image of self that incorporates sensitivity, new feelings, and intimate relationships. However, chaos prevents the abuser from achieving these objectives because all his energy goes into addressing crises. He must start changing behaviors one at a time that create chaos in his life. Self-care, which is usually deficient, must also increase. Things as simple as getting eight hours of sleep, cutting his workload, and spending more time with family may greatly reduce the stress level of his life and make it more enjoyable. During the group process, it is helpful for men to find a couple of these behaviors to focus on at a time. Once the chaos lifts and life is more manageable, the abuser can put his energy into more permanent change.

Communication and conflict skills must also be presented so that the abuser can replace power and control with personal empowerment in relationships. Abusers tend to view conflict as competition—there is always a winner and a loser. Actually, in this scenario, both parties lose because intimacy and trust are destroyed. Conflict must be reframed as an opportunity for both sides to win. With much input from the group, the men may learn listening, assertiveness, and negotiation skills to achieve this objective.

Finally, alcohol and illicit drugs must be addressed. These play a significant part in domestic violence. It was pointed out previously that these serve more as an excuse for violent behavior than as a cause. However, the use of alcohol and drugs perpetuates the chaos in an abuser's life and keeps him from remembering and applying material from the group. The drinking and drugs must stop at the onset of treatment. The Amend program has developed domestic violence groups that also address alcohol and drugs simultaneously. The substance abuse batterer should be in some sort of program that addresses this problem.

Though the task of holding the abuser accountable is full of frustrations and pitfalls, it also has rewards. These may include the restoration of a sinner to right relationship with God and others. Even if his marriage fails, intervention with the abuser may give hope for his future—one of harmonious relationships minus the abuse. Men who batter can change, some more readily than others. The call of the church is to be a place of healing for all hurting people, including the man who abuses his wife.

A Prison Epistle

Thomas

The least likely place for me to be that August night in 1988 was lying on a sweat-stained, rancid bunk in an overcrowded cellblock in county jail. As I lay on my back with my eyes closed, something prickly landed on the bridge of my nose. I quickly swiped at it as I bolted up in time to see the huge cockroach hit the rugged concrete floor and scurry for a crack between the floor and the block wall. I stared into the unfocused muddle. My chest tightened, and between the stacked bunks I cast a glance at my cellmates. Then my hand touched the cold steel bunk frame. The reality of county jail came down on me like a crushing ocean wave that sent me to the bottom of the sea. The filthy mattress I sat on was light-years from my comfortable, upper-middle-class queen-sized Stearns and Foster. The cold, damp floor didn't compare to the thick high-low carpeting to which my feet had become accustomed. Tears surfaced as I slung my body back down on the thin mat and turned to face the filthy wall once again. It was a ritual that had taken place several times a day for nearly two weeks. I hid my tears from the men crowded in that cell. I hated to keep crying, but each convulsive sob reached for a God I could no longer touch. My sin was so vile that I was sure he would never again listen to me. Torment slowly ebbed the life out of me, oozing painfully into the perverted atmosphere of this sex-offender's cellblock. The black specter of death hung over me and I desired nothing less. It would be sweet relief.

A Scripture verse plagued my mind: "It would be better for him to have a large millstone hung around his neck and to be drowned in the depths of the sea" (Matt. 18:6 NIV). My sobs and intense search for the God I once knew so intimately negated the din of jailhouse chatter from the twelve men cramped into a cell designed for no more than eight.

Day after endless day I cried out, repented, quoted bits of Psalm 51, and sank deeper into depression. The days were empty and the nights hollow in cellblock 23A. Then while reading my Bible the afternoon of September 5, 1988, God seemed to speak to my spirit. I stopped everything and waited. My mind couldn't comprehend it at first. But, there . . . there it was. Yes! I sensed his presence. It was God! Teardrops hit the printed page and I closed my eyes breathing deeply. Yes, God was there, there in that cell, there with the stench and dregs of humanity. "Jesus," I muttered. "Jesus." My lips were suddenly parched and I could hardly make the words come out. Tears flowed freely as he pierced the brokenness of my life. I could do nothing more than continue to whisper his name. Closing my Bible, I hugged it to my heaving chest. A peace enveloped me as the men of the cell went about their card games and foul conversation in the perverted atmosphere of homosexual undercurrents. Without words, God covered my shattered life with nothing less than his amazing grace. I wanted to shout, "I'm forgiven!" but *they* wouldn't hear it. Forgiven for what? Forgiven for—something I didn't want to face—sexual battery perpetrated against my loving grandchildren. As I considered my crime and God's forgiveness, hot tears of a new sort cascaded down my cheeks and dripped off my chin. I was *forgiven!* I *was* forgiven! God had accepted my repentant prayers! I experienced a wonderful sense of elation, yet there was no one with whom I could share my euphoria. Deep within me I worshiped him.

My mind felt scrambled into an incomprehensible maze of questions, statements, and unintelligible fragments of thought. I'd been taken to the depths of despair—so much so that my wife had hidden the pistol we kept in our home. She feared I'd take my life that terrible night my sin was revealed. To fall to such depths, then, without advance notice, and then now, in this rotten jail cell, skyrocket to ecstasy beyond comprehension was almost more than my mind could handle. I fell back on the bunk as though I were home, and sobbed myself into a sound sleep, the first time I'd slept like that in over 330 hours.

Within another two weeks I requested and was granted incarceration in a cell normally used for incorrigibles. It was across from the office, a single-man cell with a private shower. God's favor was evident even to the hundred-plus inmates on the wing. Sitting on the edge of my bunk in that isolated cell offered a semblance of quiet that gave me the opportunity to begin a daily journal. I suspect that, had I known the emotional upheaval such writings would bring, I wouldn't have started that diary. Yet, I'm a writer, and possibly that penchant for prose overpowered my desire to hide my past, my failure, my sin.

Why didn't I have some answers? What happened to make me treat my family with such shamefulness? What about my grandchildren? What would happen to them? How could I undo what I'd done? The same questions plagued me again and again. Why had I perpetrated such evil within my own family—the family I loved, and the children I cherished?

I withdrew my legal pad and wrote. Shortly my mind raced back to the "playtime" with my grandchildren. Even though there were strong sexual overtones and wrong touching, the laughter that permeated the air made everything all right. At least that's the lie into which I tried to escape while rationalizing my actions.

I put the pad away and spread my body out on the bed and stared at the nicotine-stained ceiling. It hadn't been washed in years. I glanced around the cell. The walls were supposed to be off-white but they were yellowish-beige. Without further concern for my journal, I bounded off the bunk and called to the guard to ask for a rag, bucket, and some detergent. It was as though this task demanded my immediate attention. I told the uniformed man I planned to "clean this filthy house."

It took three days to clean that stinking film off the walls and ceiling, and twice during my intense wiping, rinsing, and changing the water, a sudden overwhelming urge to cry convulsed my body. Here I was, half a century old and out of emotional control.

At those times, I reached through the bars and caught the big steel door and pulled it shut. I could close out the world and simply kneel at my bunk and cry and pray. It was at that time that I learned what it was to "offer up the sacrifice of praise." Up to that point, I'd wondered how praise could ever be considered a sacrifice. To sacrifice is to give something of value. It also carries the connotation of giving something we really don't want to give. When despair would break me, I really didn't want to praise God. It became a sacrifice that I poured out of the depth of my spirit. This was jail, and I was facing life with a mandatory twenty-five years in prison. Did I really feel like praising God for *that?* When childhood recall plunged me into the pit of despair, praising God was a distant consideration. Yet in that isolated cell, on my knees, with my hands raised and tears flooding my face, I got real with God. "Father, I hate myself. As Job has put it, 'I abhor myself.' I hate this cell. I want to be home. Oh, please undo this nightmare!" Then as I slumped down, I'd catch myself muttering, "Nevertheless, I worship you. Let your will be done in my life."

The night before I was arrested, three men came to our home—two of my sons-in-law and another man. They'd been drinking. In the depth of me I knew the "secret" was out, but as long as no one stated it, I refused to believe anyone really knew. That night, however, the three pushed their way through my front door armed with a club. My two sons-in-law beat me unmercifully. I was knocked to the floor, kicked in the face, and beaten with the club until parts of my body were as black as charcoal. They shouted obscenities at me, venting their anger, hatred, and the fact that they felt as violated as the children because I had broken the inherent trust unspoken among family members. They finally quit their tirade and stormed out of the house.

After they left, my wife hid our pistol. She saw my state of mind and my physical brokenness and realized I might do just about anything at that moment. I was a completely shattered man.

After getting me cleaned up, the questions surfaced. She was deeply wounded, yet she remained kind as we talked. She didn't interrogate me, rather stated, "You must have lived in torment." Then she added, "I should have known something terrible was wrong when your drinking got out of hand." Ultimately she asked,

"Why?" I had no answer. I, too, wanted to know why I'd destroyed the loving relationship I had with my grandchildren. We discussed the children and what would become of them. My mental state was in such disarray that I couldn't cry at that moment. Never in my fifty-one years had I experienced such guilt, depression, mental turmoil, pain, confusion, and emptiness. I had to assure my wife continually that she was not to blame.

The next day I was arrested, charged, booked, printed, and mugged. I was taken to cellblock 23A where all types of sexual deviants were held. It was there that I broke. The tears flowed as I lay on my bunk facing the wall while all around me homosexuals, pedophiles, female impersonators, and husbands and fathers like myself mingled, chattered, or sat blankly staring into unfocused mental disarray. It was there that I had to take a look at myself and ask the same question over and over again: *Why?*

(As I reread the above paragraph, I analyzed the fact that I listed myself with the "husbands and fathers," not with the homosexuals, pedophiles, and female impersonators. I wonder if that's some protective device within me. Is it a form of denial? I'm in prison because of *perversion*. Am I denying that I should be labeled a *pervert*, or is my act due to traumatic stress disorder—therefore labeled aberrant behavior? I wonder if there is a definitive answer, or simply clinical assumptions.)

Why did I molest the very ones I loved so much? Why? Although I couldn't even consider an answer at that time, as I lay on my back in my single-man cell, I enumerated the events that led to my withdrawal from the normal, loving relationships I'd had with my grandchildren to what eventually can only be called perversion. But other factors entered the picture.

In late 1981, I founded a Christian-oriented magazine. My desire was to help Christians who felt God's call in a specialized area of ministry. Because of circumstances that can only be labeled "miracles," I *knew* God was sanctioning this project. The first year it was one miracle after the other. Oh, there were struggles, times when all appeared lost, moments of fear and unbelief, but when the end of 1982 came, the miracles had pulled us through. Unfortunately, in 1983 the pressure and financial strain grew and the miracles seemed to be fewer. Around that time, I assured myself a glass of wine with my evening meal would serve me well. As the years flicked by, the debt from the magazine grew along with the pressure to succeed, and my wine consumption increased to inordinate proportions. By 1986, I held a debt of $272,000 and realized everything I owned was at stake. For my wife, losing our home would be a blow that could destroy our lives.

The wine dulled my sense of responsibility to the subscribers of the magazine. Somewhere in the midst of my irrational thoughts and clouded sensibility, the first encounter with my oldest granddaughter took place.

Although I sold my magazine and was relieved of the debt, by then the drinking was used to cover the reality of deviance that spread to my other grandchildren.

When I was arrested, I felt compelled to confess my sins and exonerate my sons-in-law from prosecution for their felonious assault. Later I had flashes of regret for signing that waiver. I could have used that beating as a tool to secure a lesser sentence. Then, as I considered the harm I'd done and the conflict that would have arisen from my battling for my rights, I'd relent and admit I was glad I didn't press charges against the parents of my grandchildren—they'd been through enough. When I had the opportunity to defend myself by going to trial, I chose not to put my family through such an ordeal. I certainly didn't want the trauma of a sexual abuse trial impressed into the minds of my grandchildren. The wire services had picked up the story and I wasn't going to put my family into the media spotlight. I decided on a plea bargain instead. To save my wife further problems, I urged her to divorce me. I told her I'd not contest it and she could have everything. It was the least I could do. I'd hurt everyone I loved. What could I do to replace what I'd taken? How could my unfaithfulness, by secret abduction of the children's innocence, ever be salvaged enough to remove the destruction I'd done? What restitution could there be?

Yet, after going through all that reasoning, times of remorse hardened into self-preservation. Blame-finding surfaced once again, and I wrote a long letter to my attorney to tell him of the fact that the parents of these children had contributed to their "sexual aggression." They allowed the children to view sexually explicit videos, actually had hard-core pornographic magazines in their home, all in the context of a very casual attitude toward sexuality. My mind willfully forgot who initiated the contact with the children, and I told the lawyer how *they forced me* into sexual games in the pool many times. Or, simply driving along with the two girls in the car, how the older, more aggressive one took off all her clothes while I protested. The other girl simply laughed as she crawled over and sat on my lap in her nakedness as I drove. At the time I felt the urge to alleviate my responsibility; I could recall so many instances where the children were extremely aggressive. But who created that monster?

Now that I look back on it, I realize the children initiated sexually explicit play only *after* I'd broken down the natural sexual barrier that stands between adults and children. Once that invisible wall is destroyed by a perpetrator, the children feel comfortably safe with adult/child sexual play, so at times they will naturally initiate it. As my innate desire to squirm out of the pain of incarceration periodically overwhelmed me, I wanted to rid myself of the anguish and guilt.

Now that I've been in prison for nearly six years, I find that most men choose relief from the discomfort of prison over forgiveness for sin. While lying on that bunk in cellblock 23A, I'd confessed my sin. I'd reestablished my relationship with God. Yet, the natural instincts within me screamed for relief from my guilt. It led to entertaining the idea of strategically placing the blame—first on my upbringing, then on various family members, on my childhood environment in a tough area of Detroit, even on my abused grandchildren.

Oh sure, I *was* molested as a child. That's a given. But does that really carry any weight of comfort, of mitigating evidence, of pardon for my sin? Some may point to the statistics and say that most molesters were molested when they were young. I point to the statistics and ask, "What about those who were molested when they were young who *haven't* molested others?" How do those statistics fit into the picture? I'm certain there are plenty of men and women who were treated terribly as children and have grown up to abhor molestation and have never considered such acts.

It all makes me wonder whether the Freudian concept that the child is the father of the man is correct. Was I so weak, so out of touch with myself, so completely lacking in self-control that I was forced into perversion by the things that happened to me thirty-five, forty, forty-five years ago? Was I searching for lasting comfort in the refuge of fault-finding patterns through which I could hide the responsibility for my actions, instead of searching for a lasting relationship with God? Was I really "overcome" by some evil within me? Did those much-maligned endorphin levels really numb my sensitivity to right and wrong, carrying me beyond the brink of control? Does that line up with God's Word?

I have a problem trying to hide behind the "I couldn't control myself" concept because of my relationship with God. During the time of my sinful behavior, I was stepping into the shower late one afternoon, and as surely as I've ever heard that inner voice of God, I heard the urging of the Holy Spirit warn me to "Stop what you're doing." I didn't have to ask what he was speaking to me about. In fact, as I turned on the water I muttered, "Yes, I have to take control of the situation." And I really meant to, but when the time came to take control, I made a conscious choice to continue in sinful behavior and rebellion.

I didn't hear that voice once or twice. He spoke to me three separate times over a one-year period. On the third time, the impression was most emphatic, "This is your last warning." Again, I didn't have to ask what the warning was about. I knew it was the voice of God within me and I realize to this day that he would never have told me to stop if I could not have taken control. Therefore, through my many steps of therapy, I've come to take full responsibility for my actions. Forget my sister and her friends. Forget the fact that I'd had other encounters with older kids and adults when I was young. Forget the pressure of losing my magazine, the financial load, the supposed loss of face. Forget the numbing effect of heavy alcohol intake. I *sinned!* I was a Christian capable of being directed by the Holy Spirit of God when I yielded to him. But I chose *not* to yield to him when I got into the deeper pressures of life. In fact, I rebelled. I chose to drink. I chose to escape the pressure of adult life by becoming the sexually active *child* I once was. I refuse to place the blame on anyone.

To me the blame-finding alibi is valid only in the thinking of someone who is considering the preservation of his or her own skin. But when I take full responsibility for my own actions, I am concerned first for the well-being of the other party or parties involved. So, I can't blame others for my choice to sin by rebelling against God. I made those choices because I believed God wasn't working out my life just the way I thought he should. I decided to "show him a thing or two" that would make him sorry for not answering my prayers the way I wanted. *I made a choice to sin.* No one can be blamed for the decision to rebel except me. I'm ashamed of the fact that I did what I did. When my sin was brought to light, for nearly twenty-four hours a day for fourteen days I cried convulsively as I sought God's mercy through my repentance. Like King David when he was confronted with murder and adultery, I realized I'd sinned against God. I hate my sinful self. Upon my arrest, I understood David's position and his torn relationship with God. And like him, my resistance crumbled like the walls of Jericho and I offered a complete confession of my guilt to God and the authorities.

Here in prison, I talk with those who have no relationship with God; blame-placing prevails. Even those who profess a real and vital witness refuse to say, "I, and I alone, am guilty." Blame is placed on myriad things. Few seem interested in taking responsibility for their actions. Most simply look for a loophole in the system in order to get back into court to get a reduction of sentence.

God has definitely dealt with me about taking responsibility for my actions. I've discovered that finger-pointing is unacceptable in the kingdom of God. Each of us is responsible for his or her behavior—no exceptions.

The greatest area of growth in my life came when I stopped blaming others for my failures and confessed that I, and I alone, made the choice to rebel, and took full responsibility for my own lack of self-control.

God's Purposes in the Midst of Human Sin

Catherine Clark Kroeger

undamentalists have long recognized that the Bible places a very strong emphasis on human sin and its tragic consequences: "All have sinned and come short of the glory of God. . . . The wages of sin is death. . . . All our righteousness is as filthy rags. . . . We have all gone astray" (Rom. 3:23; 6:23; Isa. 64:6; 53:6). Long ago, St. Augustine observed the doctrine of sin within the Scriptures and built a theological system that acknowledged its presence in every human heart.

Human sin is a major plank in the doctrinal treatise of the Epistle to the Romans. Paul wrote that he knew that in his heart dwelt no good thing (Rom. 7:18). He was well aware that out of the flesh, even the flesh of believers, came animosity, discord, fits of rage, selfish ambition, dissensions, factions, and envy (Gal. 5:19–21). Furthermore, Christians must be careful not to put an occasion for stumbling in the path of a weaker brother or sister (Rom. 14:13; 2 Cor. 6:3).

I suggest that the doctrine of family hierarchy—as commonly expounded—is fertile ground for precisely such a stumbling block, capable of leading people into animosity, discord, fits of rage, selfish ambition, dissensions, factions, and envy. Many who propound the doctrine emphasize that the husband must exercise a humble, Christlike attitude. Advocates of hierarchy state that they have no intention of promoting any kind of abuse. Still, the system affords an opportunity of which we sinful human beings all too often avail ourselves. Even an individual made new by the power of the Holy Spirit may succumb to temptation (1 John 1:7–10).

How often we have heard that power corrupts and that absolute power corrupts absolutely! The husband who is told that he is to be the boss in the home often finds within this statement warrant to carry things too far. A major flaw in the system is that it does not recognize the propensity to sin that lies within the human heart.

Marxism in its early form contained the same error. It set forth an ideal—in some ways very similar to the sharing of all things in common that characterized the early church in Jerusalem (Acts 2:44–45; 4:34–35). Alas, the Marxist system failed to reckon with human greed and corruption. More and more repressive measures had to be used to enforce the envisioned good of the state, and more and more evil was spawned.

In the same way, there is great danger in a theological doctrine that places one human being in subordination to another, that puts decision-making power in the hands of one and deprives the other of control over her own life or that of her children. That system ignores the checks and balances that God has built into human relationships.

There are over fifty instructions in the New Testament as to how Christians are to treat one another, each employing the term *allēlos,* meaning "one another" (Mark 9:50; John 13:14, 34, 35; 15:12, 17; Rom. 12:5, 10, 16; 13:8; 14:13, 19; 15:5, 7, 14; 16:16; 1 Cor. 7:5; 11:33; 12:25; 16:20; 2 Cor. 13:12; Gal. 5:13, 15, 26; 6:2; Eph. 4:2, 25, 32; 5:21; Phil. 2:3; Col. 3:9, 13; 1 Thess. 3:12; 4:9, 18; 5:11, 15; 2 Thess. 1:3; Heb. 10:24; James 4:11; 5:9, 16; 1 Peter 1:22; 4:9; 5:5, 14; 1 John 1:7; 3:11, 23; 4:7, 11, 12; 2 John 5). The first great safeguard against improper behavior is that Christians reprove, admonish, and instruct one another when someone gets out of line (Col. 1:28; 3:16; 2 Tim. 4:2). Many of us have made a wrong turn with an automobile onto a one-way street only to be corrected very quickly by the reaction of other motorists. The Bible says that if a brother or sister is overtaken in a sin, other spiritual believers are to restore the individual in the spirit of love and humility. Yet much current literature tells wives simply to endure rather than to reprove, to talk to God about mistreatment rather than discussing it with the offender. This advice may be the best strategy in an unsafe situation, but it deprives the husband of the godly counsel that lies most closely at hand.

Although every other major institution has a system of checks and balances, certain individuals would deny this grace to the Christian home. Pastors must be accountable to the deacons and elders of their church, and frequently to the larger connectional units within the denomination. In the business world, even the president of a corporation must answer to the board, and the board to the stockholders. An employee who is unjustly treated may report the abuse to duly constituted persons charged with policing unfair labor practices. Government administrators may be examined by special investigative committees, the Congress, the courts, and so forth.

If a believer is overtaken in a fault, those who are spiritual are to restore such a person (Gal. 6:1). If a believer sins against us, we are to go to that person and discuss the matter. If the conduct continues, other people should be involved; then, if the behavior still persists, the church is to take appropriate action (Matt. 18:15–17). Christians are enjoined to turn sinners from the error of their ways (James 5:19–20). Even an elder is to be corrected, gently to be sure, by entreaty rather than by stinging reproof (1 Tim. 5:1). Believers are repeatedly commanded to warn those whose behavior is unseemly (1 Thess. 5:14; 2 Thess. 3:15). Timothy is advised that those who sin are to be rebuked publicly, so that others may take warning (1 Tim. 5:20).

Why is a husband unique in often being exempted from this sort of correction? You may say that the elders of the church should offer the reproof to him, but all too often the reproof is given to the wife instead. She is told to go home and mend her ways, while the husband is affirmed as having the right to deal with his family as he deems appropriate.

If a sinful human being may lunge toward an improper use of the power that has been allotted to him by theological sanction, the less powerful person may also be overtaken by sin. She may harbor grudges, resentment, hostility, bitterness, and despair. She may be overtaken by fear, frustration, and depression. Because she does not understand God's call to full personhood, she may put her own life and that of her children at risk. Although she may wish to do God's will above all things, she may instead be reduced to the role of enabler in her husband's abusive conduct.

Let us make no mistake: Her submission to sinful behavior perpetuates her husband's problem and puts him in spiritual and emotional jeopardy. God says that he hates a man's covering his wife with violence as with a coat (Mal. 2:16 NIV, alternate reading). According to 1 Peter 3:7, a man's inconsiderate treatment of his wife hinders his prayer life; Isaiah also said that God will not hear the prayers of one engaged in quarreling and strife who ends up striking with wicked fists (Isa. 58:4–6; see also Ps. 7:17 and Prov. 21:7). Ezekiel issues God's call to "Give up your violence and oppression and do what is just and right" (Ezek. 45:9 NIV). A fundamental theme of the Old Testament is that violence is the work of sinners, associated with wrong choices, injustice, lying, evil, and Satan (Pss. 27:12; 58:2; 140:11; Prov. 3:31; 10:6, 11; 13:2; 24:2; Ezek. 28:16; Hosea 12:1; Micah 6:12; Zeph. 1:9). Christians who construct a theological justification for such behavior cast a very large stumbling block in their brother's way.

Verbal abuse can be equally hurtful and is condemned in the most scathing tones by Jesus (Matt. 5:22). James, the brother of our Lord, likewise has much to say about the vicious use of the tongue (James 3:1–9). When the apostle Paul expands on the subject of human sin in the opening chapters of Romans, he turns to the words of the Psalms, Proverbs, and Isaiah (citing Pss. 10:7; 31:1; 140:3; Prov. 1:16; Isa. 59:7–8) in ascribing verbal and physical abuse to the wicked:

The poison of asps is upon their lips. Their mouths are full of curses and bitterness. Their feet are keen to shed blood. Destruction and misery are in their pathways and the way of peace have they not known. There is no fear of God before their eyes.

Romans 3:13–18, author's translation

The church has an obligation to stop abuse and to protect the victim (Matt. 18:15–17; 1 Thess. 5:14; 2 Thess. 3:15; 1 Tim. 5:20;

Titus 3:2–11; James 5:19–20). Do we acknowledge that the Scriptures twice tell us that battering is an automatic disqualification from church leadership? Seldom does the word "batterer" turn up in our English translations, but that is precisely what *plektes* means in 1 Timothy 3:3 and Titus 1:7. The individual must not be intemperate in the use of alcohol, greedy for gain, nor a batterer. Why are we so complacent about this last disqualification in Christian circles?

Rapists are condemned three times in 1 Corinthians (5:10, 11; 6:10), though translations frequently obscure this by speaking instead of the "rapacious" or "greedy." We tend to take rape very lightly whether in or out of marriage—and the experts tell us that rape occurs in 10 to 20 percent of all marriages. Yet the Bible says the kingdom of God is not for such as these. Rape, we must remember, is not primarily a sexual issue, but the exercise of power using sex as a weapon. This is indeed at the heart of much of the abuse of women and children.

In short, violence and abuse—whether sexual, verbal, or physical—are vehemently condemned in Scripture as a manifestation of sin. All the professed piety of the perpetrator is mere sham. Why do we continue to provide a climate where people take their justification for abuse from selective misuse of the Bible?

Looking at the Definitions

Headship

Proponents of a hierarchical view of the sexes will argue that woman is of a secondary order of creation over whom man is the "head" and that therefore she must "submit." Unfortunately, some of the contemporary paraphrases of the New Testament perpetuate this notion in a most unhealthy way. They infuse the term with meanings unwarranted by the Greek text.

The Bible does indeed say that the man is head of the woman, Christ head of the man, and God the head of Christ (1 Cor. 11:3). Saint John Chrysostom, an early Greek Father and a highly influential exegete of Scripture, was aware of the theological implications of ascribing inferiority to any member of the Godhead. Therefore he declared that anyone was a heretic who proclaimed that "head" in this context denoted superior power or authority! Rather, he said, the term should be understood as total unity, and primal cause and ultimate source. (J. P. Migne, *Patrologia Graeca* (PG) 61.214, 216. For similar concerns on the part of other church fathers, see Athanasius PG 26,740 B; Cyril of Alexandria *De Recte Fide ad Arcadiam* 1.1.5.5(2). 63; Basil PG 30.80.23; Theodore of Mopsuetia PG.66.888C; and even Eusebius *De Ecclesaistica Theologia* 1.11.2–3; 2.7.1.)

Obviously, the first meaning of *kephale* was that of a body part, one dependent on and interactive with the rest of the body. Beyond that lay a number of metaphorical usages. (See Kroeger, "Head/headship" in *Dictionary of Paul and His Letters,* IVP.) Let us be aware that a metaphor is just that—a figure of speech used to enforce a concept. Furthermore, metaphors may change meaning in different languages and cultures. In French, for instance, "head" does not have the meaning of "boss" or "chief" as it does in English. In ancient Greek, the original language in which the New Testament was written, "head" very seldom denoted a person in a position of power or superiority.

On the other hand, "head" *(rosh)* in Hebrew could hold just such a metaphorical meaning. As Berkeley Mickelsen has shown, this required an interchange of words on the part of the early translators of the Old Testament as they prepared a Greek version known as the Septuagint (third century B.C.) Where *rosh* occurred in a metaphorical sense meaning chief or ruler, the translators avoided the use of *kephale* and substituted a Greek term meaning leader or person in authority.

Nearly three hundred years before the composition of the New Testament, the Septuagintal translators exhibited this interchangeability of *kephale* (head) with *arche* (source or beginning) when they came to Isaiah 9:14–15. The Hebrew reads:

So the Lord cut off from Israel head *[rosh]* and tail,
palm branch and reed in one day—
elders and dignitaries are the head *[rosh]*,
and prophets who teach lies are the tail. (NRSV)

In order to make the meaning clear, the Septuagint rendering says

And the Lord has taken away from Israel head *[kephale]* and tail,
great and small in a single day,
the elder and those that respect them, this is the beginning *[arche]*
and the prophet who teaches unlawful things, this is the tail.

Greek writers frequently used "head" in a metaphorical sense to mean the beginning, basis, or point of origin of something, including human life. Aristotle and many another Greek believed that sperm was formed in the head, which was in consequence the very source of life itself. *Kephale* was considered by Photius, an assiduous scholar of earlier Greek literature, to be a synonym for a procreator or progenitor (*Comm. 1 Cor* 11:3. ed. Staab 567.1). Similarly, Philo, a contemporary of Paul and Jesus, declared, "As though the head *[kephale]* of a living creature, Esau is the progenitor of all these members" *[Mating* 61). The Greek fathers demonstrated the same understanding, for St. Hippolytus designated the head as the characteristic substance from which all people were made (PG 16.iii. 3138). So too Irenaeus equated "head" with "source" when he wrote of the "head *[kephale]* and source *[arche]* of his own being" (PG 7.496. See also Tertullian, *Against Marcion* 5.8).

No one was more emphatic in asserting that *kephale* (head) was synonymous with *arche* (source or beginning) than Cyril of Alexandria. He wrote of Adam:

Therefore of our race he became first *head, which is source,* and was of the earth and earthy. Since Christ was named the second Adam, he has been placed as *head, which is source,* of those who through him have been formed anew unto him unto immortality through sanctification in the spirit. Therefore he himself, our *source, which is head,* has appeared as a human being. Yet he though God by nature, has himself a generating head, the heavenly Father, and he himself, though God according to his nature, yet being the Word, was begotten of Him. *Because head means source,* He establishes the truth for those who are wavering in their mind that man is the head of woman, for she was taken out of him. Therefore as God according to His nature, the one Christ and Son and Lord has as his head the heavenly Father, having himself become our head because he is of the same stock according to the flesh. (*De Recta Fide ad Pulchr.* 2.3, ed. Pusey, p. 268, italics added)

In case you have lost count, *kephale* is defined as source *(arche)* no less than four times in this single paragraph.

Paul too utilized the concept of head *(kephale)* as source, beginning, or point of departure. Head is used in apposition to *arche* (beginning, source) in Colossians 1:18, along with a reminder that the head is the part of the body that is usually born first. As such, Christ is not only the firstborn from the dead, but also the firstborn of all creation (Col. 1:15, 18).

The Jewish Philo maintained that the head was like a spring, from which power flowed forth to other bodily organs (*Fli&Find* 182; see also Arist. *Prob.* 10 867a.). Medical writers also viewed the head as source of supply to the whole body, and the thought is twice echoed by the apostle Paul (Eph. 4:15–16; Col. 2:19). In Colossians 2:10, Christ is proclaimed the head (source) of the originative power and ability needed for the believer's fulfillment, as he himself embodies the fullness of the godhead. Recognizing man as the source *(kephale)* of woman (1 Cor. 11:3, 8, 12), and woman as the source of man (v. 12), Paul called for mutual support and interdependence in the Lord (1 Cor. 11:11–12). In a society that viewed woman as being created of material fundamentally inferior to that of man, there is great importance to the perception of woman as being drawn forth from man's very being and thus vitally interrelated with man. As with head and body, severance of the connection brings extinction for both parts.

The doctrine of headship is egregiously misapplied when it comes to assignment of decision-making roles. All too often, husband and wife both believe that the husband is to make the ultimate decisions in matters profoundly affecting the lives of the entire family. Yet this is not the way that God treats us nor the way Christ deals with his bride, the church. By God's own design, each one of us has been given free will. It is up to us whether or not we shall worship God, study the Word, follow after righteousness, do acts of kindness, lead others to Christ, and so on. If there is no compulsion in Christ's dealing with us, why do we introduce such a mandatory element into husband-wife relationships? Christ calls us not as puppets but as fully responsible persons, free and capable of making our own decisions. He says that we are not servants, but friends. He maintained that a servant-master relationship inhibited good communication. "From henceforth I do not call you servants, for servants do not know what their master does. I have called you friends" (John 15:15, author's translation). If we deprive the wife of the right to have her opinions heard and respected, if we do not encourage her to become mature in decision-making, how can we say that the marriage reflects the relationship between Christ and the church?

Submission

Even the most conservative dictionary will grant that *hupotasso,* the word translated "submit," has several different meanings. (See, for example, *Analytical Greek Lexicon,* published by Bagster and Son [now published by Zondervan], 1970 l.c.) We often fail to tell this to those who are not reading the Greek original. We must be careful how we translate the term *hupotasso* in key passages. Beside the sense of complying with the wishes of another, the verb sometimes has the concept of responsible behavior toward others. At 1 Corinthians 14:32, we are told that the spirits of prophets are subject to the prophets. This is understood by many translators as implying that prophets can control themselves and exercise responsibility toward the body of believers, just as women are asked in 1 Corinthians 14:35 to behave responsibly, to "be subject" and not to disrupt the services of worship. Both commands to be subject *(hupotasso)* may imply orderliness of conduct and proper responsibility toward others. Similarly, Christians were told to comply *(hupotasso)* with the institutions of the state (Rom. 13:1; 1 Peter 2:13). Never for a moment did they give slavish obedience or compromise themselves when commanded to worship the emperor. The contexts make clear that believers are being asked to exercise the virtues of lawful behavior and good citizenship. *Atakteo,* the opposite of *hupotasso,* meant to be lawless, to fail to discharge an obligation or to be neglectful of duty (Xenophon *Cyropaedia* 8, 1, 22; *Oecumenicos* 5, 15; Lysander 141, 18.). This antonym turns up in 2 Thessalonians 3:7 in the sense of living a disorderly life.

Another meaning of *hupotasso*, observed in Bagster's *Analytical Greek Lexicon*, is that of being brought into a sphere of influence. We encounter this concept in Romans 8:20, "Creation was subject unto vanity" (author's translation). All of us know that God, not vanity, rules the world; nevertheless, the universe bears the taint of human stupidity, greed, and pollution. Thus we find here the use of *hupotasso* in the sense of bringing something into an association. Creation was associated with vanity not willingly, but through the one who brings things under his control, with the hope that the creation itself shall be liberated from the bondage of corruption unto the freedom of the glory of the children of God (Rom. 8:20–21).

In connection with a similar use of *hupotasso*, we might consider the boy Jesus who apparently assumes that once he has made his bar mitzvah, his proper place is in the learned world of the temple. His conscientious parents must have communicated to him the promises of the angel and the mission for which he was being prepared. He is surprised to discover that Mary and Joseph, who had themselves brought him to the temple, did not expect him to continue on there. Although already a man according to Jewish law, he returns to the world of the carpenter shop in Nazareth and was, as Luke tells us, "subject unto them" (2:51, author's translation). This, I suggest, did not necessarily imply obedience, as later stories of his dealings with his mother and brothers indicate. Rather, he reenters the sphere of his parents, and identifies, associates, and integrates himself with them and their world of everyday life, rather than with the learned doctors of Jerusalem.

Paul, in thanking the Corinthians for their generosity to needy saints, says the recipients glorify God because of their submission to their profession of the gospel (2 Cor. 9:13). How, I ask, is one submissive to a profession of the gospel? In sending their gift to impoverished Christians, the Corinthians had "put their money where their mouth was." We must understand the phrase "submission to the profession" as meaning that the Corinthians brought their behavior into a meaningful adherence, identification, association, and integration with what they had already confessed. Here, as in a number of other places, the sense is one of identifying with a concept, person, or thing rather than obeying it. The Corinthians had followed through on, aligned, associated, identified themselves with their profession. They had matched their walk to their talk.

We find this sense of *hupotasso* in nonbiblical writers as well. Polybius, a military writer of the first century B.C., uses the term sometimes to denote those under the command of a leader, and sometimes also to mean his adherents, allies, or associates—those aligned with him. More interesting yet, Polybius sometimes used the word to indicate the identification, integration, or association of one person, idea, or thing with another in a meaningful relationship. One gains a better understanding of geographic locations, he said, if one associates or identifies *(hupotasso)* a given area with the cardinal directions north, south, east, and west *(Histories* III.36.6–7). Human behavior is sometimes easier to analyze if one relates or integrates *(hupotasso)* a person into a broad general category of those displaying certain common characteristics *(Histories* XVIII.15.4). The relationship gives meaning to the individual. I suggest that the concept of relating one person to another in a meaningful fashion is a highly important value.

Polybius, along with the ancient scientist Ptolemy uses a negativized adjectival form of the same word *(anupotaktos)* to designate concepts or persons who are dissociated from others, confused, or difficult to comprehend—not part of an integrated group (Polybius *Histories* III.36.4, 38.4; V.21.4; Ptolemy *Tetrabiblios* 61). The writer of the Pastoral Epistles applied the term to individuals displaying irresponsibility or lack of accountability (1 Tim. 1:9; Titus 1:6, 10).

Hupotasso in a positive sense can also mean to add or unite one person or thing with another. We may see this in the fivefold use of the verb in two verses in 1 Corinthians 15. There is a play on words, an employment of the same term with different senses attached. I suggest that we are being told not that Christ will be placed under the domination of the Father, but that the Son and those redemptive functions specifically attributed to him shall be associated, integrated, assimilated into oneness with the Father. The emphasis here is on unity rather than supremacy or subordination: "For he has set all things under his feet. When it says that all things are made subject, clearly there is an exception of the one who set all things under him. But when all things are made subject unto him, then the Son himself shall be integrated unto him who has placed all things under him that God may be all in all" (1 Cor. 15:27–28, author's translation). Christ assumes a distinctive role in order to return a rebellious world to God and then integrates himself to the Father "that God may be all in all."

In the so-called "household codes" of the New Testament, where women are told to submit *(hupotasso)*, we find the same concern with oneness in the family. From what we can gather, the family in the Roman Empire frequently fell victim to severe disintegration. The plays of Plautus and Terrence, still extant, provide literal translations of the earlier plays of Menander and give a picture of family life that is nothing short of appalling. The standard plot portrays the son, the clever slave, and the mother all conspiring to outwit the father in order to subvert the authority of the Roman *patria potestas*. These plays were said to hold a mirror up to real life, and many other pieces of evidence point as well to the fundamental disunity of the Greco-Roman family. But Paul calls upon Christians to live together as cohesive and dedicated families. Children and slaves are to "obey" *(hupakouo)*, while wives are asked to "be subject" *(hupotasso)* and to show respect for their husbands (Eph. 5:33).

The apostle began his famous call for wifely submission with a prior instruction that all believers should be subject one to another (Eph. 5:21), and continues with a challenge for husbands to emulate the self-sacrifice of Christ in loving care of their wives who are to be cherished as "their own bodies." Colossians 3:19 may alternately be translated, "Husbands, love your wives and do not make yourselves a bad taste in their mouths." Those insisting upon the biblical mandate that wives should be subject to their husbands would do very well to consider the instructions that husbands should be subject to their wives (1 Cor. 7:3–4; Gal. 5:13; Eph. 5:21; Phil. 2:3; 1 Peter 3:7). While all Christians are called to be subject to one another, Paul made it very clear that it was not right to yield the slightest submission to an individual whose behavior or communications were wrong (Gal. 2:5–6).

A usage of *hupotasso* that is often used to support an authoritarian form of marriage is found in an account of the *Life of Alexander*, erroneously ascribed to Callisthenes even though it was written in its final form several centuries later. It concerns the marriage of Alexander's parents, Philip of Macedon and Olympias. By all reports the union was a troubled one. In some accounts, Olympias, after being divorced by Philip, returned to her own family and raised an army against him. In the Callisthenes version, the youthful Alexander returns home from an Olympic victory to find that his mother has been divorced and that his father is celebrating his marriage to a new queen. Alexander is roused to anger and lays about him with his sword, wounding all within his range. While Philip is still convalescent from the fray, Alexander extracts from him a promise that he will be reconciled to Olympias. Now the young man must persuade his mother to reenter the marriage. During his speech to her he exhorts, "Be the first to go to him, for it is proper for a wife to be subject *(hupotasso)* to her husband."

It is evident that at this point Philip is not her husband. He has divorced her, and she is under no obligation to obey him. Indeed, obedience would require her to respect his wish for a divorce. It is her acquiescence to the marriage contract that is at stake. Alexander asks his mother to enter under the former husband's roof again and to attach herself to him. He is surely pleading for a form of marriage that will require allegiance to her husband rather than to those relatives who might pose a military threat to the king.

Ancient Marriage and Christian Application

In New Testament times, the terms we have been discussing may well have applied to that peculiar Roman institution of giving a woman in marriage while at the same time her family retained legal, religious, and financial claims upon her. In contradistinction to children and slaves, the wife alone was not ordinarily a member of her husband's household. Jewish marriage laws, by contrast, transferred the woman into the family of her husband. In Roman marriage, such a transfer might be arranged, but involved for a woman the loss of "head" *(caput)* (Cicero *Topica* III.18; Gaius *Institutes* I.162). First Corinthians 11:3 declares her husband now to be her head; both man and woman are called to leave their families and to establish a new household in Christ. They are to belong to one another and become one flesh (Eph. 5:31). The concept is that of unifying the two.

If we understand wifely submission as a meaningful and responsible attachment to her husband, along with an acknowledgment of marriage as the primary tie rather than to loyalties and bonds with her family of birth, we shall both enhance Christian marriage and offer a deterrent to unequal and abusive situations. Only thus can the love between Christ and his bride, the church, be mirrored to the world.

14

Theology for the Healthy Family

James R. Beck

n the past several years, the American public has learned more and more about a grim reality in American family life— namely, the extent and severity of domestic violence. Persons of conscience experience a variety of contradictory reactions as these sad and tragic facts etch themselves on our awareness. First, we feel revulsion. How could the family, that divinely ordained venue of the highest possible levels of intimacy, also be the site of the worst forms of physical violence? We want to believe that physical violence within marriage is both "contradictory and unlikely" (Martin, 1987, p. 20). But perhaps we should remember that the first family (Adam, Eve, Cain, and Abel) displayed both high levels of intimacy (they were naked and not ashamed) and high levels of violence (Cain murdered Abel). Second, we sometimes react with denial (Walker, 1986). Surely, these reported levels of domestic violence that we hear about must be exaggerated. But our denial cannot withstand the convincing incidence data that continually confronts those of us who work in the human service vocations. Our third reaction is one of determination— determination to ensure that we do all we can to minimize this

216

blight on the Christian home and to apply the sound and healthy teachings of Scripture to this tragic reality.

I propose here to examine a Christian theology for the healthy family. All too often our attempts to extract Scripture's teachings about the family rely solely on an exegesis of relevant biblical texts. As a result, theologies for the Christian family normally discuss covenant, commitment, altruistic love, and the priority of love for God. However, my strategy for discussing a theology for the healthy family will vary slightly from that standard approach. I will attempt to exegete some relevant passages of Scripture, especially in the teachings of Jesus, as well as to exegete the cultural phenomenon of domestic violence. Thus I will seek to identify a theology for the healthy family by examining, in part, how the unhealthy family operates. The deficits and lacks in the family that resorts to the use of physical violence may then help us see what should be in place in order for a family to enjoy healthy interactions. This approach is akin to learning about healthy physiological functioning by studying disease. While my strategy is only one of several for uncovering a theology for the healthy family, perhaps this search will help us understand the teachings of Jesus in new and encouraging ways.

Overview on Domestic Violence

Our first task in preparation for discussing a theology for the healthy family is to review in brief form what we have come to know about domestic violence, our chosen example of how depraved family life can become when God's grace is not fully operative in the lives of family members. Violence against women most often occurs in the home. Between two and three million women will be assaulted by male partners in any given year, with the result that between 21 and 34 percent of all American women will be physically assaulted at some point during their lifetimes (DeAngelis, 1994). Partner homicide accounts for over one half of all women murdered in the United States. Despite attempts to educate the public, the rates of occurrence continue to be high. The recent attempt to make violence against women a crime in federal statutes is an example of current efforts to curb this mounting problem in the United States.

Domestic violence most frequently takes place at night in the living room or the bedroom of a home. The home's bathroom may be the only sanctuary for a woman in danger. Often one or both of the partners involved in the violence are unemployed or are working alternating shifts. Weekends tend to be worse than weekdays, and children and finances are cited by those involved as frequent topics of dispute when the violence erupts. Pregnant women are not exempt from danger in a violent home. As the frequency of violence increases, so does its severity (Martin, 1987). Violence often continues because of the perpetrator's belief that outbursts of physical assault are the only effective means available to maintain control. Sadly, violence works to accomplish this ugly purpose, at least temporarily (Ewing, Lindsey, & Pomerantz, 1984). In addition to physical violence, abusers may also use sexual, property, or psychological abuse to reinforce their purposes.

Researchers have spent considerable time and effort on the task of identifying the major characteristics of abusive men. These men often have an inability to manage anger, an early exposure to violence in domestic contexts, a profound level of emotional inexpressiveness except through rage and violence, a low level of self-esteem, a lack of assertiveness, and a rigid approach to life and its complexities (Martin, 1987). Abusers also display unusually high tendencies toward denial of personal responsibility for the violence and minimalization of its severity (Sonkin, Martin, & Walker, 1985). Anecdotal evidence from clinicians also enumerates the impulsive qualities of abusers that, combined with a low tolerance for stress and a tendency toward possessiveness and jealousy, add to the explosiveness of the home (Star, 1983). Abusers often demonstrate little understanding of the concept of intimacy that is nonsexual; many abusers seem incapable of building genuine emotional closeness. Other factors sometimes associated with the incidence of domestic violence include psychiatric disorders, education and income levels, and substance abuse (Steinmetz, 1986).

Why do people resort to violence as a "solution" to their domestic problems? Some researchers trace the acceptance of violence as a viable means of interacting with one's spouse to the costs and rewards (social exchange theory) of the violent behavior. Gelles and Straus (1988) assert that violence occurs when three factors lower the cost of violence and increase its rewards. First, violence tends to occur when social attitudes condoning it prevail in the culture or subculture of the participants. Second, violence breaks out when the privacy of the home allows secretive or hard-to-discover behaviors to occur. Third, violence characterizes marriages when serious inequality, both in physical size and roles, characterizes the relationship.

Women who experience violence in their homes often turn to the clergy for help. All too often the response to these women in the past has been unhelpful.

> The primary responses these women received were (1) a reminder of their duty and the advice to forgive and forget, (2) a reference elsewhere to avoid church involvement, and (3) useless advice, sometimes based on religious doctrine rather than their own needs. (Pagelow & Johnson, 1988, p. 4–5)

Goodman and colleagues note that "Many authors locate the roots of violence in women's efforts to escape their historically subordinate roles in settings such as the family" (Goodman, Koss, Fitzgerald, Russo, & Keita, 1993, p. 1054). In many instances, secular authors will see this attempt to escape subordination as commendable, whereas many conservative religious leaders view the very same goal as lamentable and contributory to the problem.

Many authors note that domestic violence often occurs in cycles. Not all authors who describe the cycle theory of domestic violence enumerate exactly the same number or content of phases (Ewing et al., 1984; Martin, 1987). But for the purposes of this paper, I will use a four-stage reconstruction of the violence cycle: (1) A "normal" phase when all appears to be well in the family but when family interactions are actually incomplete and inadequate; (2) a tension-building phase in which various unresolved problems and conflicts increase and fester; (3) an acute outbreak of violence; (4) a "hearts and flowers" phase during which the perpetrator attempts to cover over the offenses and manipulate the family system back toward the "normal" phase. Although some authors question the value of the cycle theory of domestic violence because it tends to overlook the constant presence of domination in such families

(Pence & Paymar, 1993), I will utilize this outline of the cycle theory because it will enable us to analyze the various expressions of unhealthiness in violent families.

Toward a Theology of the Healthy Family

Presuppositions

Any attempt made by biblical Christians who study domestic violence must immediately address the theological issue regarding distribution of power in the marriage relationship. Otherwise we are ignoring the proverbial elephant standing in the middle of our living room. Evangelical scholars fall into one of two basic approaches to the concept of marital power differentials. The traditional approach interprets the headship concept of Scripture as indicating a difference between the husband and wife in terms of responsibility, power, authority, or some combination of these factors. Those who espouse this view often speak of a basic equality between the sexes, but also posit a distinction between the two that gives the husband greater authority in the marriage. Proponents of this view do not feel that this power differential, mandated by their understanding of the biblical text, contributes to the incidence of domestic violence. "There is nothing wrong with the 'traditional' marriage, but there is a great deal wrong with a husband who uses violence to maintain his position within the marriage" (Martin, 1987, p. 88). These authors thus feel that the normative and biblically mandated distribution of power is distinct from the abuse of that authority by some people. Traditionalists see no necessity to rethink the standard understandings of power differentials in marriage.

Most secular authors dealing with this subject disagree. For example, Beavers and Hampson (1993) describe the ideal family structure as egalitarian, with leadership shared between the parents in the family. Secular authors display little sympathy with those attempting to retain power differentials within a marriage as normative.

Those in control use societal institutions to justify, support, and enforce the relationship of dominance and make extensive efforts to obtain general acceptance of the premises that hierarchy is natural and that those at the bottom are there because of their own deficiencies. (Pence & Paymar, 1993, p. 4)

Evangelical egalitarians argue that one cannot maintain that the underlying power differential in a marriage sanctioned by a traditional understanding of Scripture is unrelated to the abuse of that power that characterizes some Christian homes (Alsdurf, 1985; Garland & Garland, 1986). Egalitarians reason that an egalitarian structure in marriage is both biblical and pragmatic in that the structure is hostile toward violence. They believe that as a married couple moves boldly into an egalitarian stance with one another as equals before Christ, the couple will begin to experience the blessing of God in their mutuality and mutual submission. And the couple will not be as tempted to resort to force and violence as a means of shoring up positions of power and authority.

This paper affirms these egalitarian assertions. I will treat egalitarian structure in marriage as a presupposition to the building of a theology for the healthy family. The scope of this paper does not allow me to focus on this important component of a biblical theology for healthy family functioning; instead, I will use this well-documented formulation as a presuppositional base for other important theological issues I wish to erect on this foundation.

Upon an egalitarian foundation, I can erect the following theology for healthy families: Building on our full equality in Christ as marriage partners, our family *communicates* fully, directly, lovingly, and honestly with one another, *confesses* to and forgives one another in the routine conflicts of life, *conciliates* when tempted to misuse authority with control or force, and *conjures* no one, but offers only authentic contrition to one another.

These four theological themes correspond to the four phases of the domestic violence discussed earlier. The table lists these four phases, the corresponding deficit characteristic of each phase, the biblical alternative to that deficit as found in the teachings of Jesus, and some corresponding themes from the secular literature on normal family functioning (see Walsh, 1993, as one example of this literature). With each of these four theological themes, we will

Theology for the Healthy Family

Domestic Violence		Teaching of Jesus	Traits of Normal Family Process
Phases	Principle Issue		
Phase 1 "Normal" interactions	Superficial interaction, Lack of connectedness	Building on our full equality in Christ as marriage partners, our family . . . *communicates* fully, directly, lovingly, and honestly with one another,	Intimacy (Beavers); Direction expression of a wide range of feelings (Beavers); Clear and direct communication (McMaster); Mature dependence and supportiveness (Olson)
Phase 2 Mounting tensions	Inability to resolve issues, to settle problems, to grant and accept forgiveness	*confesses* to and forgives one another in the routine conflicts of life,	Capable negotiation (Beavers); Little or no unresolvable problems (Beavers); Effective problem solving (McMaster); Reliability (Olson); Therapeutic role (Nye)
Phase 3 Acute outbreak of violence	Misuse of authority, resorting to violence, wrongful use of power	*conciliates* when tempted to misuse authority with control or force, and	Choice and ambivalence respected (Beavers); Effective behavioral control (McMaster); Physical safety (Olson)
Phase 4 Guilt, remorse, hearts and flowers	Insincere interaction, lack of true remorse	conjures no one but offers only authentic *contrition* to one another.	Warm, affectionate, humorous, optimist climate (Beavers); Consistent, emphatic responsiveness (McMaster); Affective responsiveness and involvement (Beavers); Pleasurable interaction (Olson)

discover that it has its roots in the very character of God, its major exemplar in the life of Jesus, and its implementation grounded in the sanctifying work of the Holy Spirit.

Communication

When Jesus taught his followers how to communicate, he was laying out a new style of relating and speaking that was well suited to subjects of the kingdom of God. His radical ideas stood in great contrast to the "normal" styles in use during his earthly life. His teachings on the subject brought his followers back toward the creation ideal for how humans are to relate to one another.

The communication processes characteristic in violent homes represent some of the tragic consequences of sin. In phase 1, the "normal" phase in the domestic violence cycle, family members interact with one another on a shallow, superficial level. Their interactions are characterized by fearful anticipations, uncertainties, and hesitancy. They relate, but they do not connect. They live in the same home, but they bear more resemblance to people stranded on separate South Sea islands than they do to members of the same nuclear family. Their communications are incomplete, timid, and often ineffective. Misunderstandings rule the day, and misperceptions rule the night.

The teachings of Jesus regarding communication stand in great contrast to the grim description above. Jesus' teachings apply to all who follow him, including all families that seek to live by kingdom values. "In the beginning was the Word, and the Word was with God, and the Word was God" (John 1:1 NIV). A communication mode has existed within the godhead since before the foundation of the world. God's desire to communicate with human creatures is so characteristic of God's being that the second person of the Trinity is named the Word. Zacharias was struck dumb because of his doubt, but when he regained his speech, he used his loosened tongue to bless God (Luke 1:20, 64), a task all of God's followers must emulate.

When Jesus healed dumb and impaired tongues so that people could speak plainly (Mark 7:31–37), he was displaying his will that all should be able to speak in that way. The language of Jesus was clear, direct, and at times confrontive (John 4:17–18), as was the language of his mother to him and of him to her (Luke 2:48). The mother of Jesus also demonstrated for us how we must use God's wisdom to know when to speak and when not to speak (Luke 2:19, 51). Jesus likewise displayed the discretion of silence for us to observe and imitate (Mark 14:61).

Communication, then, is rooted in the very character of God. Jesus demonstrated for us how to speak well and how to use communication as a means of building healthy relationships. But Jesus has not abandoned us as orphans; rather he has sent the Holy Spirit as a comforter and as a counselor to guide us into all things. The Holy Spirit equips believers by teaching them all things and by assisting them in their speech (Matt. 10:20). The entire godhead is poised to assist families in the challenging and difficult task of communicating well with each other.

Good communication is at the core of healthy family functioning.

> Family members interact through verbal and nonverbal exchanges to express their core emotions. By their expressions of love and intimacy as well as anger and conflict family members come to know each other in very intimate ways. It is basically by communicating and expressing thoughts and feelings that family relationships grow and deepen. (Balswick & Balswick, 1989, p. 197)

The centrality of good communication as a vital component of healthy family interactions is confirmed in the recent literature on normal families. Healthy families display interactions that respect individual choice and ambivalence, that express thoughts and emotions with clarity, and that convey warmth, intimacy, and humor (Beavers & Hampson, 1993). Epstein, Bishop, and Baldwin (1984) describe normal families as having the capacity to communicate with one another in clear, unmasked forms that are direct rather than indirect. Strong and effective communication is needed in families (Fisher, Giblin, & Hoopers, 1984), and should characterize the majority of their interactions (Olson, 1993).

Confession

Healthy families not only communicate well, they also confess one to another well. Violent families move from phase one of their gruesome cycle into phase two, where tensions begin to mount. Conflicts, problems, issues, and concerns arise in the routines of daily living. The violent family is remarkably unsuited to deal with them. Instead of resolution and diminution, the family atmosphere manifests escalation and exaggeration. In place of apologies, the members of the violent family blame one another and externalize responsibility for the growing and ominous tension in the house. The unresolved bickerings and disputes soon give the batterer just the "excuse" needed to lead into the violent phase three. Sometimes the second phase of mounting tensions give perpetrator, victim, and innocent bystanders an inkling of what is ahead. Like omens in a dark night sky, these unresolved issues propel the family along toward the painful phase three. This phase of growing strain and stress in violent families almost seems to fulfill the prophecy of Jesus when he said:

> From now on there will be five in one family divided against each other, three against two and two against three. They will be divided, father against son and son against father, mother against daughter and daughter against mother, mother-in-law against daughter-in-law and daughter-in-law against mother-in-law.
>
> Luke 12:52–53 NIV

Against this backdrop of mounting tensions come the radical teachings of Jesus. By life, example, and word, he taught us how to breathe into our family relationships the cool winds of confession and the giving and receiving of forgiveness. The very coming of Jesus was "to give his people the knowledge of salvation through the forgiveness of their sins" (Luke 1:77 NIV). The forgiveness of sin by the coming Messiah was at the heart of the message of John the Baptist (Mark 1:4). Jesus came to earth to call sinners to repentance (Luke 5:32).

The parable of the prodigal son illustrates a central feature of our loving God—the full and unhindered forgiveness of offenses and misdeeds (Luke 15:11–32). The loving father searches for the one lost sheep and brings it back to the fold (Matt. 18:10–14).

As God through Jesus Christ forgives us, so must we forgive one another (Matt. 5:24, 44; 6:12; 18:22; Mark 11:25). Jesus implants within us streams of living water and living bread that satisfy our deepest needs and provide life-giving strength to forgive as God forgives (John 4:13–14; John 6). The aim of Jesus is to bring peace to us as he did to the wind and the waves (Mark 4:39). Believers are to confront one another in the spirit of Christ (Matt. 18:21–35).

This ongoing rhythm of forgiveness is to characterize the lives of all family members who would seek to please God (Guernsey, 1984). As this forgiveness is extended, grudges, fears, jealousies, suspicions, hurts, resentments, and hostilities fade (Bromily, 1980).

> Reconciliation with God—the first step of restoration as the break with God was the first step of disintegration—carries with it the reconciliation with one another to which even the worst and deepest and broadest of human conflicts must yield.... New sources of hurt and irritation will constantly arise. New acts of pride, willfulness, folly, and selfishness will bring new distortion and new crises to the marital union. Yet these can no longer inflict lasting or mortal wounds on marriage partners who know that as forgiven sinners they must also forgive one another. (Bromily, 1980, p. 47)

Secular authors sometimes refer to this needed feature of family life as the therapeutic function that members within the family must sustain toward one another (Nye, 1976). Healthy families must possess the skills of capable negotiation so that the family climate contains little or no unresolvable conflict (Beavers & Hampson, 1993). Problem-solving skills, of which forgiveness is an important part, are necessary for normal family functioning (Epstein et al., 1984). Healthy families must possess a quality of reliability that can only stem from an effective conflict-reducing environment in the home (Fisher et al., 1984).

Conciliation

The third phase in the domestic violence cycle, the acute outbreak of violence (be it physical, verbal, sexual, or emotional),
denotes one of the most sinister of all the consequences of sin
among humans. While we are all sinners and are all capable of all
sins, people of conscience must still recoil from the tragedy of violence in the context of intimacy. If the violence of this phase is
not the worst of all sins, it surely ranks among those that are the
most repulsive. The issues at stake that have gone awry in the violent family and that are exemplified by phase three include the
misuse of authority, the misuse of power, the misuse of control,
and the vain belief that these abuses will yield some good result.

If the violence of phase three represents sin at its worst, the
alternatives given to us by Jesus for these sinful tendencies in all
of us are surely some of his most demanding teachings. Jesus gives
to us new standards by which we all must redefine authority,
power, and control. Nothing short of a radically new configuration of these concepts will do. The standards of Jesus are stern, but
when implemented, they yield a good result—peaceable, fulfilling, and rewarding family life.

God's standards differ from human standards. God puts down
the mighty and elevates those of low degree (Luke 1:52). When
Jesus came to earth, he came to minister to the needs of the poor,
oppressed, and imprisoned (Luke 4:18). Jesus not only directed his
ministry energies toward the needy, he came to earth to bring peace
to those of good will (Luke 2:14).

By contrast, those who stoop to violence are roundly condemned
in the New Testament (Matt. 2:16; Mark 1:21–28; 6:12–29; Luke
3:14). Acts of anger and even harbored thoughts of anger are unlawful in the kingdom of Jesus (Matt. 5:22–26). Disciples must forego
acts of revenge or violence and seek to find peaceful solutions to
aggression (Matt. 5:38–42). The true disciple does not judge others, does not condemn, does not selfishly seek to hold on to, but
gives to others (Luke 6:37–38). Those who are happy in Christ's
kingdom are those who are poor not rich, mournful not scornful,
meek not aggressive, and hungry and thirsty not self-satisfied
(Matt. 5:1–6).

We are not to use authority, even legitimate authority, to lord it over others as tyrannical first-century Gentile rulers did (Matt. 20:25; Mark 10:42–45). Our example is the gentle and lowly Jesus (Matt. 11:28–30). In the kingdom, the greatest of all is the least of all, and the least of all is the greatest of all. Those who aspire to be great in the kingdom must become servants (Matt. 23:11). Make no mistake about it. These principles are not lofty ideas for the few; they are not ideals that cannot be attained; they are not just for apostles and prophets. They are rules for living that demand conformity from all members of God's kingdom, and these rules affect life in civil, ecclesiastical, and domestic settings. Families that seek to honor God must live by the new and radical teachings of Jesus.

Violent families, by contrast, tend to focus on hierarchy and rank. When couples build their marriages on a foundation of dominance/submission, violence can erupt if male power and privilege are challenged (Gondolf, 1985). Alsdurf found that "virtually every researcher" he consulted regarding domestic violence cited hierarchy as contributing to the susceptibility of women to mistreatment (1985, p. 38). Often pastors view the preservation of a marriage as the supreme value when dealing with instances of violence in the home. "In some sense, then, pastors are more committed to their concept of Christian marriage than they are to a Christian concept of loving nurture (the woman's physical safety)" (Alsdurf, 1985, p. 196). In contrast to Jesus, who calls every individual—including all husbands and all wives—to loving service of the other, some Christians treat the concept of submission as the exclusive responsibility of the wife. Submission almost becomes the magical cure that can correct all the problems of others in the family, including the violent husband (Alsdurf & Alsdurf, 1988; Alsdurf & Alsdurf, 1989). Jesus never taught differential responsibility in this regard; all are to obey Christ's call to gentleness, humility, service, and peaceableness.

Does violence have any place in the Christian home? No. In fact, some authors feel that violence breaks the marriage covenant (Eilts, 1988). Healthy homes are places where choice and ambivalence are respected (Beavers & Hampson, 1993), where behavior is effectively controlled (Epstein et al., 1984), and where all members live in physical safety with regard to one another (Fisher et al., 1984).

All too often, however, the evangelical Christian world simply mimics the dominant characteristic of the surrounding culture where men do not appear to understand that males abuse women in a vain effort to maintain control and authority over them ("Men on Domestic Violence," 1994). Perhaps Christian men display such misunderstandings because we have not yet ceased selling to them lines of power clothing (as available in a recent *Tooling Up* catalog) or calling men to fill their roles as protectors (as is true of Promise Keepers).

Contrition

The final theological ingredient of healthy family functioning that I will explore addresses the deficit evident in phase four of violent family functioning—faulty contrition. After the batterer has exploded in a volley of violence, a period of extensive remorse and guilt feelings often follows. These powerful feelings, when they appear, prompt the batterer to beg for forgiveness, to promise never to repeat the behavior, and generally to engage in behaviors designed to move the victim quickly toward the "normal" phase once again.

Observers of this process are hard-pressed to determine the validity and genuineness of the emotions in phase four. Is the feeling of guilt real? Is the remorse genuine? Is the perpetrator actually behaving to the best of his capacity? Or is the guilt phony? Is the remorse shallow and unmeant? Is phase four just a con game? Only God knows the answers to these questions in any given case as well as in the sum total of cases. Yet we do not have to wrestle with the issue if we apply one simple test: Do the behaviors and emotions of phase four lead to the total cessation of all violence in the home? If so, they must be genuine. If not, these phase four characteristics fall under the category of the inauthentic, and must be replaced by the new and different behaviors that Jesus introduced to us.

In the Gospels we find that Jesus clearly called his followers to authenticity of life and thought. John the Baptist was the first to sound this note. He roundly condemned the religious leaders of

229

his day for their ill-thought-out behavior. "You brood of vipers! Who warned you to flee from the coming wrath? Produce fruit in keeping with repentance" (Matt. 3:7–8 NIV). John would have nothing to do with emotion or attitude that was not accompanied by matching behavior. He warned that Jesus would continue to preach these same themes. "He will baptize you with the Holy Spirit and with fire. His winnowing fork is in his hand to clear his threshing floor and to gather the wheat into his barn, but he will burn up the chaff with unquenchable fire" (Luke 3:16–17 NIV). Those within earshot of John the Baptist could not miss his point: Jesus would demand genuine and authentic fruit in the lives of his followers. Jesus would not tolerate the chaff of inauthenticity, falsity, or deceit.

Jesus demands that his followers not engage in verbal games and meaningless oaths; instead they must speak and act directly and clearly. "Anything beyond this comes from the evil one," said Jesus (Matt. 5:37 NIV). Careless words will condemn us; those who utter them will have to give an account on the day of judgment "for every careless word they have spoken" (Matt. 12:36 NIV). The outer life and the inner life must conform one to the other (Mark 7:1–23). If Jesus excoriated any human behavior, it was hypocrisy. On repeated occasions he confronted religious people with their hypocrisy (Matt. 23:15, 23, 25, 27, 29; Luke 12:1–2; 13:15). Those who trivialized the things of God, as exemplified by false contrition or meaningless remorse, received the strong condemnation of Jesus. What Jesus truly wants from his followers is exactly what he demonstrated for his disciples on the last night of his earthly life. He served them in a loving manner to demonstrate with his behavior the true emotion of his heart by washing their feet (John 13:1–20).

Families are healthy when they display warm, affectionate, humorous, and optimistic environments coupled with consistent empathic responsiveness (Beavers & Hampson, 1993). In such a family, guilt and remorse that are not substantiated by heartfelt behavioral change have no place. The healthy family operates with affective responsiveness and involvement that is likewise incongruous with shallow guilt and remorse (Epstein et al., 1984). Finally, the healthy family manifests interactions that are pleasurable in a genuine sense, not misleading interactions that are inauthentic (Fisher et al., 1984).

Implementation

Having reviewed the teachings of Jesus to locate some key theological concepts that must replace the defective interactions of the violent family, I now come to the critical issue of implementation. If God wills that these standards of communication, confession, conciliation, and contrition characterize family interactions, how are they to be implemented?

Ideally, these concepts are best taught to children and adolescents as they are growing up in nurturing homes. Developmentally, these standards of Jesus for the true disciple are best learned during formative years. Before children or adolescents learn faulty and incomplete approaches to communication with others, they should learn good communications skills as modeled by their parents. Children and adolescents should learn the rhythms of apology, confession, and forgiveness as they are maturing so as to be well equipped for adult living. The same can be said for conciliation skills and for authenticity in contrition.

Yet we all know that many persons do not have the blessing of growing up in homes that faithfully teach Scripture and its truths to children. For those who approach their adult years without these healthy behaviors in place, the best hope for them is an encounter with the risen Christ who can write these kingdom principles upon the tables of their hearts. Sadly, the secular approach to domestic violence often seems to dismiss outright the possibility that religion can help attack this problem. Many authors simply repeat the contention of Walker (1979) that it is a myth that religious beliefs will prevent battering (Gondolf, 1985; Goodman et al., 1993; Pagelow & Johnson, 1988). We cannot let this pessimism deter us from the conviction that an encounter with Jesus Christ, who moves people from the kingdom of darkness into the kingdom of light, can dramatically change a person's life. As the indwelling Christ and the sanctifying Holy Spirit work to reshape fallen and broken people into the image of God's own Son, family life can be transformed from danger to delight, from violence to victory.

Epilogue
What Can Churches Do?

gain I looked and saw all the oppression that was taking place under the sun: I saw the tears of the oppressed—and they have no comforter; power was on the side of their oppressors—and they have no comforter" (Eccles. 4:1 NIV).

Often we simply look the other way when we are aware that abuse is happening within the household of God. Why do we continue to provide a climate where people take their justification for abuse from the Bible? Even among godly, Bible-believing folk, it is all too easy to develop stereotypes in our minds. We consider what "Dr. So-and-so" says rather than what is truly spoken by Scripture.

It is part of God's own nature to deliver from violence (Ps. 11:5). "The wicked lie in wait for the righteous, seeking their very lives; but the LORD will not leave them in their power" (Ps. 37:32–33 NIV). Make no mistake about it—the purpose of God is to deliver believers from the hands of violent men. If you don't believe it, read Psalm 140. Read through the entire psalm and keep on reading Psalm 141, 142, and 143. See also 2 Samuel 22:3 and Psalm

10:17–18. Psalm 18:48 declares, "You exalted me above my foes; from violent men you rescued me" (NIV).

In the prophecies concerning the Messiah, it is predicted that the righteous king will defend the afflicted and crush the oppressor (Ps. 72:1–4). "He will rescue them from oppression and violence, for precious is their blood in his sight" (Ps. 72:14 NIV). For the acts of another righteous king, see Jeremiah 22:15–16. God calls his people to do likewise.

"Do what is just and right. Rescue from the hand of his oppressor the one who has been robbed. Do no wrong or violence to the alien, the fatherless or the widow, and do not shed innocent blood in this place" (Jer. 22:3 NIV). See also Jeremiah 21:12. These passages, and many other similar ones, might be utilized to let the Word of God speak to us about the responsibilities of the church.

Yes, God stands ready to deliver, but well-meaning pious folk sometimes obstruct the purposes of God. Specifically, God commands his people to rescue the helpless from the abuser (Isa. 58:6; 61:1). Are we being obedient? God has given to us the helpless and the oppressed as a special trust. Believing communities are bidden to take appropriate action when those within their midst are involved in abuse, incest, battering, neglect, or sexual assault (Matt. 18:15–17; 1 Cor. 5:1–13; 1 Thess. 5:14; 2 Thess. 3:6, 14–15; 1 Tim. 5:20; Titus 3:2–11; James 5:19–20).

Our first action must be believing, fervent prayer. A congregation faced with an abusive situation needs to pray earnestly and powerfully. Violence is specifically said to be associated with Satan (Ezek. 28:16), and only by prayer can his stronghold be assailed.

A series of sermons or Bible studies would be a good second step. A church might well lead off with a consideration of verbal and emotional abuse (see Matt. 5:21–22; 12:34–37; 15:18–20; Eph. 4:29; James 2:2–10) before moving on to sexual harassment and abuse (Eph. 5:4–5; Col. 3:8). Many pastors fear to preach about incest because they do not wish to face their responsibility when victims come forward to tell of the treatment they have received at the hands of some of the strongest church members. This is nothing short of a failure to exercise our prophetic mandate in the midst of an enormous spiritual and moral crisis.

We need to be honest when a crisis arises in one of our church families, and secrecy may simply play into the hands of the perpetrator. One of the major hazards is that abusers are often very persuasive, presenting themselves as the true victims and skillfully eliciting the sympathies of the church. Credence should not be given to individuals whose behavior or communication is wrong, even though they manage to appear very pious (Gal. 2:5–6). Despite their professed righteousness, their ways are far removed from the paths of God. In the days of Isaiah, there were also those who sanctimoniously kept the fast but failed to keep God's law: "Your fasting ends in quarreling and strife, and in striking each other with wicked fists. You cannot fast as you do today and expect your voice to be heard on high. . . . Is not this the kind of fasting I have chosen: to loose the chains of injustice and untie the cords of the yoke, to set the oppressed free and break every yoke?" (Isa. 58:4, 6 NIV).

One of the devil's stratagems may be to tempt persons in the congregation to provide counseling or other services which lie beyond their own competence (see, for example, Satan's inappropriate suggestions in Matt. 4:3–10; Luke 4:2–12). Well-intentioned advice that a wife should return to her husband may be issuing her a death warrant. Couple counseling too is fraught with dangers and is usually inadvisable. Inappropriate shelter arrangements may lack proper security and thereby endanger the lives of all those involved in the effort. Most pastors—and indeed many Christian therapists—do not have the professional experience and expertise to counsel in a seriously abusive situation. Furthermore, ministerial ethics dictate that the pastor should provide no more than four to six counseling sessions before referring a parishioner to someone else.

While a congregation may not have within its membership persons capable of counseling or of providing a safe shelter, the church can seek out such facilities and make them available to those in need. Prayerful and constructive support can be offered to all members of a troubled family. The abuser may well be helped by an accountability group. The victims, too, should know that they have their own support network that allows them time to work through the many issues at their own pace. Forgiveness should not be forced or hastened.

A list of resources could be compiled and kept available before any known need exists. Emergency phone numbers could be displayed on a bulletin board. Persons engaged in children's, youth, and women's ministries should be provided with information about abuse and be encouraged—should they be approached—to believe the victim's story even if it implicates the prize deacon. They should also be instructed as to the recommended steps that they should take, including reporting to the authorities, according to the legal requirements of the state in which they reside. No matter how high the position of the abuser, their primary obligation lies with the victim.

The church's support of a battered women's shelter, counseling service, or batterers' group might be one indication of its concern that violence will not be tolerated or condoned. Through prayer, action, study, and planning, we can create an environment within our churches that communicates our repudiation and abhorrence of abuse in any form within the household of God.

Let us pray with David, "O righteous God, who searches minds and hearts, bring to an end the violence of the wicked and make the righteous secure" (Ps. 7:9 NIV).

Appendix
Some Biblical Thoughts on Physical, Sexual, and Verbal Abuse

The Law of Israel on Household Violence

"If a man hits a manservant or maidservant in the eye and destroys it, he must let the servant go free to compensate for the eye. And if he knocks out the tooth of a manservant or maidservant, he must let the servant go free to compensate for the tooth" (Exod. 21:26–27 NIV).

The Prophets on Violence

"'*I hate a man's covering his wife with violence* as well as with his garment,' says the LORD Almighty. . . . You have wearied the LORD with your words. 'How have we wearied him?' you ask. By saying, 'All who do evil are good in the eyes of the LORD, and he is pleased with them' or 'Where is the God of justice?'" (Mal. 2:16–17 NIV alternate translation).

"Give up your violence and oppression and do what is just and right" (Ezek. 45:9 NIV).

"Your fasting ends in quarreling and strife, and in striking each other with wicked fists. You cannot fast as you do today and expect your voice to be heard on high.[1] . . . Is not this the kind of fasting I have chosen: to loose the chains of injustice and untie the cords of the yoke, to set the oppressed free and break every yoke?" (Isa. 58:4, 6 NIV).

The Destructive Effects of Violence on the Batterer

"The trouble he causes recoils on himself; his violence comes down on his own head" (Ps. 7:16 NIV).
"The violence of the wicked will drag them away, for they refuse to do what is right" (Prov. 21:7 NIV).

Violence Associated with Wrong Choices, Injustice, Lying, Evil, and Satan

The violent devise injustice (see Ps. 58:2).
"Their hearts plot violence" (Prov. 24:2 NIV).
The violent bear false witness (see Pss. 27:12; 140:11; Prov. 10:6, 11; Hosea 12:1; Micah 6:12; Zeph. 1:9).
The violent are associated with Satan (see Ezek. 28:16).
"Do not envy a violent man or choose any of his ways" (Prov. 3:31 NIV).

Stalking and Verbal Abuse Condemned

"All day long they twist my words; they are always plotting to harm me. They conspire, they lurk, they watch my steps, eager to take my life" (Ps. 56:5–6 NIV).
"They have tracked me down, they now surround me, with eyes alert, to throw me to the ground" (Ps. 17:11 NIV).
"In his arrogance, the wicked man hunts down the weak. . . . He lies in wait near the villages; from ambush he murders the innocent, watching in secret for his victims. He lies in wait like

a lion in cover; he lies in wait to catch the helpless; he catches the helpless and drags them off in his net" (Ps. 10:2, 8–9 NIV).
See also Psalm 37:33; 59:3; Jeremiah 5:26; Micah 7:2.

God's Purpose Is to Give Deliverance from Violence

"From violent men you rescued me" (2 Sam. 22:49; Ps. 18:48 NIV).
God will judge the violent (Ps. 11:5) and deliver the oppressed who cry out to him (2 Sam. 22:3).
"Rescue me, O LORD, from evil men; protect me from men of violence. . . . Keep me, O LORD, from the hands of the wicked; protect me from men of violence who plan to trip my feet. . . . May disaster hunt down men of violence" (Ps. 140:1, 4, 11 NIV).
"You hear, O LORD, the desire of the afflicted; you encourage them, and listen to their cry, defending the fatherless and the oppressed, in order that man, who is of the earth, may terrify no more" (Ps. 10:17–18 NIV).

Jesus on Child Abuse

In that hour, the disciples came to Jesus saying, "Who then is the greatest in the kingdom of heaven?" Calling a little child, Jesus set her in their midst and said, "Truly, truly I say to you, unless you repent and become as little children, you shall not enter into the kingdom of heaven. Whosoever therefore shall humble themselves as this little child, these are the greatest in the kingdom of heaven. And whoever receives one such little child in my name receives me. *Whosoever shall give offense to* (cause to sin, shock) *one of these little ones who believe on me, it would be better for the offender that a millstone would be hung about his neck and he were sunk into the sea"* (Matt. 18:1–6).[2]
Whoever shall offend one of these little ones who believe on me, it would be good for the abuser rather if a millstone lay about his neck and he were cast into the sea (Mark 9:42).

It is unavoidable that offenses (literally, *that which causes revulsion*) should come; but woe to him by whom they come. It would be better for him if a millstone lay about his neck and he were thrown into the sea rather than that he should offend one of these little ones (Luke 17:1–2).

Jesus on Verbal Abuse

You have heard that it was said in the olden days, "Do not kill; and whosoever shall kill shall be liable for judgment." But I say to you that anyone who is angry with his brother shall be liable for judgment. And whoever shall say to his brother, "You numbskull," shall be liable to the council. Whoever shall say, "You imbecile," shall be in danger of hellfire (Matt. 5:21–22).

How are you able to speak good things when you yourselves are evil? For out of the abundance of the heart, the mouth speaks. Good persons bring forth good things out of the good treasure within themselves, while evil persons bring forth evil things from the evil storehouse within themselves. I say to you that for every evil word which people speak they must give an accounting on the day of judgment. You shall be justified by your words, and you shall be condemned by your words (Matt. 12:34–37).

It is not what goes into the mouth which defiles a person, but what proceeds out of the mouth—this defiles a person. . . . The things which proceed forth out of the mouth come out of the heart, and they defile a person, for out of the heart come forth disputes, evil thoughts, murders, adulteries, sexual exploitation, robberies, false witness, abuse, and blasphemy. These are the things which defile the person (Matt. 15:18–20).

The Epistles on Sexual Abuse

I wrote to you in a letter not to associate with those whose sexual conduct is improper—but by no means with the immoral of this world, or the exploitive, or the rapists,[3] or idolaters, since then you would be obliged to leave the world. But now I write to you not to associate with any who, though they call themselves sister or brother, yet engage in sexually inappropriate behavior,[4] or are exploitive, or idolatrous,[5] or verbally abusive, or drunken, or rapists. Do not share the fellowship of the Lord's Supper with such persons.[6] Why should I judge those who are without? Rather judge those who are within,[7] and God will judge those who are without. *Cast out the evil person from among you*[8] (1 Cor. 5:9–11).

The Conversion of Rapists

Neither thieves, nor the exploitive, nor drunkards, those who are verbally abusive, nor *rapists* shall inherit the kingdom of God. And such were some of you; but you are washed, but you are sanctified, but you are justified in the name of the Lord Jesus Christ, and in the Spirit of our God (1 Cor. 6:10–11).

The Apostle Paul Calls upon the Church to Assume Responsibility in a Known Case of Incest

It is commonly reported that there is inappropriate sexual behavior among you, and of such a kind as is abhorred by the heathen, that a man should have his father's wife. And have you not been arrogant when you ought rather to have mourned, so that the one who did this deed may be removed from your midst? But I, though absent as to my body and yet present in my spirit, have already come to a judgment against the one who committed this outrage. In the name of our Lord Jesus Christ, when you are gathered together with my spirit, in the power of our Lord Jesus, I decree that you give such an individual over to Satan for the destruction of the flesh so that his spirit may be saved in the day of the Lord. Your smug complacency is not good. Do you not know that a little yeast leavens all of the dough? Purge out the old yeast so that you may be a new dough without leaven. For Christ has been sacrificed as our Passover, so that we may keep the feast not with the old leaven of wickedness and guile, but with unleavened sincerity and truth[9] (1 Cor. 5:1–8).

The Epistles on Verbal Abuse

If any consider themselves to be religious while their tongues are unbridled, they deceive their own hearts, and their religion is at this point an idle sham. . . . If anyone does not sin in his or her speech, this is a fully mature individual, able as well to bring his or her entire body under control. If we put bits into the mouths of horses in order to make them obey us, we can move and turn their whole bodies. Behold how great ships are driven by strong winds, and yet are guided by the smallest rudder wherever the impulse of the helmsman wills; just so, the tongue is a small member and yet has great things whereof to boast. Behold how small a fire sets a whole wood ablaze, and the tongue is a fire. The tongue constitutes a world of wickedness among our members, polluting the whole body and inflaming the cycle of existence; it is set on flame by hell. For every sort of beast and bird and reptile and sea creature is tamed and has been controlled by humanity. But no one can tame the human tongue, an unruly evil and full of deadly poison. With it we bless our Lord and Father, and with it we pour invective upon people who have been made in God's likeness. From the same mouth come forth both blessing and abusive cursing. Brothers and sisters, this ought not to be so (James 3:2–10).

Let no evil communication come forth out of your mouth, but rather that which upbuilds in a helpful way, so that it may give grace to the hearer (Eph. 4:29).

The Epistles on Sexual Harassment

All filthiness and foolish jesting—let it not be named among you as befits the saints (Eph. 5:4).

Now put away all wrath, venom, evil, blasphemy, and dirty jokes from out of your mouth (Col. 3:8).

Batterers Disqualified from Church Leadership

A bishop should be above reproach, the husband of one wife,[10] sober, discreet, honorable, hospitable, apt to teach, not given to wine, *not a batterer*, but meek, peaceable, handling the affairs of his own household well, with children who behave in a responsible fashion (1 Tim. 3:2–4).

It is necessary for a bishop to be of irreproachable character, as the steward of God, not arrogant nor quick-tempered, nor given to strong drink, *nor a batterer,* nor greedy for financial gain (Titus 1:6–7).

The servant of the Lord should not become embroiled in fighting (2 Tim. 2:24).

Biblical Antidotes

Thy gentleness hath made me great (2 Sam. 22:36; Ps. 18:35).

Depart from evil and do good. Seek peace and pursue it (Ps. 34:14).

There is a future for the man of peace (Ps. 37:37).

There is deceit in the hearts of those who plot evil, but joy for those who promote peace (Prov. 12:20).

Make your souls holy in obedience to the truth, and with unfeigned affection love one another steadfastly with a pure heart (1 Peter 1:22).

Be devoted to one another with kindly affection, in honor advancing one another (Rom. 12:10).

As much as it is possible for you, be at peace with everyone (Rom. 12:18).

Let us therefore make every effort to do what leads to peace and to mutual edification (Rom. 14:19).

Be angry and do not sin. Do not let the sun go down upon your angry mood, lest you give an opportunity to the devil (Eph. 4:26–27).

Let all bitterness and anger and rage and angry shouting and blasphemy be put away from you, along with all wickedness. Be

243

kind to one another, compassionate, forgiving one another just as God in Christ has forgiven you (Eph. 4:31–32).

Let your forbearing spirit be known to all people (Phil. 4:5).

Seek peace with everyone and holiness, without which no one shall see the Lord (Heb. 12:14).

The Call for God's People to Deliver the Oppressed from Violent Oppressors

"Again I looked and saw all the oppression that was taking place under the sun: I saw the tears of the oppressed—and they have no comforter; power was on the side of their oppressors—and they have no comforter" (Eccles. 4:1 NIV).

The righteous king will defend the afflicted and crush the oppressor (Ps. 72:1, 4).

"He will rescue them from oppression and violence, for precious is their blood in his sight" (Ps. 72:14 NIV).

"Thus says the LORD: Act with justice and righteousness, and *deliver from the hand of the oppressor* anyone who has been robbed. And do no wrong or violence to the alien, the orphan, and the widow, or shed innocent blood in this place" (Jer. 22:3 NRSV).

"He did what was right and just, so all went well with him. He defended the cause of the poor and the needy, and so all went well. Is that not what it means to know me?" declares the LORD (Jer. 22:15–16 NIV).

"Thus says the LORD: Execute justice in the morning, and deliver from the hand of the oppressor anyone who has been robbed, or else my wrath will go forth like fire, and burn, with no one to quench it, because of your evil doings" (Jer. 21:12 NRSV).

The Need for Believing Communities to Deal with the Problems Associated with Abuse

See Matthew 18:15–17; 1 Thessalonians 5:14; 2 Thessalonians 3:14–15; 1 Timothy 5:20; Titus 3:2–11; James 5:19–20.

Submission should not be given to individuals whose behavior or communication is wrong, even though they pretend to be very pious (Gal. 2:5–6).

Notes

1. The concept of abuse as nullifying the prayers of the abuser is also found in 1 Peter 3:7.

2. Unless otherwise indicated, all translations are those of Catherine Clark Kroeger.

3. The word used here *(harpax)* can refer to anyone who seizes by force against the will of another. Translators usually render this "robber" or "rapacious," but the term is used specifically of rapists. In a passage on sexual immorality, this is the most appropriate meaning.

4. The Greek adjective used here *(pornos)* and the related noun *porneia*, cover a wide range of sexually inappropriate and exploitive behaviors, such as obscenity, prostitution, indecent exposure, rape, fornication, incest, and pederasty. No one English word implies the whole cluster of activities. This means that we often fail to understand the strength of the biblical condemnation of abuse.

5. Idolatry in the ancient world was frequently associated with explicitly sexual behavior.

6. Such behavior is unacceptable within the believing community.

7. Here the church is specifically charged to deal with sexual misbehavior within the congregation. The believing community is responsible not only to protect the victim, but to condemn the perpetrator.

8. This is an Old Testament quotation. See Deuteronomy 17:7; 19:19; 22:21, 24; 24:7.

9. In this extended passage, the sacrifice of Christ, the Lamb unblemished with evil or hypocrisy, is specifically set against the wickedness and deceit of incest.

10. During the New Testament period, it was legal for a Jewish man to have more than one wife. A series of documents discovered in the Dead Sea area reveal that the practice was more widespread than previously thought. Bigamy was certainly not acceptable for leaders within the Christian community.

Prepared by Catherine Clark Kroeger. Please send suggestions or corrections to:

Christians for Biblical Equality
P.O. Box 7155
St. Paul, MN 55107-0155
Telephone 612-224-2426, FAX 612-224-3504

245

Reference List

Adorno, T. W., Frenkel-Brunswik, E., Levinson, D. J., & Sanford, R. N. (1950). *The authoritarian personality*. New York: Harper.

Alexander, P. C., & Lupfer, S. L. (1987). Family characteristics and long-term consequences associated with sexual abuse. *Archives of Sexual Behavior, 16*(3), 235–245.

Allen, R., & Allen, B. (1985). *Liberated traditionalism: Men and women in balance*. Portland, OR: Multnomah Press.

Allender, D. (1990). *The wounded heart: Hope for adult victims of childhood sexual abuse*. Colorado Springs, CO: NavPress.

Allport, G. W. (1954). *The nature of prejudice*. Reading, MA: Addison-Wesley.

Alsdurf, J. M. (1985). Wife abuse and Christian faith: An assessment of the church's response (Doctoral dissertation, Fuller Graduate School of Psychology, 1985). *Dissertation Abstracts International,* 8518437.

Alsdurf, J. M., & Alsdurf, P. (1988). A pastoral response. In A. L. Horton & J. A. Williamson (Eds.), *Abuse and religion: When praying isn't enough* (pp. 89–99). Lexington, MA: Lexington Books.

Alsdurf, J. M., & Alsdurf, P. (1989). *Battered into submission: The tragedy of wife abuse in the Christian home*. Downers Grove, IL: InterVarsity Press.

American Psychiatric Association (1993). *Let's talk facts about depression*. Washington, DC: APA.

Aneshensel, C. (1986). Marital and employment role-strain, social support, and depression among adult women. In S. Hobfoll (Ed.), *Stress, social support, and women* (pp. 99–114). Washington, DC: Hemisphere.

Bacchiochi, S. (1987). *Women in the church*. Berrien Springs, MI: Biblical Perspectives.

Balswick, J. O., & Balswick, J. K. (1989). *The family: A Christian perspective on the contemporary home*. Grand Rapids, MI: Baker Books.

Bandura, A. (1977). Self-efficacy: Toward a unifying theory of behavioral change. *Psychology Review, 84,* 191–215.

Beardsley, L., & Spry, T. (1975). *The fulfilled woman*. Irvine, CA: Harvest House.

Beavers, W. R., & Hampson, R. B. (1993). Measuring family competence: The Beavers systems model. In F. Walsh (Ed.), *Normal family processes* (2nd ed.) (pp. 73–103). New York: Guilford Press.

Belenky, M. F., Clinchy, B. M., Goldberger, N. R., & Tarule, J. M. (1986). *Women's ways of knowing: The development of self, voice and mind*. New York: Basic Books.

246

Benson, C. K. (1994). The Mindset of Women Today. Presented at the Women's Ministries Symposium. Pasadena, CA. Used by permission of the author.

Berger, P. (1969). *The sacred canopy: Elements of a sociological theory of religion.* Garden City, NY: Anchor Books.

Bilezikian, G. (1990). *Beyond sex roles: What the Bible says about a woman's place in church and family* (2nd ed.). Grand Rapids, MI: Baker Books.

Blumstein, P., & Schwartz, P. (1983). *American couples: Money, work, sex.* New York: William Morrow.

Bromily, G. W. (1980). *God and marriage.* Grand Rapids, MI: Eerdmans.

Bryer, J. B., Nelson, B. A., Miller, J. B., & Krol, P. A. (1987). Childhood sexual and physical abuse as factors in adult psychiatric illness. *American Journal of Psychiatry, 146* (5), 640–644.

Brym, R. (1993). Why sociology? In R. Brym (Ed.), *New society: Sociology for the 21st century* (pp. 6–7). Toronto: Harcourt Brace.

Campbell, A. (1981). *Rediscovering pastoral care.* Philadelphia: Westminster Press.

Chambers, O. (1935). *My utmost for his highest.* New York: Dodd, Mead & Company.

Chodorow, N. (1978). *The reproduction of mothering.* Berkeley, CA: University of California Press.

Christenson, L. (1970). *The Christian family.* Minneapolis, MN: Bethany Fellowship.

Claes, J., & Rosenthal, D. (1990). Men who batter women: A study in power. *Journal of Family Violence, 5,* 215–224.

Clarke, R. L. (1986). *Pastoral care of battered women.* New York: Free Press.

Clebsch, W., & Jaekle, C. (1964). *Pastoral care in historical perspective.* New York: Jason Aronson.

Cohen, T. (1983). The incestuous family revisited. *Social Casework, 64* (3), 154–161.

Cole, P. M., Woolger, C., Power, T. G., & Smith, K. D. (1992). Parenting difficulties among adult survivors of father-daughter incest. *Child Abuse and Neglect, 16,* 239–249.

Connell, R. W. (1987). *Gender and power: Society, the person and sexual politics.* Stanford, CA: Stanford University Press.

Cooper, D. B. (1974). *You can be the wife of a happy husband.* Wheaton, IL: S. P. Publications.

Coopersmith, S. (1967). *The antecedents of self-esteem.* San Francisco: W. H. Freeman.

Coopersmith, S. (1968). Studies in self-esteem. *Scientific American, 218,* 96–106.

DeAngelis, T. (1994). Psychologists suggest ways to reduce abuse of women. *APA Monitor, 25* (3), 38–39.

DeMause, L. (1987). Schreber and the history of childhood. *Journal of Psychohistory, 15,* 223–230.

Dillow, L. (1977). *Creative counterpart.* Nashville, TN: Thomas Nelson.

Dobson, J. C. (1994). The five keys to family harmony. *Focus on the Family, 18* (3), 10–13.

Dutton, D. (1986). The outcome of court-mandated treatment of wife assault: A quasi-experimental evaluation. *Violence and Victims, 1,* 163–175.

Eilts, M. N. (1988). Saving the family: When is the covenant broken? In A. L. Horton & J. A. Williams (Eds.), *Abuse and religion: When praying isn't enough* (pp. 208–214). Lexington, MA: Lexington Books.

Elliot, E. (1976). *Let me be a woman.* Wheaton, IL: Tyndale.

Epstein, N. B., Bishop, D. S., & Baldwin, L. M. (1984). Mcmaster models of family functioning: A view of the normal family. In D. H. Olson & B. C. Miller (Eds.), *Family Studies Review Yearbook*, Vol. 2 (pp. 75–101). Beverly Hills, CA: Sage Publications.

Ewing, W., Lindsey, M., & Pomerantz, J. (1984). *Battering: An AMEND manual for helpers*. Denver, CO: AMEND.

Faller, K. C. (1991). Polyincestuous families: An exploratory study. *Journal of Interpersonal Violence, 6,* 310–322.

Finkelhor, D. (1984). *Sourcebook on child sexual abuse*. Beverly Hills, CA: Sage Publications.

Finkelhor, D., & Yilo, K. (1985). *License to rape*. New York: Free Press.

Fisher, B. L., Giblin, P. R., & Hoopers, M. H. (1984). Healthy family functioning: What therapists say and what families want. In D. H. Olson & B. C. Miller (Eds.), *Family Studies Review Yearbook*, Vol. 2 (pp. 563–574). Beverly Hills, CA: Sage Publications.

Fortune, M. M. (1991). *Violence in the family: A workshop for clergy and other helpers*. Cleveland, OH: Pilgrim Press.

Fortune, M. M. (1983). *Sexual violence: The unmentionable sin*. New York: Pilgrim Press.

Fossum, M., & Mason, M. (1986). *Facing shame*. New York: W. W. Norton.

Friedan, B. (1986). *The second stage*. New York: Summit Books.

Friedman, E. (1985). *Generation to generation*. New York: Guilford Press.

Garland, D. S. R., & Garland, D. E. (1986). *Beyond companionship—Christians in marriage*. Philadelphia: Westminster Press.

Garma, J. (1991). A cry of anguish: The battered woman. In M. Glaz & J. Moessner (Eds.), *Women in travail and transition: A new pastoral care* (pp. 126–145). Minneapolis, MN: Fortress Press.

Gebhard, P., Gagnon, J., Pomeroy, W., & Christenson, C. (1965). *Sex offenders*. New York: Harper & Row.

Gelles, R. J., & Straus, M. A. (1988). *Intimate violence*. New York: Simon & Shuster.

Getz, G. (1972). *The Christian home in a changing world*. Chicago: Moody Press.

Gil, V. E. (1988). In thy father's house. *Journal of Psychology and Theology, 16,* 153–158.

Gilligan, C. (1982). *In a different voice*. Cambridge, MA: Harvard University Press.

Gilligan, C. (1987). Moral orientation and moral development. In E. F. Kittay & D. T. Meyers (Eds.), *Women and moral theory* (pp. 19–33). Lanham, MD: Rowman & Littlefield.

Gilligan, C. (1988). Remapping the moral domain: New images of self in relationship. In C. Gilligan, J. V. Ward, & J. M. Taylor with B. Bardige (Eds.), *Mapping the moral domain* (pp. 3–19). Cambridge, MA: Harvard University Press.

Glaz, M., & Moessner, J. (Eds.). (1991). *Women in travail and transition: A new pastoral care*. Minneapolis, MN: Fortress Press.

Goffman, E. (1961). *Asylums: Essays on the social situation of mental patients and other inmates*. New York: Doubleday Anchor Books.

Gondolf, E. W. (1985). *Men who batter: An integrated approach for stopping wife abuse*. Holmes Beach, FL: Learning Publications.

Goodman, L. A., Koss, M. P., Fitzgerald, L. F., Russo, N. F., & Keita, G. P. (1993). Male violence against women: Current research and future directions. *American Psychologist, 48* (10), 1054–1058.

Gothard, B. (1979). *Research in principles of life*. Oak Brook, IL: Institute in Basic Youth Conflicts.

Guernsey, D. B. (1984). *The family covenant: Love and forgiveness in the Christian home.* Elgin, IL: David C. Cook.

Hamburger, K., & Hastings, J. (1986). Personality correlates of men who abuse their partners: A cross-validation study. *Journal of Family Violence, 1,* 323–341.

Handford, E. R. (1972). *Me? Obey him?* Murfreesboro, TN: Sword of the Lord.

Harter, S., Alexander, P. C., & Neimeyer, R. A. (1988). Long-term effects of incestuous child abuse in college women: Social adjustment, social cognition, and family characteristics. *Journal of Consulting and Clinical Psychology, 56* (1), 5–8.

Heggen, C. H. (1989). *Dominance/submission role beliefs, self-esteem and self-acceptance in Christian laywomen.* Unpublished doctoral dissertation, University of New Mexico.

Helfer, R. E., & Kempe, R. E. (Eds.). (1968). *The battered child.* Chicago: University of Chicago Press.

Hendricks, M. (1984). Women, spirituality, and mental health. In L. E. Walker (Ed.), *Women and mental health policy,* Sage Yearbooks in Women's Policy Studies, Vol. 9 (pp. 95–115). Beverly Hills, CA: Sage Publications.

Herman, J., & Hirschman, L. (1981). Families at risk for father-daughter incest. *American Journal of Psychiatry, 138,* 967–970.

Hiebert, P. (1978). Conversion, culture and cognitive categories. *Gospel in context, 1,* 24–29.

Hinkle, J. (1989). *The meaning of pastoral care* (Rev. ed.). Bloomington, IN: Meyer Stone.

Hochschild, A. R. (1983). *The managed heart: Essays on belief systems in action.* Athens, GA: Southern Anthropological Society, University of Georgia Press.

Hoorwitz, A.N. (1983). Guidelines for treating father-daughter incest. *Social Casework,* 515–524.

Howard, C. (1993). Factors influencing a mother's disclosure of incest. *Professional Psychology: Research and Practice, 24* (2), 176–181.

Hubbard, M. G. (1992). *Women: The misunderstood majority.* Dallas: Word.

Hull, D., & Burke, J. (1991). The religious right, attitudes toward women, and tolerance for sexual abuse. *Journal of Offender Rehabilitation, 17* (112), 1–12.

Huntington, S. P. (1981). *American politics: The promise of disharmony.* Cambridge, MA: Harvard University Press.

Hurley, J. B. (1981). *Man and woman in biblical perspective.* Grand Rapids, MI: Zondervan.

Jack, D. C. (1987). Silencing the self: The power of social imperatives in female depression. In R. Formanek and A. Gruion (Eds.), *Women and depression: A lifespan perspective* (pp. 161–181). New York: Springer.

Jack, D. C. (1991). *Silencing the self: Women and depression.* Cambridge, MA: Harvard University Press.

Jackson, J. L., Calhoun, K. S., Amick, A. E., Maddever, H. M., & Habif, V. L. (1990). Young adult women who report childhood intrafamilial sexual abuse: Subsequent adjustment. *Archives of Sexual Behavior, 19* (3), 211–221.

Jaffe, P., Wolfe, D., & Wilson, S. (1990). *Children of battered women.* Newbury Park, CA: Sage Publications.

Janeway, E. (1971). *Man's world, woman's place: A study in social mythology.* New York: Delta.

Janeway, E. (1975). *Between myth and morning: Women awakening.* New York: William Morrow.

Jehu, D. (1990). *Beyond sexual abuse.* New York: John Wiley & Sons.

Jewett, P. (1982, June). Theological issues in domestic violence. *Theology News and Notes,* 8–11.

Johnson, M. (1988). *Strong mothers, weak wives.* Berkeley, CA: University of California Press.

Jordan, J. V., Kaplan, A. G., Miller, J. B., Stiver, I. P., & Surrey, J. L. (1991). *Women's growth in connection.* New York: Guilford Press.

Kahr, B. (1991). The sexual molestation of children: Historical perspectives. *Journal of Psychohistory, 19* (2), 191–214.

Kandel, D. B., Davies, M., & Ravels, V. (1985). The stressfulness of daily social roles for women: Marital, occupational and household roles. *Journal of Health and Social Behavior, 26,* 64–78.

Kaplan, A. G. (1986). The "self-in-relation": Implications for depression in women. *Psychotherapy: Theory, Research, and Practice, 23,* 235–242.

Keener, C. (1991). . . . *And marries another: Divorce and remarriage in the teaching of the New Testament.* Peabody, MA: Hendrickson Publishers.

Kessler, R. C., & McRae, J. A. (1982). The effect of wives' employment on the mental health of married men and women. *American Sociological Review, 47,* 216–277.

Koss, M. P. (1990). The women's mental health research agenda: Violence against women. *American Psychologist, 45,* 374–380.

Kwentus, J. A., Hart, R. P., Peck, E. T., & Kornstein, S. (1985). Psychiatric complications of closed-head trauma. *Psychosomatics, 26,* 8–14.

LaHaye, B. (1976). *The Spirit-controlled woman.* Irvine, CA: Harvest House.

Landers, A. (1994, 3 April). *Toronto Star,* p. C3.

Leehan, J. (1989). *Pastoral care for survivors of family abuse.* Louisville, KY: Westminster/John Knox Press.

Lindsey, M., McBride, R., & Platt, C. (1993a). *Amend: Philosophy and curriculum for treating batterers.* Littleton, CO: Gylantic Publishing.

Lindsey, M., McBride, R., & Platt, C. (1993b). *Amend: Workbook for ending violent behavior.* Littleton, CO: Gylantic Publishing.

Litfin, A. D. (1979). Evangelical feminism: Why traditionalists reject it. *Bibliotheca Sacra 136* (543), 258–271.

Llaboe, G. (1985). The place of wife battering in considering divorce. *Journal of Psychology and Theology, 13,* 129–138.

Long, V. O., & Heggen, C. H. (1988). Clergy perceptions of spiritual health for adults, men, and women. *Counseling and Values, 32* (3), 213–220.

Martin, G. L. (1987). *Counseling for family violence and abuse.* Waco, TX: Word Books.

McGrath, E., Keita, G. P., Strickland, B. R., & Russo, N. F. (1990). *Women and depression: Risk factors and treatment issues.* Final report of the American Psychological Association's national task force on women and depression. Washington, DC: APA.

Men on domestic violence: Prevention easier said than done (1994). *Bulletin of the Colorado Psychological Association, 27* (3), 4–5.

Miles, J. M. (1975). *The feminine principle: A woman's discovery of the key to total fulfillment.* Minneapolis, MN: Bethany Fellowship.

Miller, J. B. (1984). The development of women's sense of self. *Work in progress, no. 12.* Wellesley, MA: Stone Center.

Miller, J. B. (1986). *Toward a new psychology of women.* Boston: Beacon Press.

Mollerstrom, W., Patchner, M., & Milner, J. (1992). Family functioning and child abuse potential. *Journal of Clinical Psychology, 48* (4), 445–454.

Neff, D. (1991). Women in the confidence gap. *Christianity Today, 35* (8), 13.

Nelson, J. (1983). *Between two genders.* New York: Pilgrim Press.

Nosko, A., & Wallace, B. (1988). Group therapy with abusive men: A multidimensional model. In G. S. Getzel (Ed.), *Violence: prevention and treatment in groups* (pp. 33–52). Binghamton, NY: Haworth Press.

Nouwen, H. (1972). *The wounded healer.* New York: Doubleday.

Nye, F. I. (1976). *Role structure and analysis of the family.* Beverly Hills, CA: Sage Publications.

Olson, D. H. (1993). Circumplex model of marital and family systems. In F. Walsh (Ed.), *Normal family processes* (2nd ed.) (pp. 104–137). New York: Guilford Press.

Pagelow, M. (1981). *Woman battering: Victims and their experiences.* Beverly Hills, CA: Sage Publications.

Pagelow, M. D., & Johnson, P. (1988). Abuse in the American family: The role of religion. In A. L. Horton & J. A. Williamson (Eds.), *Abuse and religion: When praying isn't enough* (pp. 1–12). Lexington, MA: Lexington Books.

Pancheri, P., & Benaissa, C. (1978). Stress and psychosomatic illness. In C. Spielberger & I. Sarason (Eds.), *Stress and anxiety,* Vol. 5. Washington, DC: Hemisphere.

Park, R. (1927). Human nature and collective behavior. *American Journal of Sociology, 32,* 739.

Parsons, T. (1947). *Max Weber: The theory of social and economic organization.* New York: Free Press.

Pence, E., & Paymar, M. (1993). *Education groups for men who batter: The Duluth model.* New York: Springer.

Perry, W. (1970). *Forms of intellectual and ethical development in the college years.* New York: Holt, Rinehart & Winston.

Piper, J., & Grudem, W. (Eds.) (1991). *Recovering biblical manhood and womanhood: A response to evangelical feminism.* Wheaton, IL: Crossway Books.

Pratt, L. (1992). The lost coin. *Daughters of Sarah, 18* (1), 16–18.

Ramsay, N. (1991). Sexual abuse and shame: The travail of recovery. In M. Glaz and J. Moessner (Eds.), *Women in travail and transition: A new pastoral care* (pp. 109–125). Minneapolis, MN: Augsburg Fortress.

Rice, J. R. (1941). *Bobbed hair, bossy wives and women preachers.* Wheaton, IL: Sword of the Lord Publishers.

Rosenthal, H. G. (1986). The learned helplessness syndrome: Specific strategies for crisis intervention with the suicidal sufferer—Emotional first aid. *American Journal of Crisis Intervention, 3,* 5–8.

Ross, C. E., & Mirowsky, J. (1988). Child care and emotional adjustment to wives' employment. *Journal of Health and Social Behavior, 19,* 127–138.

Ross, C. E., Mirowsky, J., & Huber, J. (1983). Dividing work, sharing work, and in-between: Marriage patterns and depression. *American Sociological Review, 48,* 809–823.

Russell, D. E. H. (1983). The incidence and prevalence of intrafamilial and extrafamilial sexual abuse on female children. *Child Abuse and Neglect, 7,* 133–146.

Russell, D. E. H. (1986). *The secret trauma: Incest in the lives of girls and women.* New York: Basic Books.

Sanford (1994, March). Letters to the editor. *Interest,* 30.

Scharfenberg, J. (1980). *Pastoral care as dialogue.* Philadelphia: Fortune Press.

Shulman, B. H. (1968). *Essays in schizophrenia.* Baltimore: Williams & Wilkes.

Shuster, M. (1987). *Power, pathology, and paradox.* Grand Rapids, MI: Zondervan.

Sirles, E. A., & Lofberg, C. E. (1990). Factors associated with divorce in intrafamily child abuse cases. *Child Abuse and Neglect, 14* (2), 165–170.

Smalley, G. (1989). *Love is a decision.* Dallas: Word.

Smalley, G., & Trent, J. (1992). *The hidden value of a man.* Colorado Springs, CO: Focus on the Family.

Soelle, D. (1975). *Suffering.* Trans. E. R. Kaplin. Philadelphia: Fortress Press.

Sonkin, D., & Durphy, M. (1989). *Learning to live without violence.* Volcano, CA: Volcano Press.

Sonkin, D., Martin, D., & Walker, L. (1985). *The male batterer: A treatment approach.* New York: Springer.

Sorensen, A., & McLanahan, S. (1987). Married women's economic dependency, 1940–1980. *American Journal of Sociology, 93* (3), 661–662.

Stacy, W., & Shupe, A. (1983). *The family secret.* Boston: Beacon Press.

Star, B. (1983). *Helping the abuser: Intervening effectively in family violence.* New York: Family Service Association.

Stark, R., & Bainbridge, W. S. (1985). *The future of religion: Secularization, revival and cult formation.* Berkeley, CA: University of California Press.

Steinmetz, S. K. (1986). The violent family. In M. Lystad (Ed.), *Violence in the home: Interdisciplinary perspectives* (pp. 51–67). New York: Brunner/Mazel.

Straus, M. A., Gelles, R., & Steinmetz, K. (1980). *Behind closed doors: Violence in the American family.* Garden City, NY: Anchor Books.

Surrey, J. L. (1985). Self-in-relation: A theory of women's development. *Work in progress, no. 13.* Wellesley, MA: Stone Center.

Tournier, P. (1964). *The whole person in a broken world: A biblical remedy for today's world.* New York: Harper & Row.

Trepper, T. S., & Barrett, M. (1989). *Systemic treatment of incest.* New York: Brunner/Mazel.

Turner, R. (1976). The real self: From institution to impulse. *American Journal of Sociology 81,* (5), 989–1016.

van der Kolk, B. A. (1988). The trauma spectrum: The interaction of biological and social events in the genesis of the trauma response. *Journal of Traumatic Stress, 1,* 273–290.

Van Leeuwen, M. (1990). *Gender and grace: Love, work, and parenting in a changing world.* Downers Grove, IL: InterVarsity Press.

Vanderbilt, H. (1992). Incest: A chilling report. *Lears, 4,* 49–77.

Wahl, B. (1990). Pastoral management of domestic violence. Research Paper for D.Min. program, Denver Seminary, Denver, CO (Denver Seminary Library).

Walker, L. (1979). *The battered woman.* New York: Harper & Row.

Walker, L. E. A. (1984). *The battered woman syndrome.* New York: Springer.

Walker, L. E. A. (1986). Psychological causes of family violence. In M. Lystad (Ed.), *Violence in the home: Interdisciplinary perspectives* (pp. 71–97). New York: Brunner/Mazel.

Walsh, F. (1993). Conceptualizations of normal family processes. In F. Walsh (Ed.), *Normal family processes* (2nd ed.) (pp. 3–69). New York: Guilford Press.

Warren, R. P. (1946). *All the King's Men.* New York: Bantam Books.

Weber, Max. (1922, 1963). *The sociology of religion.* Boston: Beacon Press.

Weissman, M. M. (1987). Advances in psychiatric epidemiology: Rates and risks for major depression. *American Journal of Public Health, 77,* 445–451.

Weissman, M. M., Leaf, P. J., Bruce, L., & Florio, L. (1988). The epidemiology of dysthymia in five communities: Rates, risks, comorbidity, and treatment. *American Journal of Psychiatry, 145,* 815–819.

Welter, B. (1976). *Dimity convictions: The American woman in the nineteenth century.* Athens, OH: Ohio University Press.

West, C. (1993). *Race matters.* Boston: Beacon Press.

Wise, C. (1966). *The meaning of pastoral care.* Revisions by J. Hinkle (1989). Bloomington, IN: Meyer Stone.

Witmer, J., Rich, C., Barcikowski, R. S., & Mague, I. C. (1983). Psychosocial characteristics mediating the stress response: An exploratory study. *The Personnel and Guidance Journal, 62,* 73–77.

Yorky, M. (Ed.). (1990). *Growing a healthy home.* Brentwood, IN: Wolgemuth & Hyatt.

Contributors

James R. Beck is professor of counseling at Denver Conservative Baptist Seminary. He is a clinical psychologist, an ordained minister, and the author of *Dorothy Carey*. He also is a founding board member of Christians for Biblical Equality.

Mary Nella Bruce obtained her M.Div. degree from North Park Seminary. She is an ordained minister with the Evangelical Covenant Church and pastors, along with her husband, an inner-city church in south Chicago. She is a director of the Barnabas Project.

Steven R. Fleming holds an M.Div. degree from Denver Seminary. Since graduation he has worked at several treatment facilities that specialize in the treatment of male batterers. He is currently a mental health worker in Phoenix, Arizona.

Shirley Gillett works in Toronto, Canada, with Grandview Survivors, a group of women who were sexually abused while incarcerated. She is a founding member of Women Won't Forget and is herself a survivor of sexual assault, rape, and violent physical battery.

Carolyn Holderread Heggen holds a Ph.D. from the University of New Mexico. She is a psychotherapist in Albuquerque, New Mexico. Among her many writings is *Sexual Abuse in Christian Homes and Churches*. She is an elder in the Albuquerque Mennonite Church.

M. Gay Hubbard is a psychotherapist in Denver. She has taught on the faculties of the medical school at Ohio State University and at Colorado Christian University. She is the author of *Women, the Misunderstood Majority*.

Jackie J. Hudson is a licensed marriage, family, and child counselor with a private practice in Redlands, California. She has been associated with Campus Crusade for Christ since 1972 and is on the part-time faculty at the International School of Theology.

Craig S. Keener is professor of New Testament at Hood Theological Seminary. He was trained at Duke University. His publications include ... *And Marries Another; Paul, Women, and Wives;* and *The IVP Bible Background Commentary (New Testament)*.

Catherine Clark Kroeger is an adjunct professor at Gordon-Conwell Theological Seminary. She earned her Ph.D. in classics at the University of Minnesota. She is president emerita of Christians for Biblical Equality. She and her husband authored *I Suffer Not a Woman.*

Diane Langberg is a licensed psychologist with a private practice in the Philadelphia area. She authors a column in *Today's Christian Woman* and is the author of *Feeling Good, Feeling Bad* and *Counsel for Pastors' Wives.*

Alice P. Mathews serves on the academic team of the Philadelphia campus of CB Seminary of the East. She is a producer for Radio Bible Class daily broadcasts and has served as an editor of *Focal Point.* She served with her husband as a missionary in France and Austria.

David M. Scholer is professor of New Testament at Fuller Theological Seminary. He has formerly taught at North Park College and Theological Seminary, Gordon-Conwell Theological Seminary, and Northern Baptist Theological Seminary.

Thomas (a pseudonym) is currently incarcerated in a state penitentiary after he was convicted of sexual abuse crimes. He is a writer with a history of magazine publication. His interest in participating in this project stems from his desire to do all he can to combat sexual abuse.

Joan Burgess Winfrey is associate professor of counseling at Denver Seminary. She formerly served on the faculty of Metropolitan State College in Denver. She is a psychologist and serves on the staff of the Minirth-Meier Clinic in Denver.